REINVENT RICH

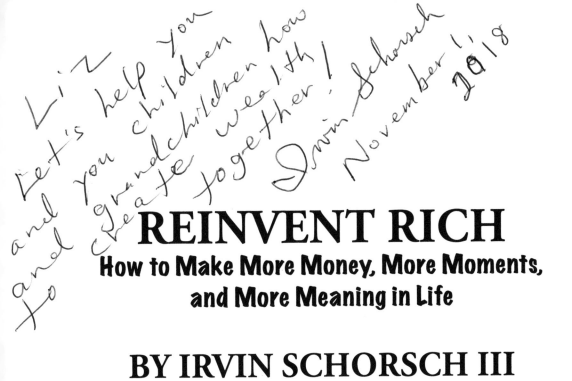

Liz
Let's help you
and you children how
and grandchildren how
to create wealth
together!

Irvin Schorsch

November 11, 2018

REINVENT RICH

How to Make More Money, More Moments, and More Meaning in Life

BY IRVIN SCHORSCH III

WITH TED SPIKER

NEXT CENTURY
PUBLISHING

Reinvent Rich
How to Make More Money, More Moments, and More Meaning in Life

Copyright ©2018 by Irvin Schorsch III
All rights reserved.
Published by Next Century Publishing
Austin, TX

www.NextCenturyPublishing.com

ISBN: 978-1-68102-105-8
Library of Congress Control Number: 2018936334

Printed in the United States of America

I dedicate this book...

To my Dad, my first client, my mentor and friend, who taught me the art of strategy, that we must trust our vision and live TODAY.

To Jack Petrosky, Myke Kanis, Myles Turtz, all leaders in their fields and great teachers.

To my wonderful wife, Marilyn, and our children Stephanie, Irvin, and Merrie, who are an endless source of courage and perspective.

I am also grateful to the many friends and clients who have shared their dreams.

Reinvent Rich

How to Make More Money, More Moments, and More Meaning in Life

by Irvin Schorsch III
with Ted Spiker

CONTENTS

Section 3
FINANCIAL FOCUS
Managing Life's Special Wealth-Building and

REINVENT RICH

Foreword
by Dr. Mehmet C. Oz

W hy is a doctor writing the foreword to a book about wealth? Good question, but one that has a very straightforward answer. Health and wealth aren't just similar in that they're one letter different from each other. They're so closely tied together that you can't—or at least you shouldn't—think about one without the other.

What do I mean by that? In today's society, there's a lot you can point to as being the source of our collective health problems. Too much sugar. Not enough exercise. The allure of the smartphone that keeps us tethered to our technology rather than lying asleep in our bedrooms. Tied to all of them, in many ways, is stress. Stress makes us eat poorly, stress keeps us from exercising, stress makes us toss and turn, and stress puts us in bad situations with the people we care for. Stress is like a carton of Twinkies—it's toxic to our bodies. And without question, financial burdens are a major source of stress for many, many people.

That's one of the reasons why I'm so excited about Irvin Schorsch's book, *Reinvent Rich*. I have known Irvin for more than thirty years, and I know that he is so passionate about helping people gain financial security and freedom to help them improve their lives. Selfishly, I love that goal because in the process of people gaining more wealth, they're also gaining better health. And that's not just good for the individual, but it's good for all of us as well.

The other reason why this book is important, I believe, is because of the theme that comes through loud and clear right from the start. Having wealth isn't just about the size of your bank account. It's about aligning your financial strategies with your passions in life. It's about having the freedom and ability and wherewithal to pursue those passions. And most importantly, it's about creating time. Time to live your passions. Time to connect with your family. Time to leave a lasting impression on those around you. Time to do what you want in life.

As Irvin says, that is what *Reinventing Rich* is all about. Ben Franklin knew what he was saying when he used the phrase "healthy, wealthy, and wise." Heck, he may have even been talking about Irvin Schorsch when he said it.

– Mehmet C. Oz M.D.

Introduction
More Wealth, Your Wealth

No matter what image you want to think about—the pot of gold, the treasure chest, the stack of Benjamins, the bank statement with a loooooooong line of digits—when we think about wealth, we think about *lots* of it. That's the financial dream that so many want to believe in. The lottery windfall, the year-end bonus, the big pile of cash that could buy you everything from a yacht to a mansion and every toy in between. And while, yes, some people will achieve that level of wealth, the reality is that's not really what most of us are after. Of course, when it comes to finances, our goal should be to amass as much money as possible to provide security and sanity to our lives, but here's where I think we tend to get it wrong.

Too many people equate wealth with dollars and cents, portfolios and percentages, charts and graphs. Yes, you need all of those elements to make millions, and you need strategies to help you get there. But what you need before any of that is an overriding principle, an overriding philosophy, an overriding question that helps direct where you go, how you build, why you make decisions, and what you want out of life. After more than twenty years of experience running a wealth-management firm, I have learned and developed an approach that is different from the majority of wealth advisors you will meet.

Simply, I believe that wealth is this: to build as much financial security and stability as you can to get exactly what you want out of life—with the people and projects and the missions that you're passionate about. Sometimes this is about being financially savvy, and sometimes this is about taking a step back and thinking about the big picture that involves you and your family. This is what "reinventing rich" is all about—understanding that wealth is more than just money.

In this book, I am going to cover the major financial principles and foundations that will help you make your millions, but I'm going to do it in a way so that you always keep in mind that the end game isn't making it to retirement with a good nest egg. In fact, I have different views on what retirement should be (see page 191). I'm going to do it so you can start this very minute, if you haven't already, to build two kinds of wealth—the financial kind and the personal kind.

That is my goal and your mission: to help you reinvent rich.

Much of my financial and personal philosophy is rooted in my three decades in the personal-wealth business and as the founder of a wealth-management firm near Philadelphia, Pennsylvania. Here's my quick story. In 1982, I had been working for Sprint for two and a half years. I was able to double my income because I was good at sales, but I was frustrated that my clients only stayed with me for three months (and then they were turned over to "house" accounts). I'd built the relationships, but then they were gone.

My father said to me, "You're good at investing. Why don't you look at the wealth management business?" So I did just that, even though I had achieved a top-10 status at Sprint nationwide. I joined Prudential Securities and was hired by Jack Petrosky, who said to me, "Irvin, you'll be one of the best. You'll make our Chairman's Council." And I told him, "Jack, I think you're nuts. But I'll give it a try."

I learned about stocks and bonds, mutual funds, real estate, and all sorts of other things that didn't mean much to a newcomer to the field. But I found that if I could build the business (meaning build a relationship with people and help them in a way that wouldn't hurt them), then I was comfortable.

I spent time training and learning the business, and I went up through the ranks at Prudential Securities, from being an advisor, to being a vice president, to being a senior vice president, to being on the president's council, to being on the chairman's council. I made the top group in the entire firm, and it was an exciting start to my business career.

In 1995, after Prudential Securities went through some legal troubles, I left at the urging of some of my best clients, who said, "Irvin, they're like a noose around your neck." I took their concerns to heart and I left. I mustered my courage and joined one of Paine Webber's affiliates to begin a new independent firm. I founded Pennsylvania Capital Management in September of 1995 with four team members to start, and virtually all of our clients left Prudential to join us. Now, we've celebrated more than twenty years in business.

But my story is more than just about building a successful business that helps clients achieve their financial goals. My story is about all of the things that have gone into building that business—specifically the family values that I grew up with. So throughout the book, you'll see tangible financial strategies, as well as "life-isms" that come from me, my father, and my mother—all of which have informed my outlook on building your wealth.

For example, my father taught me the value of surrounding yourself with smart, insightful people who can share with you rich life experiences. In fact, he said, "You are only as good as the people around you." He also taught me that we all only have so many "silver bullets" in life—so make sure you take advantage of opportunities that come your way. (Take the cookies when they are offered. Jump on them and take action.)

My mother taught me the value of informing yourself thoroughly by reading and researching as much as you can so you can learn to make wise decisions.

My wife taught me to listen beneath the surface and to be a keen observer of people.

Many of the lessons they taught me will bubble up throughout the book; their life lessons help give context and direction to the nuts-and-bolts tactics I will cover. Ultimately, I also think we have to change the way we look at money, since it's so full of emotion and angst and pressure. We have to start to strip the guilt and shame that comes from how we spend and save so we can make wise decisions, think strategically, and get what we want out of our money and our lives. It takes time, patience, commitment, and smarts to find the ways we can take the emotion out of our finances so we can make the best decisions for ourselves and our families. My hope is that this book will help you get there.

I wrote this book for two reasons. One, it is clear that many Americans are still in financial purgatory. They can't climb their way out of debt. They feel stuck. They haven't built the fortune they want and have dreamed about. And they haven't found the strategies that will work for them to achieve the goals they want. A 2012 Financial Industry Regulatory Agency study of 25,000 people found that only 24 percent of Americans were satisfied with their current financial situation (42 percent were neutral and 31 percent weren't satisfied with their finances).

Two, I believe that the path to get there isn't just about numbers, but about bridging the gap between the practical and the emotional—by finding out what our flaws are when we discuss finances (if we even do!) and by trying to think about wealth more holistically (how health, stress, and family values play a role in financial decision making, for instance).

I've structured this book in three sections to help you navigate the choppy waters of wealth. The first section covers the basic financial principles that I believe everyone should follow to establish baseline habits and provide the foundation for growing and managing wealth.

The second section simply adds more advanced strategies once you have the baseline established and your financial situation in stable shape. And the third section covers specific topics that may or may not apply to you, depending on your family, lifestyle, and interests. There I'll cover areas such as teaching your children about financial issues, saving for college, what to do if you have serious debt, and what happens if you win the lottery (literally or metaphorically). Finally, I'll end the book with a 21-Day Wealth Makeover. This plan works a bit like a diet plan (minus the Brussels sprouts). I'll take many of the major themes I discuss in the book and give you a map for how to get your financial situation on the right track. In 21 days, if you follow the guide, you'll be well on your way to achieving the wealth you want—and the fortune you deserve. Throughout the book, to help reinforce some of the main points, you'll see our version of a wise wealth owl popping up from time to time.

As we get started, I think it's important to go through some of my major life and wealth principles. They serve as a sort of personal foundation (before the financial foundation) that will help you make millions. Remember, these are based on my thirty years of experience working with hundreds of personal wealth clients and millions and millions of dollars. I've seen the good, the bad, and the ugly, and I've spent my entire career not just as a lifelong advisor, but as a lifelong learner—culling the wisdom not only from my wide range of clients, but also from everyone I interact with. This has allowed me to better serve my clients, and it will now serve you too.

Above all, I hope this book gives you exactly what you want—a healthy mix of tools, information, and motivation. When you put everything in motion, that's when your wealth—and ultimately your freedom and happiness—builds and builds.

That's when you learn how to *Reinvent Rich*.

So what do you say? Let's jump in.

SECTION 1

MASTERING YOUR MONEY

Baseline Principles for Building Your Wealth

Chapter 1
Strength in Your Core

The 13 Principles for Finding Wealth and Happiness

Recently, my wife and I hosted a birthday for our youngest daughter, Merrie. She invited her friends, of course, and we invited the parents to come along to a local youth center that's filled with trampolines. During the party, all of the kids did what kids do: they jumped into the action—leaping, flipping, laughing. Without missing a beat, I did the same.

Here I was, a man in my fifties, bounding around the trampolines like a teenager. And you know what? I was the only parent who did. Oh, I asked my peers (many of whom were younger than I am) to join in the fun. They looked at me like I had four tongues. Don't want to get hurt, they said. Don't want to be embarrassed, they said. Don't want to take any risks, they said.

Nonsense, I thought.

I had a blast. So did the kids—and all I could think of was how sad it was that my fellow parents didn't want to engage in life for this reason or that. They had missed the point—that living, engaging, interacting, laughing, jumping, flipping was what life is about. And ultimately, that's exactly what wealth is about too.

Yes, I know I may seem crazier than a rabid raccoon by suggesting that an afternoon of trampoline hopping is the secret to building your financial fortune. But hear me out.

In all likelihood, most of you reading this book have a similar—and singular—goal when it comes to wealth: you want more money. Now, we all may differ in what we want to do with it—whether it's saving for the future, buying a boat, taking a trip to Tuscany or the Caribbean, reducing financial stress by getting rid of debt, or doing any number of things you can do when you have financial stability and security.

The thing I hear over and over from clients, friends, or people who ask me questions on the radio is that most people want a quick fix. They want instant wealth. There's nothing wrong with wanting that, of course, because that's human nature. But unless you're a Powerball winner, a Facebook founder, or have some other secret path to a pile of cash, the process is never as fast as we want it to be. I don't want to put a damper on your dream that somehow you'll walk away from this book with a cool mil in your pocket by the time you get to page 132. (Just kidding!) I do want to tell you that gaining wealth is not only possible, but it's also probable if you take the steps that I outline.

How? Throughout the book, I'm going to give you hundreds of little strategies that you can use to accumulate wealth (and subsequently life satisfaction). I also firmly believe that this process isn't just about following these tips and tricks; it's about establishing a core foundation of principles that give you the strength to make smart decisions. These principles are your road map, your constitution, your headlights when it's dark; they give you the power to get the most out of your life by having the financial security and savvy to do the best things for you and your family.

Let me be clear: despite all the talk that the American dream is dead, I disagree. Yes, we have acquired some bad habits, and we have our challenges. But the American dream—whether it comes in the form of a nice house, a sound career, or whatever else you think of it as being—is alive. It's manageable. It's doable. It's attainable. In fact, if you follow what I lay out in this book, you can achieve it faster than you think. How do I define that dream? By being financially independent and secure at as young of an age as possible—to give you the freedom to live your life to its fullest.

We crawl before we walk. We build cement foundations of houses before we paint the walls. We practice before we play the game. Life is all about processes—about establishing baseline skills, habits, behaviors, and principles. You establish them, and then you build on them. Example: Eat your vegetables before you get to the meat on your plate and you will fill up on more nutritious food groups first. The same holds true for wealth. You don't just wake up one day with an inch of one-hundred-dollar bills under your pillow. You crawl, you build foundations, you practice, and when you do those things, *that* is how you build your wealth.

So where do you start? For me, I believe it's about having those overriding principles that guide you throughout your financial life. Some of those principles are nuts-and-bolts tactics about money, but some of them are about attitude, and some of them are simply how you approach life. Why? Because we have to look at wealth holistically. Wealth isn't just about bonds and bills, dollars and debt, savings and social security. Wealth is about those things, yes, but it's more about psychology, behavior, emotion, relationships, health, and all the things that influence how we live every day.

So before we get started in the details of how you're going to save and make money, let me outline my principles that will help you get there. To keep in line with the holistic approach I have to wealth, I've broken them down in three areas—psychological, behavioral, and financial—though they are all related and work together. Keep these in mind as you make decisions, and watch your wealth rise to levels you may have never dreamed of reaching.

PSYCHOLOGY OF WEALTH: The Mind Matters

Know that your most important asset is time, not necessarily money. Funny for me to say this, right? A financial advisor writing a finance book is telling you that your most important asset *isn't* money? That's right. Time is what you're after. Time is freedom. Time is happiness. Time is security. Having the time to do the things you want in life is what this book is all about. Now, don't get me wrong...I'm going to be giving you the financial strategies to enable you to take control of your life, but when it comes down to it—and this comes from me dealing with hundreds and hundreds of clients, many of them multi-millionaires—they all say that what they want more of... is time. To get that time, we have to make money, we have to save money, and we have to make smart money and investment decisions.

But money isn't the end game—money is the means to the end game: loving your life and the people around you. That's what reinventing rich is all about. You want to think of it not just in terms of dollar signs, but also levels of happiness. When you keep that goal in mind, the process of getting there looks a little clearer. I'll come back to this principle often throughout the book, but I do think it helps keep your goals and decisions in perspective.

What you're trying to do is not only to make money for the sake of making money, but also to live the life you want. That's a function of time as well as money. After all, what I hear over and over is that people are just too busy these days—too busy to do everything that comes with a career, a family, and all of the stresses associated with them. Because of those burdens, we're losing time (and perhaps money)—and that is decreasing the quality of our lives.

Gaining time back isn't just about stealing a few minutes to yourself to watch your reality show of choice or to surf the web. It's about providing some mental clarity to your life—to put things in order and regain control of how you live. To do that, it means that you have to define your priorities and also be willing to delegate some of the responsibilities to people you trust. It takes some creative thinking to see how you can save time and money. Life is so cluttered these days that we need to find ways to relieve that burden—not just to free you up to make more money, but really to establish the importance of that time as a form of wealth itself.

You must have courage. This is one of the first things I tell my clients. Why? Because many times they're scared—scared of their futures, scared of their situations, scared of making mistakes, scared of taking chances, and scared of how to handle money. To make money you have to be willing to take chances (i.e., there is some level of risk). And I understand that, because, as we all know, financial stability and security is one of the necessary goals in life.

But courage isn't just for fire fighters or characters from *The Wizard of Oz*. Courage is for everyone who wants to make and save the most money they can. That means you have to have courage in many different areas—whether it's demanding the most from a financial advisor if you're not getting the service you expect or having an open and honest conversation with your partner about some source of financial tension. Some of these situations aren't easy, but making a commitment to be courageous is one of the tenants you'll see over and over in this book. This isn't about having the courage to make rash decisions or impulse buys, but rather about having the courage to confront sticking points and stumbling blocks rather than ignore them.

The harder you work, the luckier you get. In my experience, a lot of people think that investing is some mysterious experience in which the deities of stocks and bonds somehow decide whether you're going to make or lose money. All about the markets. All about the economy. Nothing we can do about it, right? While that's certainly true to some extent, I've also found that the adage my father taught about hard work creating luck is true—that is, when you invest time in understanding your financial situation, what's happening in the world, and which investments may be best for you, then you actually get "luckier."

So yes, chance does play a role in investments, but over time, the savvy person usually wins. Does that mean you have to know about every single stock or bond? Of course not.

Perhaps it means finding a trusted advisor, or perhaps it just means getting up to speed on key financial issues, which you're doing right now by reading this book. But I want to reinforce that you're not done when you're done with the book. This is only the beginning.

Bottom line: learn more, get disciplined, make more.

The outcome: As you work hard and accumulate wealth, your money is eventually what ends up working hard—that is, that *money* starts making money, through disciplined savings, dollar-cost averaging, compound interest, and other smart ways. This gets us back to one of our original concepts of giving you some of your time back. See how they all work together?

Be grateful for every new day—and savor them all. I know this isn't a concept you will find in most financial books, because it doesn't seem like it has a lot to do with finances. It's been clear to me for years, but it was reinforced on a recent cross-country flight. The attendants on this particular flight were above-and-beyond pleasant, friendly, helpful, and kind. I spoke to one of the flight attendants about it, and she responded, "That's just the way we do it here." I began thinking about this concept of having gratitude and sharing it, and I realized that this appreciative attitude is a core component of how I work with my clients and everyone I come in contact with. It often pays off, even if it's only worth a smile. Many people have this notion that finances have to be about shark tactics—crushing people who are in the way to make a buck. But the reality is that the opposite is true. Treat people fairly and thoughtfully, and you'll get the value back in spades—whether it's with having your team members work better with you, someone being more willing to negotiate with you, or someone offering to provide an extra service at a fraction of the cost. I'm not saying that you'll make millions by being nice to the barista who makes your morning coffee, but I am saying I don't want you to think that aggressive approaches to finances require in-your-face interpersonal tactics. I wish more people would realize that if they calm down and stop thinking that everyone is out to get them, they'll actually benefit more over the long term.

You live longer—and better—when you take care of your business. According to a *Money* magazine survey, the one thing that couples fight over more than anything is money. Yes, more than sex, more than the kids, more than what show to watch, more than who does the dishes on Thursday (70 percent of couples fought over money more than any other subject). There's good reason for that: money problems create gargantuan levels of stress. It's also no secret that stress is one of our biggest healthcare issues today—not just for how it makes us feel and how it's related to heart issues, but also how it's related to other health problems as well (when you're stressed, you eat more, and that, of course, is linked to obesity).

So wealth isn't all about making gobs and gobs of money; it also has the very beneficial effect of prolonging your life by increasing your health and happiness. And really, that's what we're all after, more so than some big-screen TV, designer purse, or twelve-dollar appetizer of fried nastiness. And the two things really work hand in hand. When you lighten the financial stress, you can focus on what really matters, like health, diet, and exercise—so that you can better enjoy whatever wealth you've accumulated in the form of both time and money.

THE BEHAVIORS OF WEALTH: Make New Lifelong Habits

You should think of wealth creation as a team sport. Look, I get it: money is about the most private thing in your life, besides maybe your health and your sex life (though an argument can be made that more people share more info about those two things than they do about their financial situations). And that's fine; you shouldn't be broadcasting your money matters to the world. While some people can do it alone, many people can't. So a financially savvy person makes sure to have a good team (this is the subject of the next chapter).

As my father always said, "You're only as good as the people around you." So that may include such pros as a financial advisor, an accountant, and a lawyer, but more importantly, it means that you take a team approach with your spouse or partner if you have one. You work together, you strategize together, you make decisions together, you work through conflicts together, and you do so because you share a common goal—to be healthy, happy, and secure. I hope this book helps release some of the stigma and tension that often comes when we talk about finances. The more you can include the people close to you when thinking (and making decisions) about finances in a non-confrontational way, the more likely it is that you will make smarter, more beneficial life and financial decisions.

Make finances a family affair. This, of course, is related to my previous point that we shouldn't be afraid to articulate goals and strategies with our team around us, especially the familial team we have. In this book, you'll see a lot of references to how families can work together to achieve goals, but for starters, it's important to keep in mind that finances should take a multi-generational approach.

Example: You should start teaching your kids about money from an early age. (You'll make a decision for yourself about how much you want to share with your children, if you have them, but I'll detail those strategies a little later in the book.) How do I do it? For my children's birthdays, I buy them a smaller amount of toys or trinkets—which quickly wear out or are lost—and then buy them a share of stock in a company that they can relate to. They become invested in learning how companies operate (more on this in Chapter 14).

I also teach my clients' children to take a unique approach to money they make—one-third of it goes to the piggy bank for long-term savings (a car or college), one-third goes to charity, and one-third is for fun and spending. That way, they learn the value of money and the different strategies for saving. Parents usually have no clue how to do this because they think that finances should be so secretive, but the fact is that you should be teaching your kids major principles about money, just as you would about health, or the world, or your community. You don't have to give details of your accounts, but you should teach them the value of dollars and having their own savings/investment accounts. I also think it's important to involve the grandparents in teaching the grandchildren their success stories and good financial habits. Remember, modern-day schools are often weak in their financial curriculum in educating your children.

In my mind, the goal is not about accumulating wealth so you can simply leave it for your children and your grandchildren. It's so you can have experiences with those grandchildren and leave a legacy. For example, I have clients who take trips with each of the grandchildren or the whole family so that they can not only build the relationships, but also have common experiences they can share in the moment and talk about in the future. So these folks take one grandchild to a baseball camp, another to driving school, another to a course for a culinary experience. They created each trip to that grandchild's specific interest. And those trips are special moments that both generations will remember for the rest of their lives.

This is a meaningful use of wealth, but these kinds of things only happen if there's a lifelong commitment to ensuring that we're in a financial state to do so. Without that, it's much harder to do these kinds of things (though admittedly, there are plenty of ways for families to connect without involving elaborate trips or experiences). In any case, grandparents can also be involved in other ways, not just buying toys and games for birthdays, but also contributing to a savings account to help teach children about money—and help them establish a baseline foundation for their financial future. My point is that finances shouldn't be taboo with families. The topic should be something that families talk about, help each other with, think about, and plan—with the goal of bringing everyone closer together to improve our children's futures and create memories (and wealth) that will last a lifetime.

You must use tools. Too often, I've found, people go into financial decision making a little willy-nilly—not thinking about numbers, not thinking long term, and not strategizing about what works best. Some of this is because of what I just said about courage (being too timid when it comes to finances), and some of it stems from the fact that many of us find math about as comfortable as a granite sofa. That's okay.

In this book, I'm going to give you many tools to help you understand finance, but I don't expect you to master everything. Use the tools for the purpose in which they're intended—to make your job easier. I'll have some fun ones that you can use—wait until you see the mind map on page 39—as well as some easy ways to wrap your head around concepts that you may not understand. Above all, you shouldn't apologize at all for using any kind of financial tool. Some of us are good at sports, some are good at music, or art, or math, or cookie-making.

The point isn't that you need to be an expert in any of this; it's that you need to feel comfortable using the tools that will help you navigate through unfamiliar waters. Also, tools can also mean people. You should leverage the knowledge of others on your team for your advantage, whether it's understanding tax laws that will benefit you, finding expenses that could be written off, or making investments that you wouldn't typically come across. If you've picked up this book, then you've already made the first step in that you're comfortable enough to talk about and think about financial issues. Now, if you don't like math and percentages and statistics, I just want you to take it one step further. You don't need to be a whiz; you just need to be willing to dip your toes into the mathematical waters. A person who accumulates wealth doesn't need to know everything, but he or she also isn't afraid to find someone who does.

Be strategic about expenses, no matter your income. One of the main dilemmas I see people face is that when they start accumulating some wealth, or see nice bumps in salary, their tastes change to the more expensive. The more expensive hotels, more dinners out, private schools for the kids, you name it. There's nothing wrong with spending money on things that are your priorities—or that give you or your family joy. And I want to make that clear: wealth isn't about being a miser and never enjoying anything in life. But wealth is about making sure you don't live beyond your means. If you live beyond your means, you will never get wealthy!

Example: One of my clients, a lawyer, saw an incredible bump in pay from when he first started out, to the point where he's making around $400,000 a year. Sounds nice, huh? But what if I told you that he's up to his eyeballs in debt because his expenses shot up at a higher pace than his salary—to the point where he has to dip into savings just to pay the bills.

So while it's easy to say, "If I made that kind of money, I'd never do those things," the truth is that it is very easy to overspend, no matter what your income bracket, whether you make $50,000 a year or ten times that. So what savvy investors know to do is prioritize their expenses. They also often break out their bank/investment accounts and shift funds to invest immediately after they pay their bills to make it hard to get the money back out (i.e., no checkbook or online access to the investment accounts—merely transfer the bill-paying money into the accounts). They transfer funds to pay the bills in the bill-pay account and transfer funds into the investment accounts to get the excess funds working harder immediately. What do they want? What do they need? What can they live without? What is just a fleeting impulse that will pass?

This takes some doing—and some discipline. So many companies are making millions because you're not really thinking about what you need. Do you need a gas-guzzling car, or can you find one that saves you thousands of dollars in gas over the long term? Do you need coffee brewed in a shop as opposed to some brewed at home, which will save you hundreds every year? So the question is: Who deserves that wealth—you or them? You do. But you're only going to get it if you're more strategic about your everyday expenses. I can also tell you that I know many people with very high salaries who are *not* wealthy because they have not taken care of this piece of the puzzle. It's an absolute must if you want to see any kind of long-term wealth in your future.

THE FINANCES OF WEALTH: Common Starting Points for Everyone

You need to develop your game. Many times, my clients think that wealth just happens over time, that years of working and saving will lead to wealth. But ten or fifteen years later, they wake up and realize that too much money went to bills, not enough went to saving and investing for retirement, and now they're scrambling to figure out how to make up for lost time. Bottom line: money begets money. The more you make, the more you make.

But if all of that gets spent in bills or frivolous expenses, your earned money never gets a chance to, well, earn money. So the first financial strategy you should have is to make sure you don't just sit passively, hoping that wealth will just appear. You need to have clear goals and objectives, discipline when it comes to avoiding impulse and frivolous buys, and a clear structure of where your income needs to be budgeted (more on that in a moment). So my point here is that creating wealth requires strategy—and requires you to think, plan, and attack—just in the way, say, a team would do in a sporting event. Are you going to play to win?

You should save ten cents of every dollar before you pay your bills. I will pepper you with lots of financial tips throughout the book. All of them will be little insights and strategies that will help you achieve whatever specific goal you're pursuing (whether it's reducing debt or saving for your kids' college). But if there's one financial tip that I think every person should follow, it's this one that my father taught me at a very early age. Before you spend, pay yourself 10 percent. Save it. That tip alone—especially if you start early—is your path to financial security. It doesn't matter if your savings start with a small amount because you're twenty-two and in your first job or doing quite well for yourself in your mid-forties. It will help you develop the cushion you'll need for retirement, for emergencies, for giving you the freedom to do what you want most in life. This is a bit of a fluid number based on what you have saved already, of course, and what age you are. And there is ample evidence to suggest that you can and should save more if you can.

For example, a study by the Center for Retirement Research at Boston College looked at the required savings to replace 70 percent of an individual's income at age sixty-five, and found that across all income groups, the required savings rate was 14 percent per year. The percentage varied for different income groups, and one of the biggest factors in the study was the age at which an individual began saving. Individuals who began saving at age twenty-five needed to save 10 percent of their income annually, while those who delayed saving until age forty-five needed to save 27 percent of income in order to replace 70 percent of their income at age sixty-five. But for starters, especially if you're a novice, if there's one thing you can change right now about your life, make it this: save ten cents for every dollar you earn (as for where you should put it, I'll cover that in Chapter 5). If you need just one starting point when it comes to managing your money, this is the biggest change you can make in saving for your future and accumulating wealth.

Sketch out your proper percentages. One of the tricks with writing a financial book is that everybody's situation is different—income, savings, expenses, and so on. It's hard for an advisor like me to prescribe a one-size-fits-all protocol the way a doctor may prescribe 800 milligrams of a certain prescription. There are just too many moving parts to make any two situtations the same. So the best I can do is provide a framework to allow you to plug in the specifics. And one of the first frameworks you should think about is the one that addresses how you allocate your income.

The principle applies whether you make a lot or a little (which is also relative as well). Another factor that influences your budgeting is how much risk you're willing to accept; that varies from person to person and family to family. So take my following recommendation knowing that you should adjust it based on some personal factors. But if I had to outline the ideal way to divvy up your income, it would look like this—to provide a cushion in times of emergency, save for the future, and to allow you to pay your expenses.

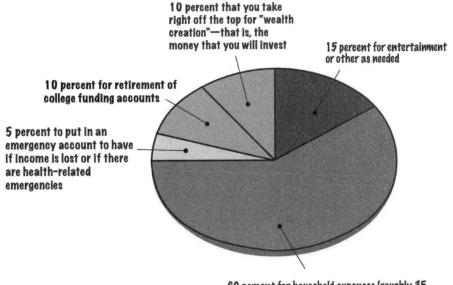

Don't fall prey to the muffin. You like your muffin. You buy your muffin. You eat your muffin. Every day. And every day, your muffin (or latte or doughnut or vending machine snack) is costing you millions. How could that be? It's only a couple of bucks, so what's the big deal? Here's the big deal: if that muffin and coffee costs you $5 a day, that's not just $150 per month on snacks. It's much more than that. If you take that same five bucks—which is really eight or so dollars in pre-taxed earned income—and put it into a retirement account, that muffin a day turns into more than a million bucks after forty years. That's right. When you account for the money invested plus the interest made, that muffin is costing you a million dollars in retirement. So for that much money, those muffins better be diamond flavored. What's my point?

Not to deny you a treat or something you enjoy, but to make sure you ask yourself if that treat is worth it. Is that habit you have—whether it's to decrease stress or give some emotional pick-me-up in the middle of the day—worth what you could save over time? If the answer is yes, then that's fine. But if the answer is no, then you need to start thinking the way a savvy investor would—by taking that same five bucks for a muffin and coffee, investing it for the long term, and watching that money grow. And think about what happens if two of you in the same family have the same habit? That same ten bucks a day over forty years could yield over $800,000 (assuming an average stock market return of 7 percent). I'm pretty sure that when all is said and done, your dream trip to wherever you want when you retire (or even before that) is worth more than those muffins.

I'm not saying that you have to nickel-and-dime everything, but I am saying that you should evaluate all of your expenses and ask if that money is better off working for you, rather than in some corporation's pocket. So can you cut your five bucks a day to two? Or make it a twice-a-week treat instead of every day? Or do you need it at all? Or, can you make a plan to start with a dollar a day for a year, then double it every year for three years? There are lots of ways to make a new habit that has nothing to do with sugar-bombs and everything to do with giving yourself financial security. In any of those cases, you end up making gobs of money over the long term by redirecting those expenses into investments.

The financial lesson here is simple: your money makes money, and makes a lot of money over time. The more you can cut truly frivolous expenses—from the big to the small—the better the likelihood you will gain wealth faster than you ever could have imagined. This holds true whether you're just starting out at an entry-level salary or have a well-established career.

The fact is that no matter your job or your income, you can find a way to take a few bucks a day and invest it this way—meaning that everyone has the potential to become a millionaire. Certainly, you'll make more money the more time you have invested and the more money you make, but let's put it this way: it's never too late to start. And it's never ever too early to start. How about replacing one money spending habit with an investing habit, such as exchanging your daily muffin or favorite coffee drink for a wealthy habit of investing that same money in a personal brokerage or retirement account?

How Much is That Muffin Costing You?	
If you saved the $5 each day, and invested it at 8 percent, you would be able to accumulate the following amounts over the following periods:	
5 years:	$11,218
10 years:	$27,953
25 years:	$145,713
50 years:	$1,222,162

Chapter 2
The Golden Tools

The Faster, Simpler, and Smarter Ways to Make Millions

In a dieting dream world, we could take a magic pill and appear ten, twenty, or fifty pounds lighter. In a career dream world, we could emerge from college with a job that gives us all the power, prestige, and satisfaction we could ever want. In a fairy-tale dream world, we could meet the man or woman of our dreams and every day would be as blissful as the first time we met.

Real life isn't a dream. Everything we do takes some time and commitment to achieve our goals. That goes for everything from losing weight and finding career happiness to working through the ups and downs in our relationships. Does that mean we can't have what we want? Of course not. It just means that our goals usually don't get achieved with a snap, a wish, or a hope. They come with strategy, smarts, compromise, thought, passion, and all of the other things that propel us to get what we want out of life.

Wealth is no different.

Yes, in a dream world, we'd win the lotto, or stumble across a suitcase of gold coins, or dream up the zillion-dollar idea that changes the world. And yes, there are plenty of cases of instant wealth—some achieved by luck, some achieved by inheritance, some achieved by talent or skill. But hundred-dollar bills aren't raining down on most of us, with perhaps the exception of the occasional game-show champion. And we all need to start thinking about wealth goals in the same way we think about other goals, taking smart steps to achieve them.

When you're pursuing any goal, there are plenty of factors that go into whether or not you succeed. But it's pretty standard operating procedure that most goal-seekers utilize the tools of the trade to get them where they want. Olympians may use barbells and stopwatches. Dieters may use calorie calculators and refrigerator locks. Corporate folks may use resumes, headhunters, and two-martini networking lunches. They're all the tools you use to get you where you want to go. When it comes to creating wealth, the same applies: use the tools to help you get where you want to go.

Too often, I've found, people simply don't know (or ignore) the fact that they have so many tools at their disposal to help them create wealth—and the life satisfaction that's part of having wealth. And it's my plea to them: learn the tools, use the tools, and leverage the tools in your favor. With them, you can more quickly achieve the wealth—and happiness—that you want. That's what this chapter is all about, giving you the toolbox that includes the essential utilities you need to get started and keep you going when it comes to creating a wealth system for you and your family.

Must-Have Tools to Unlock the Secrets to Wealth

Look in any tool chest, toolbox, or tool drawer, and you'll see the essentials—the hammer, the screwdrivers, the pliers, and the wrench. They provide the foundation for the box because they're the tools that are used the most often and can handle the most jobs. Versatile, effective, help you solve problems, get the job done.

The same is true for any system of tools; you'll stock the essentials before getting into the more specialized ones (the circular saws and the staple guns can come later). But we're not talking about faulty faucets or the wall that Junior just dented because he thought it would be funny to shot-put a Tonka truck. We're talking about the tools that will help you manage your money. So everybody—no matter your age, stage, income, or expenses—should have a basic set of tools that you use to manage your money. Here are my must-use tools for creating wealth. (Quick note: If you use a professional wealth advisor, that person will often create these for you and with you, but there's nothing saying that you can't create them on your own as well.)

The Stomach Ulcer Index: No, this has nothing to do with how many jalapenos you've inhaled, but rather it's to help you identify how you approach your investment strategies and how much risk you can handle (and yes, we actually call this the Irvin Stomach Ulcer Index in my office). You probably have a pretty good idea of your overall risk threshold... but perhaps not. Are you the kind of person who has taken risks in your life—cruising down a hill on a mountain bike or signing up to skydive, approaching a stranger to ask for his or her number, trying the frog legs on the menu, speaking up to challenge the boss, skinny dipping at midnight at the lake? By nature, you probably already have a sense of whether you fall into the "play it safe" or "what the heck, go for it" category (of course, there are many varying degrees of risk on both sides of that spectrum). But risk is a whole different ball game when we're talking about your money.

So the main question you have to ask yourself before really thinking about your investments is this: How much risk can you handle when it comes to finances? Truth is, most couples that I work with actually have no clue about how to do this or what it really means. That's because risk comes in several different forms (I'll explain those in a moment), and because it's hard to speculate about what you think you can risk until you actually experience it. With some areas of life, it's a lot easier to visualize the risk. You know the potential consequences of driving one hundred miles per hour in a driving rain. But what is the equivalent in finances? And in many cases, the riskier behavior in finances is actually the smarter one. But the risk and reward benefits when it comes to your money might be a little harder to visualize than in other areas of life—and maybe that's one of the reasons why people so blatantly ignore them in the first place.

The risks you take with your investments have many variables, mostly depending on your age, income, and how fast you need access to your investments. What it does is provide a starting point for how aggressive you want your investments to be. Important note, which I'll go back to many times in this book: There's no such thing as low risk and high return. If you want safe investments, you simply won't get as much return as you would with riskier ones. Over the long run, that's fine, because you will make money. Over short periods, it's tougher because you do risk losing your principal, especially if you need periodic access to portions of your nest egg. One recent study found that only 17 percent of respondents were willing to take some risks with their financial investments, while 35 percent said that they were not willing to take financial risk at all.

But the reason why risk is both relative and complex is because there are different kinds of risks you should think about. In the financial field, we generally think in terms of eight major risks, but for our purposes, the main four are:

Principal Risk: This is exactly what it implies. How much risk do you want to accept in the loss of principal over time? That is, do you invest in safer things like bonds or higher-risk areas like stocks and real estate? Over the long haul, the riskier areas will likely provide more return, but you'd have to be able to stomach seeing some of your principal ebb and flow as markets change. Not everybody can handle that—and if they don't have a lot of time until they need access to their assets, it's understandable. But if you start early and understand how the markets spike and dip, it makes sense to invest in higher-risk, higher-return areas.

Interest Rate Risk: So interest rates have been very low; this is a benefit for the government, because it has to pay interest on debt, so it pays for those interest rates to stay low. But when interest rates rise, bond prices fall—meaning that the value of your investment drops. And here, if you have invested in an area that is seemingly safe, but interest rates rise, you may lose principal as well.

Inflation Risk: This is one that many folks don't think about. As costs of living (such as energy, education, and general living costs) rise, what happens when income stays flat and doesn't match that inflation? You end up losing ground in your nest egg and it's hard to keep up with those rising costs. We do know that inflation rates are at about 2 to 3 percent—and that's not including food and energy (which are often not included in inflation statistics). So what does this mean in terms of risk? If costs are rising and your income is not keeping pace, then you're spending more on your lifestyle costs and not able to use as much income for new investments in those important wealth-creation areas.

Volatility Risk: This is the biggie. How much are you willing to stomach when it comes to the highs and lows of investing? The question that financial advisors often ask is, "Do you want to eat well or sleep well?" That is, eating well has nothing to do with a six-ounce sirloin or a lobster tail. It means that you're willing to experience higher levels of volatility to get more investment returns from riskier investments. And sleeping well has nothing to do with down comforters and sweet dreams. It means that you earn relatively little in terms of higher growth but have less relative risk of losing that principal. I would argue that the "sleep well" mentality will eventually catch up to most folks—you'll end up creating less wealth and you have to be willing to accept higher degrees of volatility and some fluctuation in your principal if you want to maximize your potential for income and wealth. But not everyone can handle those dips and losses in their portfolios in the short term, and those ongoing decisions are a challenge we all have to decide for ourselves.

So back to the question. How much risk are you willing to stomach? Do you get those ulcers, not from chili, but when you hear those talking heads on television see dips in the market? Do you panic when your quarterly statement comes back smaller than the month before? Oftentimes, with the clients I work with, it takes up to a year for us to really know the answer—once you see how your investments are working and what keeps you up at night. So keep in mind that this Ulcer Index may change over time, and keep in mind that your Ulcer Index could change based on the state of the markets.

If you try to assess your Ulcer Index during a good time (say, the 1990s), when virtually everything grew, then you may think that you have a high tolerance for risk. If you're measuring your index based on a bad market (say, 2008), that feeling may change. No matter, I do think it's smart to initially assess your willingness to take financial risks. To start, pick a number on the scale below that best describes that willingness when it comes to investing your money. You should do the same for everyone in your family who has a financial stake in the family, primarily your partner. Is this a hard and fast number that you'll be locked into? Of course not, but it's a starting point for discussion with your partner, or if you're by yourself, to help you articulate some of what you want out of your investment strategy.

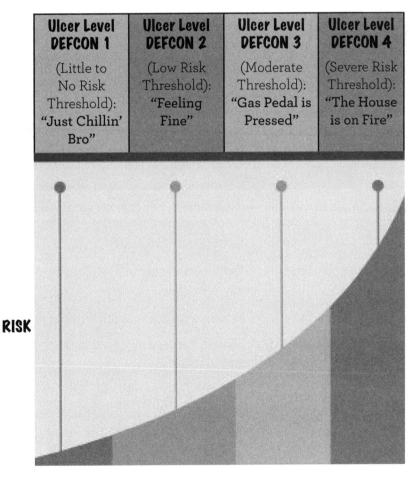

Ulcer Level DEFCON 1	Ulcer Level DEFCON 2	Ulcer Level DEFCON 3	Ulcer Level DEFCON 4
(Little to No Risk Threshold): "Just Chillin' Bro"	(Low Risk Threshold): "Feeling Fine"	(Moderate Threshold): "Gas Pedal is Pressed"	(Severe Risk Threshold): "The House is on Fire"

RISK

RETURN

Can I tell you what the right answer is? Of course not. Because this is your decision, not mine. But I can tell you that whatever number you choose influences how the rest of your financial future plays out, and the most successful people typically fall into DEFCON Levels 3 and 4 (provided they have enough years to let the investments do their work).

Make no mistake. I'm not suggesting that you take your money and throw it into Uncle Charlie's sure-fire idea of turning swampland into a reptile rodeo, and I'm not suggesting that having a high-risk threshold means you ought to invest in the Vegas slot machines. I am suggesting that if you can handle some level of risk in the areas of investment I will be detailing in Chapter 5, then you'll wind up with more money than you probably ever thought was possible.

An Outline of Family Values: Does it seem odder than a three-headed fish that I'm recommending you write down your family values? Perhaps. But when it comes to figuring out how to save, how to invest, and how to spend, family values serve as the thread that holds everything together. So what I'd like you to do is look at the following questions, let the answers simmer, then write them down (yes, I want you to write them down, not just think about them; writing them down is an important part of the process to get you to articulate some of these things that you may not have thought much about).

Question	Sample Answers
What are you saving for?	Retirement, education, vacation...
What do you most like to spend your money on?	Eating out, travel, gadgets...
What most worries you about finances?	Debt, retirement, health, unexpected emergencies...
Where is most of your debt?	Home mortgage, credit card debt, student loan debt...
What are your family's financial strengths?	Shared values among all members, good and stable income
What are your family's financial weaknesses?	Not paying off credit cards in full, not taking full advantage of investments
Briefly describe how you define wealth.	We, as a family, want to have enough wealth to pay for our kids' college educations, live in retirement comfortably, give to charities, and save enough to spend money on experiences that will give us rich memories for our lifetime, such as travel.

This may all seem like it's obvious, because you know what *you* feel. But I can't tell you how many times couples don't agree on some very basic principles, and they go for years or even decades without ever articulating that they have slightly (or sometimes majorly) different priorities when it comes to spending and saving. This exercise in writing down family values gives you a document to refer back to when you're making decisions.

What was your last impulse purchase? For example, perhaps it was a new sound system. You ask yourself if that aligns with your family goals and if the need/desire for a surround-sound system and a sub-woof this-or-that really is enough to trump what you've articulated as being a family priority. A good way to test this process is to ask yourself six months later whether you're happy you bought it or whether you regret it—that will give you some kind of barometer of your purchasing habits. Maybe it is and maybe it isn't something you end up regretting or appreciating; the point is that you have common ground as a talking point when discussing these decisions.

Having this document also allows you to revisit these values as life changes (and yes, life changes—whether it's from job changes or health situations or any number of things that may make you rethink priorities). Most of all, it allows you to do what I outlined in the previous chapter: communicate with each other openly and honestly about finances, something that most families don't do enough.

I truly do believe that if you do not have this statement of family values, you're doomed to failure. When you integrate family values with your pursuit of wealth, you create connections and meaning—and a purpose. That underlying purpose drives your decision making. Above and beyond that, creating this value system—I would argue—means that you can take financial planning away from the stigma of being drudgery and turn it into a vibrant and exciting process, one that helps you feel satisfaction and build relationships.

You should also make sure you can differentiate between a value and a dream. A value is something very specific in terms of what you prioritize in life (and it can be connected to a goal that you have), as in valuing travel or valuing education or whatever it may be. And ideally, these are shared values within the family. If you have that value system, it's much easier to make decisions and settle conflicts because you go back to a shared value system that you've all agreed on (the commercial espresso machine for your home doesn't fit into your value of travel, for example, so maybe you decide that you really don't need it). Dreams, on the other hand, are a little different—they're those things on your bucket list. So they may be things you're striving for, if you have the finances in place to take care of them. Dreams are the answer to the question "What else do you want to accomplish or do?"

One of the most powerful exercises I have my clients do is draw a picture of what retirement looks like—that is, what is their version of financial independence, passion, and freedom. Some may draw a beach or a bigger home or spending time with their families. It's a great way to start the conversation about how your values, goals, and dreams all come together through your financial strategies.

Lifestyle Expense Overview/Budget: I know that budgets sound about as fun as scrubbing grout, but sometimes things have to get a little uncomfortable for you to, well, get comfortable. Consider this fact. A 2014 survey of financial literacy by the National Foundation for Credit Counseling found that 61 percent of American adults admit that they do not have a budget. This is a huge mistake—and I'd argue the reason why so many people are in financial trouble, have financial stress, live beyond their means, have massive debt, or can't achieve their financial goals. They don't know where they stand. So if you don't have a "Lifestyle Expense Overview" already, then you need to make a list of all of your expenses—what they are and how much they cost per month (or quarter, or year, in some cases). Oftentimes, credit card companies will do this by category, and there are plenty of software programs or websites such as Quicken.com or mint.com that will help you itemize your expenses.

The other alternative is for you to gather your receipts, bank statements, and online payment receipts, and create a spreadsheet on which you put all of your expenses into major categories (mortgage, household bills, car payments, gas, education, insurance, kids' supplies, entertainment, travel, etc.). When you add them all up, they, of course, need to be less than your income, but they should also total only 75 percent of your income. (Remember from the previous chapter that the other 25 percent is for retirement/education, an emergency account, and wealth creation.) While there's really no academic research on the ideal budget, many financial pros break it down to a 50/20/30 rule. Fixed costs such as rent or mortgage payments, utilities, and car payments, as well as any other recurring monthly charges should account for no more than 50 percent of take-home pay. Then 20 percent of take-home pay should be allocated to financial goals such as retirement, emergency accounts, and paying down debt. The remaining 30 percent can be allocated to flexible day-to-day expenses like food, shopping, hobbies, and gasoline.

Once you know where you stand, you can make decisions on where you can cut if you need to or even whether you can redirect more money to those investment accounts that will allow you to create more wealth. Your goal should be to hit that 75 percent number. One of my main mantras, and a mantra of every financial guru, is this: pay off those credit cards every month so you don't waste money on non tax deductible interest and avoid the habit of living beyond your means. I'll spend a whole chapter on dealing with debt, but for these purposes, your goal is to set up a budget with those parameters—and then use a tool that will help you stick to that budget. That can come in the form of Quicken, a self-made Excel spreadsheet, or any number of online budgeting tools.

The point is, if you're honest about your expenses and make sure they align with your income, you'll have given yourself perhaps the jackhammer of financial tools, It's powerful, and it's a game-changer when it comes to creating financial security and building your self-confidence. And it's also the place where you can identify any problem you're having. When families get into trouble, the reasons are usually found in the lifestyle expense overview (one person wanting a department store credit card, one person spending too much on a particular hobby, or whatever the case may be). By looking at the expenses, you can find your traps and make adjustments that will get you out of your hole and prevent you from digging a bigger one.

Now, make no mistake, if you don't do this already, it's going to take some time to set up—and it may be painful to discuss if there are cuts to be made. Once you create and list those family values, it's a lot easier to have what might seem to be difficult financial discussions. If something doesn't fit into your values and you can talk about how it doesn't, it's a lot easier to think about trimming that item from your expense list. (Remember my muffin rule, page 22.)

See how this all comes together? Let's say you take a look at your expenses and realize that—oh my gosh—you spend more than $100 a month on ice cream outings with the family. If your family values include health and not wasting money on frivolous things, then maybe you look at that and determine that you really don't need to overdose on butter pecan or mint chocolate chip every few days, and that same hundred bucks can be spent elsewhere. (Keep in mind that $1,200, if invested in something that grows 6 percent a year such as a retirement account, would be worth about $48,000 in twenty years.)

Now what if your kids are growing and they're getting ready to leave home in a few years? Perhaps these ice cream outings are some of the few times when the whole gang gets to spend time together? In this case, these outings may truly be something that nobody can put a price on. My point isn't to judge how you spend your money. My point is for *you* to judge how you spend your money. Your family values greatly influence this lifestyle expense overview and your prorities.

Sample Lifestyle Budget

The following budget is based on national averages.

Category	Percent of Overall Spending
Housing (mortgage/rent, real estate taxes)	24%
Utilities (water, power, garbage collection)	8%
Food	14%
Clothing	4%
Medical/Healthcare	6%
Donations/Gifts to Charity	4%
Savings and Insurance	9%
Entertainment and Recreation	5%
Transportation (car payments, gas, service)	14%
Personal/Debt Payments/Misc.	12%

Source: Leavedebtbehind.com

A Financial Plan: The three tools I just outlined are really just the warm-ups for the main act: the financial plan. Those previous things help get you started talking and thinking about your whole financial picture, but the financial plan is the living, breathing document that hopefully puts it all together.

Advisors often put one together for their clients, and the document includes everything from the investment portfolio to the long-term projections of income earned based on those investments. Basically, it acts as the car manual for your money—it's got everything in it about your current financial status and your financial future. The professional ones look slick, glossy, and cool (think lots of charts and graphs). They can serve a wonderful purpose of helping the clients visualize where their money is and where it's going. But you don't need all the bells and whistles of a professionally made plan (unless you prefer that way); you can do it yourself.

Here's how I would advise my clients to create one for themselves by including these things. You can do it in a simple Word document and import your own charts and graphs, or, if you're more technologically savvy, there are plenty of other programs that can make it look fancier.

Statement of Family Values	You can take this right from the statement you created.
Annual Goals/ Priorities	These are often good to revisit once a year, especially because life does change and your situation may change.
Life Goals/ Priorities	Broad picture of what you're saving for, what you want out of your wealth, perhaps even a tangible number for what you want your retirement account to have and by what age.
Income	List all non-investment-related income from jobs or other areas.
Income Needs	Do you need your accounts to create income for the short term or the long term? And what level of risk are you willing to assume?
Snapshot of Budget	You don't need to import the nitty-gritty of your whole budget, but it's a good idea to include a chart or graph of your typical yearly expenses and how you allocate your income to them.

Listing of Retirement/ Education Accounts	Simply list all of your accounts (such as IRAs, 401(k)s, 403(b)s, 529 plans, state pre-paid college accounts, etc.) and their balance at the beginning of the year. You can add columns to them each year, so you can see their growth from year to year.
Listing of All Investment Accounts	Same as above, but do it with all stocks, bonds, and other investments. List whether they're growth oriented (high returns over the long term) or income oriented (designed to pay you money in the present but don't have higher rates of return).
Listing of Other Assets	Include a list of real estate properties, fine art, antiques, or other assets that have significant value.

So what's the point of having a plan like this all in one place? Foremost, it allows you to see the data, track the progress, and analyze the comprehensive picture. You can see where things are working and where they're not, or if some accounts are or aren't properly aligned with that Ulcer Index I explained a few pages ago. You don't need to spend a ton of time with the plan (though it may take a few hours or a weekend to create it). But it's a good idea to revisit it quarterly or annually at minimum.

I will also say this: If you don't have a plan, that's when things fall apart. A plan forces you to look in the mirror and see how your income, expenses, and investments all merge together. It allows you to identify problems and opportunities so you can work on both ends of the wealth picture (reducing unnecessary expenses and having your money make you money). You can then attain everything you want in life.

Picture This: A Total Family Profile to Make Wealth

I'm guessing that the last thing you'd expect to see in a book like this is me telling you to break out the colored pencils or markers and a whole bunch of blank paper ("You think this is kindergarten, Irvin?"). However, I do think that part of unlocking your preconceived notions and stress about money and your finances is to open your mind. And there's no better way to do that than by unleashing your artistic side (even if you don't think you have one). I'm not suggesting you try to Picasso up a portrait of a stack of dollar bills (although I won't hold it against you if you do). What I do want you to do is to draw what's called a mind map.

A mind map is essentially a diagram used to visually illustrate a data set or block of information. In this instance, we are going to use it as a visual approach to assessing all of the different financially related data in your life. The gist of it is this: Take a central theme. Write it down in the center of a piece of paper, then use spokes to add sub-themes. Then you can create additional sub-themes that map back to the primary themes you selected.

So as an example that has nothing to do with money, let's say you're trying to concoct a new recipe with chicken and are looking for a little inspiration. You'd put chicken as the central hub on your mind map. Coming off the word chicken, you'd write things like "spicy," "crunchy," or "grilled"—whatever came to mind. Then take "spicy" and create words from there—"jalapeno," "salsa," or "pepper."

Pretty soon, your paper would be filled with all kinds of words, ideas, and inspiration. Doodle in drawings too. It really is a piece of word art. Now, when you've filled in many different areas and words, you can look at that paper, see things across different hubs and spokes, and then create a chicken dish that you may never have dreamed up if you just sat at the table and tried to use your brain alone. It's an exercise in creativity, brainstorming, and unlocking parts of your mind that you may not typically use, but when it applies to your financial life, it's more than that. It helps you think about strategy in new ways.

Why does it work? Well, I like it because I think many of us are visual learners (one of the reasons why we have illustrations throughout the book). And I also like it because it helps you design your goals, see context, and think about your financial matters in a way that's different from how you have before. The advantage to creating a mind map is that it makes your goals and your information a little easier to recall and to think about—and really to strategize about. So when you take a topic that can be really confusing and lay it out visually, you've broken down one of the barriers that may be holding you back. It simplifies things and allows your mind to think in new and creative ways.

My friend Rob O'Dell, an accomplished financial advisor, introduced the concept of the mind map as it relates to finances by explaining how you could use the technique for all of your financial documents and to help you strategize. He argues that because it uses both analytic and artistic skills, it engages your brain more fully, which allows you to be more productive. And then ultimately more successful. So, let's take a look as to how it works with your financial plan.

See all the things I listed above as being part of your financial plan? You can take those elements and create that central hub with spokes coming out of it. Put your name and family values in the center—and then have all the other items spring from it. But the beauty of the map is that you can then have each of those things serve as a hub. So your investments hub can have spokes coming out of it that deal with all of your investments (from your long-term retirement accounts to your stock portfolio). And then you can take your stock portfolio and make that a hub, with spokes coming from that for all the different stocks you have. See how it just expands and allows you to see the global picture in one (or a few) pages?

Here is an example of how I like to use mind maps and what they might look like:

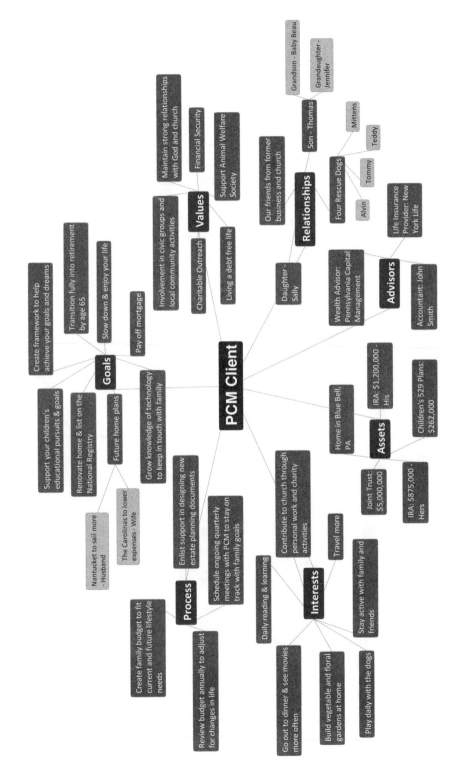

CEG Worldwide 2017

Before you start with your financial plan, I'll give you an exercise to just see how it works. Take a piece of paper and write in the center the word "Expenses." Now think of all of the things you spend money on. Take one or two of those words and think of three or four words for ways that you could save money on that particular expense and write them around that word. When you're done, take a look at your map. Did anything inspire you or give you something to think about? In just a few minutes, I suspect, you may have come up with some words that gave you something to think about—and perhaps even a tangible thing to act upon right now.

Now think about what happens if you apply that to many different areas of your financial life? That's right. So much potential. Is a mind map necessary in the way a budget is? Of course. You'll never know what you'll find out about yourself and what you can do about creating wealth without it. And really that's the whole point of the mind map anyway. It's not a working document, it's not law, and it's not your official plan. It's a way to think differently, to see differently, to create differently.

Cool Tools for Fine-Tuning Your Finances

Mint: An online budgeting tool, Mint connects to your banking and other accounts to help organize and categorize spending and income. Their tool will allow you to set budgets for various categories of spending, and will notify you when you have exceeded the budgeted amounts. They also offer a number of charts and graphs to monitor spending over time. https://www.mint.com/

Robo-Portfolio Platforms (WealthFront, Betterment, SigFig, Personal Capital, etc.): A growing presence in the investment world, these web-based investment platforms develop portfolios based on a client's risk tolerance, which is established by completing a questionnaire. They then offer to manage the portfolio, generally composed of index funds, for a percentage of assets charged each year. https://www.wealthfront.com/, https://www.betterment.com/, https://www.sigfig.com/, https://www.personalcapital.com/

TurboTax: Many people who do their own taxes turn to TurboTax, the best-selling tax software in the United States. They attempt to simplify the tax filing process by asking a series of questions about your finances, and have the ability to auto-import W-2 data for a number of companies. TurboTax has a variety of solutions available depending on the complexity of your tax return at varying price levels. https://turbotax.intuit.com/

LegalZoom: For individuals who need estate planning documents such as wills, trusts, or power of attorney (both medical and financial), LegalZoom offers a number of solutions. For a flat fee, they will ask questions about your specific situation and prepare documents based on the laws of the state in which you reside. http://www.legalzoom.com/

LearnVest: LearnVest offers financial planning services for a monthly fee, as well as some free do-it-yourself tools to track spending. Depending on the level of service you select, they will help with issues such as budgeting, developing spending and goal plans, reviewing your insurance and estate planning needs, and creating investment strategies. https://www.learnvest.com/

ReadyForZero: A debt management tool, ReadyForZero allows you to track your debts by linking credit accounts, develop a plan for paying off debt, and monitor your progress. They also allow you to set reminders for upcoming payments. For a fee, you can also get access to your credit score on a monthly basis and other added features. https://www.readyforzero.com/

AnnualCreditReport: The only site that is directed by federal law to provide free credit reports, this site allows you to obtain reports from all three of the major credit reporting bureaus (Experian, TransUnion, and EquiFax) once every twelve months. This can be valuable for people seeking to monitor their credit. https://www.annualcreditreport.com/

CreditKarma: CreditKarma is a newer, ad-supported site that provides access to an individual's credit score for free. They also offer tools to track debt, and will give recommendations for ways to manage your debts more effectively. https://www.creditkarma.com/

ShoeBoxed: For people drowning in receipts, ShoeBoxed offers the ability to scan and archive your receipts digitally. They also offer services for people who travel for business, including GPS-based mileage tracking, the ability to scan business cards, and creating expense reports based on receipt data. https://www.shoeboxed.com/

Sample Budget

Income: $100,000

Family: Married Couple with two children both under age 17

			$			$			
		Income	$	100,000					
					Standard Deduction		$	24,000	
		Taxable Income (Income Tax)	$	76,000					
		FICA Taxes	$	7,650					
		Federal Income Taxes	$	4,739	*assumes child tax credit of $2,000 per qualifying child				
		State Income Tax	$	1,900	*assumes 2.5% income rate on taxable income				
	15%	Total taxes	$	14,289					
		After Tax Income	$	85,711					
	10%	Retirement Account Contributions	$	8,571					
	10%	Personal Savings	$	8,571					
	5%	Emergency Account	$	4,286					
25%		Total Savings	$	21,428					
	18%	Mortgage (Principal and Interest)	$	15,428	*assumes $240,000 mortgage, 30 year fixed rate at 5%				
	5%	Property Tax	$	4,286	*assumes $310,000 home value at 1.38% tax rate (US average)				
	1%	Homeowner's Insurance	$	857					
	6%	Utilities	$	5,143					
	2%	Home Repairs	$	1,714					
32%		Total Housing Expenses	$	27,428					
	6%	Car Payment	$	5,400	*assumes $450/month				
	2%	Gasoline	$	1,500	*15,000 miles per/ 25mpg/ $2.50/ gallon				
	2%	Auto Insurance	$	1,800					
10%		Total Auto Expenses	$	8,700					
	10%	Food	$	8,571					
	2%	Clothing	$	1,714					
	2%	Recreation/Entertainment	$	1,714					
	1%	Cell Phone	$	857					
	4%	Travel	$	3,428					
	3%	Other Expenses	$	2,571					
22%		Total Personal Expenses	$	18,856					
	6%	Medical/Dental	$	5,100					
6%		Total Medical/Dental	$	5,100					
	5%	Charity	$	4,200					
5%		Total Charity	$	4,200					
100%		TOTAL OUTFLOWS	$	100,000					

** Subject to Change

Chapter 3
Honey Money

Creating Your Own Dream Team of Wealth Starts at Home

There are some things in life that are better done solo. Like reading. Maybe meditating. Definitely using the restroom.

But in virtually all facets of life, the best approach is a team one. We see it in health and medicine: you have a general doctor for most things, but you may also have an eye doctor, a private-parts doctor, and a surgeon if you need one. We see it in the workplace: there are big bosses, middle managers, worker bees, and interns. We see it in sports: athletes, coaches, and trainers.

We see this kind of team philosophy everywhere, so much so that it's simply assumed that your life revolves around all kinds of group structures and units, from your personal to your professional life. Work as a team, assume different roles, and achieve the objective in the best possible way. Why? Because not only is there power in numbers, but also because a team allows specialists to contribute their expertise to the greater whole. It's how we do just about everything.

Except finance and wealth.

When it comes to money matters, many of us squirrel away in a hole—not wanting to talk about them, think about them, or strategize about them. Many of us consider finances more private than our sex lives, and for good reason, because your financial situation is nobody else's business. But that mentality also causes a problem: private doesn't mean solo.

See the difference? It's fine to be private, because nobody needs you announcing your 401(k) balance on the street corner every quarter. But actually doing everything by yourself is one of the biggest mistakes you can make.

And I will also tell you this: this mistake really lies at the root of nearly all financial troubles I see when it comes to couples and families. Team starts at home, and very few of us actually think about our spouse or partner as part of the team. So if there's one thing I can get across about stabilizing and improving your financial situation, it's that if you are going to begin to create a so-called wealth team, you must first start at home. And only then will you better equipped to add more members to the team.

This chapter is all about trying to create the team of people who can help you achieve your financial—and life—goals of creating wealth and happiness. Most importantly, they can help you reform bad habits to create the new habits that I outlined in the previous chapter.

After all, when you have a great team in place, you're not only more likely to win whatever it is you're trying to achieve, but you're also more likely to have a lot of fun while doing so.

MVP: Most Valuable Partner

You talk politics and the weather. You recap last night's episode of *Homeland*. You laugh and clap and coo together when Junior takes a first step or says "Mama" for the first time. You cuddle, snuggle, and do all kinds of other verbs in the privacy of your own home. You're together. You're partners. You share life's ups and downs, and you do your best to find as many ups as you can—and weather the downs. But the one thing that so many of us won't do as couples is talk money. Oh, we fight about money. We disagree about money, and we huff and puff about who spent way too much on that piece of jewelry or power tool.

According to a study conducted by American Express, 30 percent of couples say money causes the most stress in their relationship, more than intimacy issues (11 percent), children (9 percent) and in-laws (4 percent) combined. And a survey by the American Institute of CPAs found that on average, married adults argue about financial matters three times per month. Among those aged forty-five to fifty-four, the average number of arguments was four per month. And National Marriage Project data shows that couples who argue about finances at least once a week were 30 percent more likely to get divorced. Why is this so? I believe it's because very few couples have learned to talk about money, stripped of its emotion and empowered with pragmatism.

Assuming you're in a relationship—whether you're not yet married (see sidebar, page 50) or have been so for decades—this is the one thing that most of us can do a better job of: making finance a team sport in the family. Share goals and information (not necessarily advice). When you can have frank and honest discussions, articulate goals, and work together to solve (or compromise) on financial issues, not only does your wealth improve, but so does your relationship—and your overall life satisfaction. Especially when you get started, there may be some uncomfortable moments and disagreements, but that's okay. Finances can be messy at times. The point isn't that you're trying to avoid conflict; it's that you're trying to talk about it to improve your chances of solving the conflict efficiently and wisely. Here's how to best approach the situation, no matter what stage of your relationship you're in:

Acknowledge Differences: Too often, we assume that if we're together, we share the same values. And while that may be true in a lot of areas (whether it be religious, political, or moral issues), there's usually more diffrences when it comes to financial backgrounds and priorities. I've seen it so many times. People forget that their partners come from different upbringings with different family values and financial approaches. One person may come from a family in which one partner handled all the finances, while the other may come from a family in which his-and-her finances were kept separately. Or perhaps there were differences in spending habits—one family spent at will, while the other family saved every last dime and didn't spend money on anything that wasn't absolutely necessary. Neither side of the spectrum is wrong per se. The point is that they're different, so we all come into relationships with different experiences, values, habits, and backgrounds. And we can't assume that we all think about money in the same way.

These backgrounds and foundational financial habits need to be acknowledged, and then you need to acknowledge that differences are okay (assuming that they are okay and not deal-breakers in the relationship). Once you talk about financial values and goals, you should also talk about what each other agrees with and disagrees with in terms of those financial values. If someone's family was uber-frugal growing up, does that mean the person will be the exact opposite when they become an adult? Or the same? Again, there's no right or wrong; it's just the process of laying it out all on the table. Information is one of our greatest allies, so be open about exchanging it (that is, presuming this is someone you're in a long-term relationship with).

A funny thing happens when a couple comes in to me for advice and guidance. I ask many deep and meaningful family priority questions, and while they should be interviewing me about my capabilities and services, they actually find out a lot about each other—because it's very often the first time they've actually talked about finances together in a meaningful way. As couples, we're used to relating to each other interpersonally, sexually, as fathers and mothers, professionally, and in all kinds of ways, but I'm stunned—time and time again—by how many spouses overlook each other when it comes to the talents, creativity, and ideas they have in the finance field. I don't care if you've been together for a few months or a few decades, you probably could stand to get to know each other a little better when it comes to what you think about wealth.

Quiz: What's the best place to have a discussion about finances with your partner?

a. In the bedroom after sex when you're both feeling connected

b. At the kitchen table

c. On a long walk in the park

d. At a romantic candlelight dinner

e. During the commercials of *The Voice*

Well, the real correct answer is "anywhere that you'll have it," so technically all could be correct. But if you ask me, the best answer is B—at the kitchen table. Why? You want some level of both seriousness and informality, and the kitchen table is usually a good place to strike that balance. You want to have license to get as granular and practical as you need to every given month, so romantic spots may not be the ideal environment. And a nice walk in the park might be good for talking about dreams and goals, but the best bang for the buck, in my opinion, is a place that allows you to be comfortable but get the job done.

Hold Monthly Money Meetings: Sounds a little goofy to the families that don't do this, perhaps. But this strategy is one of the most effective things you can do to improve your financial situation—and make the most of it. In this meeting, you should discuss income, expenses, goals, and financial priorities—and help each other keep on track with what was discussed at the previous meeting. This accountability works and helps you avoid conflicts, because there are no surprises. Does that mean you have to agree on everything? Of course not. And that doesn't mean that you have to have an equal-responsibility assignment. If one person loves finances and the other hates it, that's fine, but that doesn't mean you should avoid doing a spot check once a month.

The point is that you have a regular forum to talk about all things pertaining to your wealth, big and small. You can also outline responsibilities, divvy up who's in charge of what, and try to anticipate any roadblocks that may come up. This is something you would absolutely do if you were running a business, so why not do it while mutually running a household? Again, your goal is to strip away some of the tension associated with the secrecy of family finances and deal with it practically. What makes sense? What's best for the long term? See, this is why the previous point is so important—to make sure that your values are similar enough to avoid conflicts long term.

If you're at completely opposite ends of your life and financial priorities, that very well could mean you have problems that are much tougher to solve, whether they come up now or in the future. You'll never reach that common ground when financial conflict comes up because something is off at the core—what you believe in, what you want to invest in, what you value.

Keep the Big Goals in Mind: Too often, couples get into silly fights about money. Do I mean that the fight is silly? No, because if you have a disagreement, it's best to talk it through. What I mean is that too much energy is spent on arguing over little things, little items, little purchases, rather than really thinking through what the whole point is—to dream big. That is, will you and your partner have created enough security and cushion to allow yourself to enjoy life?

Remember, our most valuable asset is time, and the older we get, the faster life travels. So wasting our time on little arguments not only leads to major stress and sources of contention but also takes your eye off what's really important. So in any financial discussion you have (once a month, at least!), you should start by rearticulating the big goal: create wealth not to buy possessions, but to create happiness, whether that comes in the form of stuff, or trips, or quiet time, or earlier retirement, or whatever it is that you and your partner value most. When you lay out the big picture, it's much easier to agree on the smaller points.

The Support Crew: Specialists as Needed

Our world is filled with all kinds of systems of support. The neck supports the head. The concrete foundation supports the house. The pit crew supports the driver. Your kids seemingly single-handedly support Instagram and Snapchat. And that's the way you should view the rest of your financial dream team—as support for the goals of you and your family.

Now, let's be clear. Not everyone will have or be able to afford some of these pieces of the team, so it may take some time before you consider adding them. What I want to do is give you the options, the plusses and minuses of adding such folks to your financial team. All of these people can serve important roles and contribute to your level of wealth, decrease your stress levels, and help you achieve your family goals. The reason why: they're specialists, and they know the nuances of their trade better than you. They're often better equipped to directly help you make decisions that will either increase your income or save you money, even if their services cost you some money upfront or during the process.

The way I like to look at the team is as a wagon wheel. You're the hub and each of the spokes represents a specialist. They're united by you—the hub in the center—and they all come together to work toward your goals. So no matter what members of your team you add, you always have to remember that everything should revolve around your goals. Above all, the main advantage to adding team members is that they can act as your third-party advocates in a variety of situations. They're devoid of the emotion, and they can navigate the complexities that come with financial and legal issues. Many times, that is a service that's worth paying for. But yes, you do have to be smart, and perhaps you're in a situation where you don't need that extra team member. This section will help you figure out who you can add to your team and the best reasons for doing so. (To see best questions to ask when trying to identify members of your team, see sidebar on page 51.)

Personal Wealth Advisor: Outside your family, this will be the most important person (or group of people) you'll deal with when it comes to your wealth—namely because they're the Swiss Army knife of advisor in that they can (and should) do a lot of things well. While some of the other members of your team (see below) have very specific roles and responsibilities, your personal wealth advisor, or PWA, should be able to not only know the ins and outs of laws and investments and things of that nature, but they also need to be creative and think outside the box too. Right brain and left brain wrapped into one advisor. That's because you not only want someone who can handle specific questions and tasks, but someone who also treats money a little bit like an art, finding solutions others may not have thought about. Think of your PWA as the quarterback of your team. You trust that person to make good decisions and lead your family down the field (but you're still the coach, and the quarterback should operate under your preferred system).

So what should your PWA be able to do? Track your progress including gains and losses, advise on the best investments given your goals and assets, understand changing tax laws, make recommendations about tax minimization strategies and trusts (one of the ways to help protect your assets. I'll discuss more on this topic on page 121.), help advise on financial matters involving family situations such as health or divorce issues, advise on charitable donations, manage cash flow coming in from investments, set up "having fun" funds, and so much more (for example, I negotiate major purchases on behalf of my clients; I'll show you how you can too, on page 96).

Depending on your assets, you should expect to talk or meet with your PWA as you need them, typically monthly or quarterly (remember, communication and confronting problems and challenges head on has to be a priority both inside the family and when you involve your whole team).

Not everyone will be able to afford a PWA, depending on what stage of life and financial health you're in, though they're probably not as expensive as you may think (and the return on that investment can make it well worth it). Once you establish some baseline assets, it is smart to include this person on your team—because you will end up saving money and making money in the long run. Typically, PWAs collect fees based on a percentage of your assets. This generally works out well for both the client and the advisor; for example, if the advisor is able to make significantly more on investments than you would do on your own, that's a win for you the client, and the advisor makes his or her money based on that amount. Some advisors do charge by the hour or by an annual fee.

Here's another reason to look into a wealth advisor: preparing for an emergency. I have one couple as a client—he's a corporate attorney and she's been a stay-at-home wife for many years. He handled all of the finances in their marriage (though he had an advisor to assist, because he needed some help for asset allocation and in other areas). He made enough money to establish trusts for his kids (he had more than $5 million saved up). Sadly, he developed Alzheimer's, and his wife had to learn to handle the finances, his care, and other areas that she wasn't used to. Our firm was able to help with all of those responsibilities and the complexities of their financial picture without missing a beat, because we've been involved with the couple for many years. Nobody wants to encounter those types of situations, but having a trusted advocate who knows the ins and outs of your family and finances can help relieve some of the burden that comes from difficult health (or life) situations.

Accountant: Many young people operating on shoestring budgets can file their taxes with inexpensive DIY-type programs like TurboTax. So you may not need an accountant, but as your assets become more complicated—involving not just income, but also investments, expenses to write off as deductions, and many other factors, it's smart to bring in a professional to handle your tax documents. You'll typically want a certified public accountant who is well versed in current tax laws; this person may also be able to offer advice on deductions that you never thought of and on times you should invest in qualified retirement accounts, which will help you save for the future without a heavy tax burden.

Many accountants are backward looking (i.e., the client gives them W-2s and 1099s, and out comes a tax return). Ideally, the accountant is working with a PWA to minimize the costs and impact of taxes for you and your family.

Lawyer: Confession: I used to be wary of dealing with lawyers. I thought they were often very expensive. But I've changed my mind. At times when you need a lawyer to handle a specific situation, that person is worth his or her weight in gold. Especially

Question: What if we're not married yet?

Answer: Then absolutely sit down and have a convo about the cashola. Talk about values and goals, and talk about how you'd budget, what you want to spend money on, and all of that good stuff. You can disagree, of course, but if you are so far apart about values and approaches to money, it should give some pause. Maybe we could decrease the 50 percent divorce rate if we had these conversations before marriage, rather than in the thick of a crisis or conflict. Just as you'll likely talk about family plans, dream vacations, religious ideals, and where you want to live, you need to have a meaningful discussion about money.

if you've amassed some wealth, you'll want to find an attorney who knows how to handle various issues, especially when it comes to protecting your assets in trusts (that is, if you're sued, creditors can go after all of your assets, but lawyers can advise you on how to best protect those assets). I also think lawyers should be consulted when dealing with your PWA, because it's often your lawyer who will be able to advise on such things as what type of ownership and registration should be used on an investment (such as a joint account with a spouse or grown child, and what techniques can be used to have some flexibility on the management or taxation of those accounts).

Another thing that lawyers can really assist with is helping the financial head of the family make decisions about distributing assets—to protect children from not only each other but also from themselves. For example, a lawyer can help set up a trust in which a grown child retains some control and becomes a co-trustee at age twenty-five and then gains increasingly more control as he or she grows older, as opposed to just unleashing the entire trust on a kid, who may make poor and whimsical financial decisions at a younger age.

And, of course, a lawyer can help set up all of the vital financial documents needed, including wills, trusts, codicils, and any other directives you need for your family. As I said, I do think it's really important that your lawyer and PWA work hand-in-hand so that everyone is communicating and working toward common goals.

Others: There are also some people you may need at various points in your life. For example, I think it's wise to have a mortgage broker that you work with on your property purchases and refinancings. A good broker will help you get lower interest rates on your mortgage. But better yet, he or she will be able to advise you about refinancing your mortgage or mortgages when rates come down, because if you can get a lower rate over the long term, you'll save money (money that you can then invest and make more wealth from it). You also want to develop professional relationships with insurance pros, personal bankers, and successor trustees (someone who will manage your estate when you die).

Sleuth or Consequence: The Best Questions to Ask the Experts

The minute you decide to add members to your team, you're going to want to treat the process of finding those members with the same standards you would if you were interviewing someone for a job. Because that's what you are doing! Don't just take the first recommendation, and don't just sign on to the first person you meet because they have a good bedside manner. Do your due diligence on the front end to pay dividends on the back end. Whether you're interviewing an accountant or lawyer, you should go through the same basic process. Here are the guidelines:

➤ Get referrals. Personal referrals from people you trust are the best ways to get your starter list of the people you want to consider.

➤ Ask about level of experience, certifications, college education, and membership in professional organizations. Once you get those credentials, you can research them online to determine their credibility.

➤ Ask if they do continuing education. If so, it's a sign that they stay atop of a very changing and dynamic field and aren't stuck on the way they did things five, ten, or fifty years ago.

➤ Ask if they consult with others. Your instinct may be to want someone who doesn't consult with others—someone confident enough to know it all. But actually, I prefer if someone says, "Hey, I don't know everything, but I know people who know something about every area we're going to deal with." In a way, this extends your team even more—and it can be an incredibly valuable asset.

➤ Ask them for referrals. They should be able to provide you a list of folks (who aren't their cousins) who can vouch for their expertise. Is that list stacked, in that they're going to give you only people who would say positive things? Of course, but you can still ask those people tough questions, like if there was ever a time they regretted hiring so-and-so, or if they ever felt there was a time they wanted to change service providers.

➤ Ask yourself how they project to the outside world. Are they polished and professional? I don't want to say that appearance should be a huge factor, but we all want professional people—maybe not only for dealing with us, but for how they'll deal with others on our behalf. Your gut is a good guide. Follow it.

➤ Ask this doozy: "How do you create a wonderful client experience?" If they don't know how to answer it, you're probably in trouble. And if they do, at least they've given it some thought—and the answer will give you some fodder to think about and follow-up with.

➤ Ask about fees, both upfront and hidden. Of course, this has to be a major consideration. And you should know not only the fees but also what you're getting for those fees, in order to make a fair assessment of that person or company.

Interviewing a Wealth Advisor

If you're in the market for a wealth advisor, that person will likely ask you lots of questions about your financial situation—to provide you an overview or report in their goals and vision for how you can build your wealth. But before you jump in with the first advisor you meet with, you should do your own homework about that person or firm. Some things to ask directly:

1) *The Fee Structure:* Do they charge a percentage of your assets to manage them or is there a set annual fee or hourly rate?

2) *Credentials:* No matter their background (advisors come from all walks of the financial arena), you want to make sure the firm offers qualified and knowledgeable Certified Financial Planners (CFP) or Chartered Financial Analysts (CFA).

You want a professional who delegates a majority of the work to team members.

3) *Services:* Does the firm focus mostly on comprehensive wealth management services including financial planning or just sell products?

4) *The Plan:* Ask for a sample plan and what kind of software is used. You'll see how thorough and clear a plan can look—and if it meshes with your own personality and helps you understand your situation the best.

5) *Interaction/Contact Intervals:* What's the typical amount of contact they'll have with you—and will you be handled by that one person or a team of professionals?

Take a look at the inset to the left and decide whether you think it is a fact or a myth. The answer is . . . FACT! Surprised you, huh? Here's the reason. Sometimes, the best of the best are really expensive to hire—so much so that it's out of your price range. But if they delegate some of their support work to other people in their company (at a lower per-hour fee than the head honcho), your overall price comes down. The elite person may be available for the crucial decisions, answering tough questions, and things of that nature, but you end up not having to pay as much as you might for a solo practitioner who has to do every single aspect of the job, where the price goes way up.

I use this tactic a lot—hiring people who are specialists in their fields, but who can offer discounted work because I only use that person's work when it's absolutely necessary and more run-of-the-mill work can be billed at a lower cost. So go ahead and ask a potential team member if they "delegate down," which allows you to get high-end service at a lower price. That's a good situation, because remember, you may also not want the cheapest of the cheap, because that may mean inferior quality. This tactic allows you to strike a balance between high-end talent and middle-of-the-road costs.

Chapter 4
A Million-Dollar Body

To Have True Wealth, Your Priority Should Be Optimum Health

I'm going to take a wild guess here. You may be looking at this chapter—a chapter about health—and thinking, *Hmmm, this belongs in a finance book as much as a snow shovel belongs in Florida.* In a way, you'd be right. Why am I qualified to talk about health, nutrition, and exercise the way a doctor would? I'm not. But as someone who has experienced thirty years of war stories from clients, I see the truth day in and day out: stress (self-generated worry and responses to financial problems) and poor health can ruin lives—not just through the most obvious means, but also in so many ancillary ways, ranging from damaging relationships to destroying wealth.

That's why I believe I'm in a position to help you understand that wealth and health influence each other in a yin-yang kind of way. I don't have a prescription pad or a medical degree or any kind of stethoscope to gauge how well your anatomical ticker can handle the stock ticker. Still, I believe that I am qualified to take the position that many financial advisors won't—that is, your health is as much of a contributor to your wealth as is your investment portfolio.

How so? For starters, I hope you have learned my main thesis by now: that wealth is far more than the money in your bank or investment account. It's also your quality of life and how much you're able to enjoy and revel in the things you love, using the money that you've earned. Wealth—as I define it—is as much about having quality time and making the time to enjoy it as it is about having quality capital gains. And that's not even mentioning the fact that staying healthy allows you to do more, avoid medical expenses, and save time managing chronic diseases. The freedom you get from this—time-wise and money-wise—is enormous.

If you get one thing out of this book, or at least this chapter, I hope it's this: you've missed the boat if you find yourself, at fifty-five or sixty years old, with all the money in the world but hampered by heart disease, diabetes, high blood pressure, or other conditions that you may have been able to prevent. Just in the way that money can't buy happiness, it can't buy you a well-functioning body either. A stockpile of cash with a stockpile of health issues isn't what we're after.

If, however, you find yourself in the position of having money *and* health, then you've figured out what matters. You can live life and bathe in all the goodness it has to offer. With security. With strength. With satisfaction. Anything less would mean you have missed the point on what it means to create wealth.

All it takes to get this point is to think about your dreams, your desires, and the extraordinary things you want out of life. Maybe it's taking a dream safari, or staring a new hobby, or spending quality time with your grandkids who may live a plane ride away, or taking a chance and starting the business of your dreams. And let's assume that you've built the wealth to do the things that you want. That's great. But how are those dreams affected if you have trouble walking around for more than a few minutes at a time, or if you don't have the energy to travel across the globe or work long days in a dream job, or your body simply can't keep up with those dreams? That's right. Money can't make it all better. That's why I'm so passionate about trying to help people see that you must concentrate on both aspects of your life, and when you do—not to get all Disney on you—magical things can happen.

Remember what my friend Dr. Oz said: health and wealth are joined at the hip in so many ways. The connection is real, and it is powerful. For example, the American Psychological Association study of stress found that 75 percent of Americans cited money as a significant source of stress; other money-related issues were also stress-inducers, such as the economy which stressed 67 percent and job stability and housing costs which caused stress responses or stress-like responses for 49 percent of Americans. Chronic stress has been linked to both short-term ailments (irritability, fatigue, headaches) and more serious long-term diseases.

I didn't always understand this. When I turned forty, I almost felt embarrassed that I had reached the age, and I didn't want to tell anyone. I wanted to keep it a secret that I was getting older. But when I turned fifty, things changed. With age, I grew to appreciate the importance of maintaining my health. I wanted to tell the world that I hadn't felt this good in years. I realized that I had to make health a priority—not just for myself, but also to help teach my kids about the importance of health in their lives as they grow up.

In this chapter, I'm going to outline the five most important principles I think you must embrace when it comes to getting healthy, using my own life as an example, as well as some of the information that is recommended by the respected medical establishment. It's not meant to substitute for the advice of healthcare pros, but there are some overriding themes that you should consider as you embark on your wealth-creating journey. After all—and I'll be blunt—your pile of money will be useful for your heirs, but wouldn't it be better if you could enjoy a good chunk of it with them?

I want nothing more than for all of you to have sufficient financial gain so you can live with the more holistic definition of wealth that I use. And I do know that one part of that equation is about the foods you eat, the care you have for your body, the communication you're able to have with your partner, and all of the things that influence your physical and mental health. Here, my six main areas that you should attack as part of any personal wealth plan.

Put Yourself Under the Microscope

Remember I talked about how finance is one of those personal things that we're so afraid to talk about? It feels like it's more taboo that an eyelid tattoo. That sort of privacy is the source of a lot of conflict within families. Because spouses aren't honest about what their finances are and what their priorities are, they tend to hide, ignore, and shy away from the truth—and then conflict builds and builds until there's a financial crisis. Same holds true for our health. When we know we're in a little trouble (say our pants aren't quite fitting, or we took a look at the blood pressure and the numbers nearly broke the machine), we try to hide and ignore the clues that things aren't going well. We shy away rather than confront them head on. That's the worst thing you can do.

When I turned fifty, I took the advice of a fellow CEO with whom I was taking a program called Strategic Coach. He suggested I get a full-scale, head-to-toe health evaluation to grasp fully what was going on inside my body. I decided on the Cooper Clinic in Dallas, and I was amazed at how successfully it worked. I was tested, prodded, poked, evaluated, measured, scanned, and everything else you can think of. I got a full health picture of where I was, how I needed to improve, and what my current risk and hereditary factors were, and was given up-to-date recommendations for making changes.

Boy, did that open my eyes. While I was in very good health, understanding heredity and lifestyle issues added greatly to my knowledge and my own life.

By allowing myself to have an honest assessment, I could think about honest answers— answers that would make me healthier and happier. I've gone back every year since that first time (because one of the most important parts about health diagnostics isn't just one set of numbers or tests, but how they change over time). And I have to tell you: it's probably the most important investment I've ever made. These executive diagnostics can be expensive. Mine costs me $3,600, which is a lot of money. The knowledge I gain and the potential early detection that may arise, as well as the costs it may save because of that early detection, more than justify the price. I would also make the argument that many of us could shift funds to cover those costs. For example, I'd rather have a less expensive car and use the money in this arena to extend both the quality and the longevity of my life. And the benefits are wonderful. One of the things I get is a small data stick drive that allows me to carry my full health data with me in case of an emergency, rather than relying on different hospitals to communicate with each other's systems, especially if it's a time-sensitive situation.

Still, you don't have to have this full-scale assessment to reap the benefits of putting yourself under the metaphorical microscope. At the very least, just having an annual physical and bloodwork can help. You need to have your blood pressure measured and your cholesterol levels checked. Getting on the scale regularly may help prevent weight gain by giving you some accountability. This process of learning about your body isn't about embarrassing you, trying to scare you, or making you feel bad if you're not in magazine-cover shape. It's about learning about your body so you can make appropriate changes if necessary—just in the way you would do with a portfolio. If you saw a stock was tanking, you'd probably think about what changes you need to make to save your portfolio. Do the same for your body, because what you save is much more valuable than any share of stock.

For me, it really came down to two things that I gain out of doing this yearly assessment. One, it certainly gives me loads of data about my body, how it changes over time, and what I need to concentrate on when it comes to health, fitness, and nutrition. For example, if my bloodwork notes that my mercury levels are up, I can make efforts to avoid fish with mercury in it (like tuna, tile fish, mackerel, and swordfish). If a certain part of my body shows more weakness than others, I can include exercises that address those weaknesses. That information, especially as it's tracked over time, is invaluable—a true (and very tangible) preventative prescription.

Two, I gain something less tangible but just as vital: self-confidence. After my first assessment, the confidence that I gained knowing that I was in good shape gave me a new excitement about my life—with my work, with my family, with my leisure time, with all of my relationships. That boost of faith—inspiration, really—is something we all can use when trying to create the wealth and financial freedom we all are looking for.

Nature's Most Powerful Fuel—Food—Will Energize You

Yes, it's the subject of every diet book around—how to eat better and how to exercise more. There's plenty of quality nutrition and exercise information out there; however, I recommend the nutrition prescriptions from Dr. Oz and Dr. Michael Roizen, chief wellness officer of the Cleveland Clinic. I don't want to spend too much time talking about polyphenols and protein and cardiovascular exercise and the like, but I will tell you that the main principle that has worked for me is that I really learned to listen to my body. That is, how do I like to feel—and not just in the moment, but in the hours after I eat as well? What foods and activities make me feel good, give me energy, help me manage my stress, and allow me to best handle the ups and downs of life? I have found that as I make healthier food choices and eliminate foods that make me feel sluggish, my palate has changed significantly. I now crave the good stuff: greens, fruits, nuts, grains, and heart-healthy veggies that Drs. Oz and Roizen recommended.

The specific answers, of course, may vary for everyone, but I think the real message is that even though pumpkin pie and watching TV on a swallow-you-up couch may feel delightful in the short term, the real energy sources come from eating whole, clean, less processed foods and getting in a regular amount of exercise daily. That's what leaves you feeling invigorated. When I eat a salad with some raw walnuts, avocado, and fruit, I feel wonderful. And on the times when I may slip into splurging on a burger and fries, I always end up feeling like the gum on the bottom of a shoe—flattened out, stampeded, crusty, and nasty. So what did I learn? I didn't want to feel like junk, so I stopped eating the junk. I also fill up on the vegetables, salads, and fruits before I eat the less essential pastas, meats, or sauce-laden additions to most meals served at restaurants. Then there is less room in your stomach for the less healthy and processed foods.

Despite what the energy drink industry might lead you to believe (and what you may give into as a daily crutch), the real energy sources come from natural and less processed foods and getting our bodies moving.

How does this all relate to wealth? Well, for one, it goes back to what I said about being healthy so you can enjoy the wealth you've created. But more so, this natural, healthy energy that you get throughout the day better feeds your mind to be able to make smart decisions about money, handle stress, and just plain old be better equipped to think about the tough subject of money. I can't pretend that a few paragraphs here will help you flip the switch overnight if you're overweight or having trouble eating well, but I do hope that I've convinced you why it's so important in relation to your wealth.

Dr. Roizen says that it doesn't take all that much to get started. As far as activity, the best thing you can do is make a commitment to take 10,000 steps every day (all you need is a simple pedometer, app, or device that can track steps once you program it to fit your profile). That activity level, along with the intangible things that come along with it (goal-setting, for example), seems to really be the magic activity that can improve your health. Of course, you can integrate more or different activities as well, depending on your interest levels, but those 10,000 steps are a key benchmark, especially for those just getting started.

As far as the food picture goes, that, of course, is a much more difficult task, since that tends to be where most people have their downfalls that lead to poor health outcomes such as obesity and diabetes. So addressing the nutrition issue isn't an easy one for many people, but as Roizen says, it really comes down to changing the environments around you—making sure good foods are around you at home and that you know the best things to order when you're out. The simple formula goes like this: eat your meals based around the healthy ingredients like lean protein (think chicken or fish), lots of fruits and vegetables, healthy fats (think avocados and nuts), and 100 percent whole grains. And avoid processed foods, excess sugar, refined carbohydrates, and trans fats as much as you can.

If you'd like to see my typical eating and exercise plans, here's what they typically look like. And I love them. I enjoy the food I eat. Better yet, I enjoy the way it fuels me to live and love my life.

Irvin's Typical Eating Plan: "It's a good feeling when I'm done eating. I feel rejuvenated."	
Breakfast	Big bowl of fruit, with healthy granola (one made with quinoa and chia and no saturated fat, sugar, or syrup), add hemp or almond milk; big glass of water
Lunch	Large salad with kale, spinach, romaine, field greens; avocado, raw walnuts, cashews, or almonds sprinkled on; some kind of berries, figs, apples, or pears; grilled squash, zucchini, peppers; broth-based low sodium vegetable soup
Dinner	Fish (checked for mercury levels); quinoa or brown rice; beans; vegetable; small salad; hot or spicy sauce added for flavor; almonds
Snacks	Green or white tea at office (morning); pistachios or trail mix (afternoon), and German or Swiss dark chocolate

Irvin's Typical Exercise Plan: "I got more active when I turned 50."	
4-5 mornings/ week	35–60 minutes on elliptical trainer; strength and yoga exercises; stretching after all exercise routines
2 days/week	Tennis; platform tennis; hiking or fast-paced walking
Favorite exercises	Jump rope, jumping jacks, planks, bridges, arm weights, and rowing machine

Ain't No Bubble Bath Gonna Pay the Bills

There is no health subject more directly tied to wealth than that of stress. Simply, when we don't have our finances in order, our bodies are a mess, our minds are a mess, and our lives feel like a mess. And it's no secret that financial problems take a huge toll.

And you know what? I'm a realist. I'm not going to tell you that a twelve-hand massage and a morning bout of meditation is going to take your troubles away. I can tell you that so-called stress-busters may help you feel a little better acutely, but you'll never feel better chronically if you can't figure your way out of your financial issues. So the answer for how to de-stress doesn't lie in punching-bag sessions and candlelight dinners (though they can help); the answer is in using the rest of this book to get rid of the issues that are stressing you, whether it's having too much debt or too little saved. Once these big-picture issues are solved, you'll better manage your stress.

Just as the vicious cycle works in the bad way (the worse your problems, the more you're stressed), you can reverse it (the better you control your finances, the better you'll feel). So let this serve as my plea to improve your health by tackling your problems head on and getting professional financial help if you need it. When you work out many of your money issues, some of your body issues will follow.

One thing that does help me is spending some quiet time in the morning by myself. I wake up stress free, but then I have a little gratitude time—a few moments in prayer and focusing on being grateful for another day of life and what I have to look forward to. Once I establish that, I take some time to establish my priorities for the day; I develop the three most important things I have to do. And no matter what else happens, I know that those three things must get done. I believe this same line of thinking can apply to you whether you're the CEO or not; all of us in our work lives have to deal not only with our typical tasks, but other things that just "come up" during the course of the day. Prioritizing that list helps take some of the stress away, because it gives you permission to not feel as if you have to finish everything. You tackle what you can, and then move on to the next set of priorities. Of course, it's very hard for me to generalize since everybody's work situations (and bosses) are different. But for me, life is about finding a structure that helps you manage the stresses, take care of responsibilities, and win the day.

Consider using a tool called WinStreak, which is a simple app to document the three most significant wins from yesterday and plan for the three most important wins for tomorrow. I think you'll find that stress management is in some ways enhanced by time management. Give yourself the time (and resources) to take care of your tasks.

Your Mouth Is Your Sexiest Body Part

I see this firsthand all the time. Couples who aren't close are destined for financial failure because they can't communicate, they can't articulate their priorities, and they can't be united. They just fight and fight—or worse—ignore and ignore. The health of your body, mind, and portfolio depends on open and honest communication with your partner. When you do this, you solve problems, you prioritize your desires, and you work out sticking points.

By extension, your relationship, as well as your wealth, will actually improve. By developing more intimacy about financial issues, you'll actually develop more intimacy in other ways too. (Okay, if you thought it was strange for a wealth advisor to include a health chapter in a book, you probably think I'm odder than a seven-eyed monster for telling you that talking about money will help improve your sex life. Oh well, I'll live with it.) Assuming you're in a partnership in which you share your finances with your partner, you two need to be allies when it comes to finances. Why? Because the evidence is clear about the risks of not being aligned.

If it's difficult for you or don't know where to start, here are some strategies to help open up the lines of communication and instill a little more closeness in your life.

Your Other Important Docs Are Documents

Much of what we talk about in the health field is about how to prevent problems. That's for good reason. We'd all rather stop something from getting serious than have to deal with that serious consequences on the back end. Not all of us do it, but that's the ideal situation. Preventing the wound from happening is more preferable than treating the wound after it does.

Life, as we all know, is as unpredictable as the mouth of a good comedian. For that reason, we all need to be able to protect our bodies and our estates in the case of an emergency. So when it comes to health, my final recommendation is that you spend time getting all of your important health-related documents together. Details are in Chapter 9, but I'm talking about more than just insurance policies and the like. I'm talking about wills, about your car insurance (how much is covered in the event of the accident), about umbrella coverage, about long-term care, about healthcare directives, and about things like long-term disability insurance in the case that you or your partner are hurt and cannot work, which would significantly change your income, earnings, and wealth.

I suggest using the total family profile that I explained on page 39 when it comes to making sure that all of your health documents are in order. It will help you visualize everything you need. I should also say that not only is preparing the documents important, but so is making sure you have them securely stored. Some choose old-fashioned safety-deposit vaults at banks. Some use secure online systems, while others choose to make sure that their wealth advisors or lawyers have an updated copy. I recommend the latter, and you should also tell your loved ones who has them.

The main question is one that applies not only to those documents, but to anything when it comes to health: what have you done to prepare for the vulnerabilities in your life?

The Million-Dollar Body Workout

I like the idea of integrating a weights workout into my routine a couple of days a week, because it helps me stay strong, burn fat (muscle helps use more energy so that less of what you eat can turn to fat), and avoid injury. Below is a sample of how you can start lifting some weights, using light dumbbells or resistance bands, if you like. It's a variation of the programs that the head exercise physiologist at the Cooper Clinic designed for me.

Plank (works your core, specifically the muscles in your abdominals and lower back): Get on your toes and elbows and hold your body in a stable position, keeping your back straight. Try to hold for forty-five to sixty seconds. Do it three times.

Bridges (works your core, specifically the muscles in your hips and butt): Lie on your back with knees in the air and feet flat on the floor. Keep your arms to your sides. Raise your hips and butt off the ground, keeping your feet and upper body on the ground. Return to the starting position and repeat. Do three sets of twelve repetitions.

Ball Squat (works your legs): Place a stability ball against the wall and stand with your back against the ball. Lower yourself into a squat, making sure you don't go lower than your thighs being parallel to the ground. Stand back up. Do three sets of twelve repetitions. You can do this holding dumbbells in each hand. If you don't have a ball, just do the squats away from the wall, holding the weights.

Shoulder Press (works shoulders): Standing tall with your feet shoulder-width apart, hold two dumbbells at shoulder height. Press them straight up into the air and then lower them. Do three sets of twelve repetitions.

Ball Lawnmower Rows (works back): With a medicine ball, stand tall and pull the ball from your waist up toward your shoulder (like starting a lawnmower, but using both hands). Do three sets of twelve repetitions, alternating which side you pull to.

Push-Ups (works chest, arms, shoulders, core): Perform standard push-ups, or on your knees instead of your toes if you can't do traditional ones. Do three sets of twelve repetitions.

Curls (works biceps): Stand holding dumbbells in each hand to your side. Curl one weight up so that your elbow stays in the position and the weight comes near your chest. Lower, the weight, then alternate. Repeats so you do three sets of twelve repetitions on each arm.

Chapter 5
Grow Me the Money!

The Ins and Outs of Successful Investing

When you were little, you put your spare change in a piggy bank. When you became a teenager, maybe you saved your allowance so you could spend it on clothes or electronics or gas money. When you got to college, perhaps all of your money went to your sorority or fraternity. No matter what you did with your spare change as you grew up, you certainly knew the importance of collecting it, saving it, spending it, or squirreling it away for future use.

There are plenty of no-brainer choices about where you do *not* want to put your money. Your extra cash doesn't belong in mattresses, the freezer, holes in your backyard, and the "new venture" your neighbor has. But I get why some people go the conservative (the mattress) or aggressive (the new venture) route. Either they have no tolerance for risk at all—and they want to make sure that they never lose a cent of their nest egg—or they have wide eyes and open hands, putting their hope (and their nest egg) in a "sure thing" that is everything but. Neither approach is smart financially, because in either scenario, you'll likely lose out—either by not maximizing your financial opportunity or by actually losing everything you have.

Now that you're older, you still have the same choices—you take what you earn, you pay your bills, and then you have enough left over so that you have some choices about what you can do with it. You can (unwisely) spend it all. Or you can decide to save and invest. That's the smart choice—because that's where you earn money by doing virtually nothing, that's where you build financial security and freedom, and that's where you learn to get to where you want to go faster than you ever could have imagined.

After all, that's the entire point—investing is about giving yourself financial independence now and in retirement. That's why we do it, that's why we need to understand the basics (or hire a trusted manager to help us), and that's why we need to be able to make decisions about investing. Investing gives us a richness not just in terms of dollars and cents, but also in the security to be able to spend our money on what we want in life. We save and invest to make ourselves comfortable, decrease our stress, and get the most out of life. That means, as my favorite professor at the Wharton School of Business at the University of Pennsylvania, Richard Marston, says: saving is a necessity, not an afterthought.

What makes it even trickier is that for do-it-yourself people, there's always a level of angst when the market fluctuates and investments move up and down like an ocean tide. You wonder, *Is my portfolio doing poorly (or well) because of something I'm doing or because of natural circumstances in regards to how the economy is working?* That angst (or simply just the question) is at the center of whether or not you take control of your own investments or trust them in the hands of the professional. While I certainly would take the side of you always are in better hands with a trusted professional who is trained and smart when it comes to investing, I do know that some people want to tackle issues on their own. No matter which tack you decide to take, you do want to be educated in investment basics so that either you can handle issues yourself or be more aware of decisions that your advisor makes.

In this chapter, we're not going to tackle advanced issues, but rather talk through some of the most popular questions that my clients ask me—to help give you a framework how investing should work.

And when it comes down to it, the main question is this: Where do you put your money?

Investing is an area where you have to come in with a balanced, smart strategy—making sure you take enough risk to allow your money to grow, while not being so volatile that you end up with a portfolio of zeroes (with no number in front of all of them). This chapter is designed to help you navigate the often tricky waters of investing. It is not intended to be an encyclopedia of every investment option there is (there's plenty of long, mundane material that you can go through if that's what you're interested in). It's intended to give you the foundation principles that will maximize your success as an investor.

Also, I will say this: Unless you really love investing and are going to watch it every day (and feel you have talent at it, because your livelihood depends on it), I do think that most people should be turning to pros for professional wealth-management help. That way, your trusted team of advisors can really deal with the day-to-day decisions and details over what will make you the most money, with the appropriate level of risk.

The other advantage is that a professional can help you weather storms. Most people don't have the guts to stay in bad markets for the long haul, and an advisor can help give you context and frame the cost/benefit analysis when the market ebbs and flows. "Getting out at the wrong time" is one of the biggest mistakes do-it-yourselfers make, and having someone you trust helps assuage the fear and take the emotions out of investment decisions.

So where do we start?

Certainly, the most logical place is just making sure we're all on the same page when it comes to the *why*. Why do we save? Why do we set aside income now for future use? My favorite example comes from Professor Marston, who uses the analogy of a squirrel storing nuts to make the point. In his book, *Investing for a Lifetime*, he writes:

Let's imagine a squirrel is only concerned about the next 12 months and that it lives in a very cold place where winter lasts for six months. Then a good plan would be to "squirrel away" some nuts. The squirrel would like to eat one nut per day. To store up enough nuts for the winter, the squirrel has to find two nuts per day and save 50 percent of them. At the end of six months, the squirrel will have 180 nuts saved (i.e., half of the 360 days in a squirrel year)—just enough to last the winter. A 50 percent savings rate is very high, but the squirrel does not want to run short of nuts late in the winter… For the first six months, the squirrel steadily builds up its store of nuts. Then when winter sets in, the squirrel can sit back and consume them. By planning wisely, the squirrel can eat one nut per day for the whole year.

What if the squirrel lives in Pennsylvania where there are only four winter months? Then the squirrel can cut its savings rate to 33 percent since it can save nuts for 8 out of the 12 months. By working for two more months, the squirrel can eat more nuts (1 1/3 nuts per day!) and save less… Total nuts stored peaks after eight months. Then the squirrel sits back and eats his store of nuts during the remaining four months. In Pennsylvania, the squirrel has to work two months longer. But he will enjoy so many more nuts than his cousins in the cold north.

So now take the squirrel example and apply it to retirement: You enjoy more when you save aggressively (and when you work longer). You get to enjoy the riches when you're not earning the nuts. So let's say you don't put away a nut a day, you may not have enough to last the winter (i.e., retirement). Bottom line: The more you can sock away in various investments or retirement funds, and the less you throw away on unimportant "stuff," the better you will live—and the more secure you'll be the older you get.

The trouble is, as I'll repeat, we simply do not save enough or invest enough or cut our expenses enough. In fact, the Social Security Administration recently published a grim statistic: 21 percent of retired couples and 43 percent of unmarried retirees rely on

Social Security alone for 90 percent or more of their income. In other words, they have no savings.[1]

Step one is making sure we're budgeting enough money to squirrel away. It can be hard to do, when those impulse buys often seem more attractive than the far-away investments that will benefit us in the future. But when you make that commitment, you can start thinking about what to do with that money—that is, where you'll store your nuts.

In addition, we should really define where investment begins—that is, when should you be thinking about doing beyond-the-basics type of money management? Certainly, anybody can engage in investment activities, but my guideline is this: I'm really writing this chapter for the person who has a minimum of $75,000 to $100,000 to invest. So that means you have first set aside a liquid emergency fund to handle unexpected life occurrences, your personal debt is minimized (or converted it to a tax-deductible form of credit), you have maxed out your retirement accounts at work, and your lifestyle budget is under control. If that's the case, then it's time to look at the bigger picture. Is the $75,000 to $100,000 an absolute minimum? Of course not. But before you can start thinking about asset allocation and growth and investment portfolios, you do need some sense of financial stability by having your other bases covered. Now, on the larger asset side, if your potential investment amount is in the $500,000 range, then you're really in a position where professional wealth advisors may be ideal to handle the complexities and opportunities that you have.

Because this area of wealth can be so complex and detailed and as dry as a fossil, I'll be covering the highlights—focused on what you want to know most. That's why I'm tackling this chapter a little differently than most of the others in this book—with a question-and-answer format derived from the most common questions I've received about investing during my three decades in the business. But be forewarned: This chapter is not about identifying which stock is the hot stock. That kind of information changes too rapidly to handle in a book format and, frankly, chasing hot stocks is an unwise course that most often ends in tears for the average investor. My hope is that this chapter gives you the tools to help answer your investment questions, and ultimately gives you the discipline to make good choices. With discipline and stick-to-it-iveness comes freedom, and that's the ultimate goal anyway, right?

Why does investing seem so hard?

That's a good first question, because it can be hard for a number of reasons. For one, it's easy to brush off saving and investing for the future in exchange for living it up in the present. After all, that nice little ski vacation seems like a more fun way to spend your money than putting it safely away in some account you may not see for twenty, thirty, or forty or more years. It's also hard because it's something that few of us have experience with, due to schools offering little financial planning or savings and investment education. So when we see markets go up or down, we don't know if it's because of a bad choice that we made as investors or a function of the market. That's not even counting one of the main reasons why we're typically not so good at investing: We make decisions with our emotions. We get in and out of investments, or we make rash decisions, or we don't have the courage to ride out the benefits of riskier investments—and that's ultimately what gets us into trouble: investing with emotion, rather than with a sound strategy. But really, the first step in making smart decisions and coming up with a strategy for investments is addressing those weaknesses and making a commitment to save and invest smartly—not only for your future retirement, but so you can get the most out of life.

I'm a little nervous (my Ulcer Index is really high) about investing in anything. Why can't I just keep it in a safe and secure bank account?

Because doing so means you're losing out—big-time. It all comes down to saving consistently, investing strategically, and the magic of compound interest, which is the foundation for almost all financial-growth strategies. Without that compound interest, you actually lose money because of inflation—you erode the purchasing power of the money you already have. For example, let's say you have $50,000 and put it in a savngs account with a 1 percent interest rate. After 25 years, maybe you see a "big" gain in terms of absolute numbers, but if inflation is rising at 2 to 3 percent a year, your money is actually worth less in terms of what it will buy than when you started. And after 25 years, you'll have moved backwards. For those who don't know, compound interest basically means that any money you invest grows and grows—not just because of the amount you have in your portfolio, but because your interest is earning interest too, so that you gain and gain and gain money every year at an increasing rate.

SAVINGS ACCOUNT		
that you're going to put in a savings account	add each year to the account	at the end of ten years, your balance will be about
$50,000	$5,000	$108,000

So let's say you have $50,000 that you're going to put in a savings account, and that account pays 1 percent interest every year. And let's say you add $5,000 a year to that account. At the end of 10 years, your balance will be about $108,000. Now let's take that same $50,000 and $5,000 annual contributions. But if we change the formula so that your earnings average 8 percent interest, that same investment means you're now going to have about $186,000 at the end of the same 10 years in a qualified savings account. That's a huge difference, especially when you extrapolate the process out to 25 years. The difference between a 1 percent interest rate return and an 8 percent return is the difference between having about $207,000 at the end of 25 years and having $737,195 at the end. Quite a difference!

The fact is that safe and secure investments simply do not give you enough return on your principal, and you need investments with higher interest or growth rate return potential to allow compound interest to do the work and make you money. Plus, when you consider that for today's older generation, it's much harder to prepare for retirement because the days when companies offered defined benefit pensions that would finance their retirement are long over. That means that individuals (even with corporate retirement help through matching programs, for instance) must take control of investing decisions and strategies that grow their savings in much more active ways than safe strategies, which end up costing you money in the long run.

Why You Should Invest

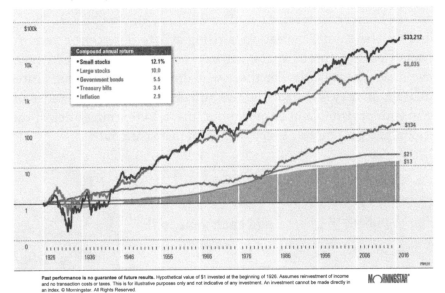

Ibbotson® SBBI®
Stocks, Bonds, Bills, and Inflation 1926–2016

Source: © 2017 Morningstar, Inc. All Rights Reserved. Reproduced with permission.

Now, I can't tell you to calm down, relax, and all of those "easy does it" type phrases—because if you can't stomach risk, it can be hard to handle. So it goes back to what I said earlier in the book. You really need the courage (and the long-term commitment) to handle the ups and downs that come with the market. The trick is that you have to stop worrying about the ebb and flow of the markets from day-to-day, month-to-month, even era to era. If you're in it for the long haul, you will always make more money with compound interest doing its job—even with riskier classes of investments. Financial author David Bach calls it being on "autopilot"—those automatic payments to long-term plans that grow and grow and grow and you don't even notice them coming out of your expenses, but you do notice the big returns as they pile up over time.

Okay, Irvin, I'm finally getting ready to get started. I have a fair amount of money sitting in a savings account ready to invest. What's the first step?

Well, you hit the first thing right on the money: You had enough sense to ask the right question. Instead of letting your money waste away in that financial purgatory known as a savings account, you're smart enough to now move forward with a strategy that will improve your financial picture—and future returns. After that, though, I think it's really about a two-step process before you do a single thing with your money. The following two documents are essential that you should draw up (in communication with your spouse or partner).

A Family Financial Agreement: In this document, you will essentially take stock of your life and define what it is that you want out of it. You should list your financial goals and priorities. And perhaps even more importantly, you should define roles: Who has responsibility for decisions and transactions? How are decisions made? Which ones are made together, and are any made separately? This may seem sillier than a four-nosed clown, but the fact is that most financial conflict in families happens when people are unclear about expectations—and there is miscommunication.

I thought you were going to put this in a college fund! I thought you wanted me to buy a new car! It doesn't matter what the responsibilities are (if one person wants to relinquish any contributions to the discussion, that's fine if you both agree). But it does matter that you do outline those expectations—and agree to revisit them every year or so. When you treat investment like a true partnership and strategy within your family, your chance of success

73

skyrockets. The other part of this statement is that you outline what happens when the unexpected happens (and it will), be it with health issues or some other type of financial strain that you didn't anticipate. Again, this is all done so that your family is literally on the same page when it comes to how to handle wealth not only in good times, but also bad (and uncertain) ones.

Investment Policy Statement: You can consider the previous document one that is big picture oriented (the macro view). It's all about your big thoughts and umbrella principles that guide not only your money decisions, but also your other decisions when it comes to your personal and family life goals. But the Investment Policy Statement gets a little more into the trenches of specific investment principles for the family.

Why is this important? Oftentimes, we're raised with very different financial values and money principles. On one extreme, one person may have grown up with a spend-it-all mentality—as families treated themselves to anything and everything they wanted, no matter how much they leveraged their future against their immediate purchases. And on the other extreme, one person may have grown up in a family where every penny was accounted for, saved, and barely saw the light of a day from a pocket because there was so much fear of losing it.

And in the big gray area in between are all kinds of families and all kinds of family financial values. So in any relationship, we come into it with very strong feelings about how we should save and spend money. In this statement, you will outline your investment philosophy (remember that Ulcer Index?). You want to outline your own tolerance for risk, whether there are certain areas you prefer to invest in, and other details about investment strategy.

Maxing Out Your Retirement: Now that you are ready to start the investing process, the first area you have to consider is the retirement account options that you have through your work. Why is this first? This is your untouchable nest egg that will ensure that you and your family have sufficient funds to live comfortably when you stop working. In addition, retirement accounts at work are often very attractive because they will provide tax deferred or tax free income and your employer will also make contributions, which is like getting free money. We all like free money, don't we?

In a way, your retirement accounts are the easiest financial planning of all. You simply start the process (as early as possible when you enter the work force). And then you don't touch it. Don't. Touch. It. Because these accounts often give you some limited options about the type of assets you can invest in, I'm including this advice in the investment chapter to give you a broad idea about how to create a diversified portfolio. But bear in mind these are investments for the very long haul—you generally can't touch them until you retire—so you want to take as much risk as you can stomach by putting most of your money in a fund that invests primarily in stocks.

The only stock I generally don't recommend is your company's own shares—that's just betting too much on one company. Remember Enron? While it topped the list of Fortune magazine's best companies for several years, it spectacularly went bust, taking the life savings of many thousands of employees with it.

Here's the retirement formula to follow: You contribute the maximum possible money you're allowed by law in whichever plan you're eligible (401(k), 403(b), an IRA); those funds being matched percentage-wise by employers, and you let the accounts grow and grow and grow throughout your life. When you're ready to retire (I do have a different take on what retirement means; see page 191), that money will be there so you can live. But ideally, those accounts (and your other investment accounts) will have grown so much that you'll not only have plenty to live on, but you'll also have plenty to pass on when you, well, do the same.

When investing through your employer, the most common plan is a 401(k) in private-sector companies, or a 403(b) plan for public employees. You can contribute up to $18,500 each year, or $24,500 if you are 50 or older. Another advantage of an employer plan is that it results in immediate tax savings. You will have to pay Social Security and Medicare taxes, but the contributions are not subject to income tax. Also, many employers will match contributions up to a certain level; for instance, the company might match 50 percent of contributions up to 6 percent of your income, which means that as long as you contribute 6 percent of income to the plan each year, you would be getting an additional 3 percent of income from the employer as a contribution. The amount matched is not included in the contribution limits listed above. Some companies also combine their 401(k) plans with a profit-sharing plan, which allows employees to receive money each year based on the overall profitability of the company they work for, and to defer taxation on the additional income.

There also are a number of tax-advantaged options for retirement savings outside of work. You can contribute up to $5,500 to an IRA account ($6,500 if you're 50 or older). You can deduct these contributions from your income tax return each year, but only if your income is below a certain level. Another option is a Roth IRA, where the money you put in is taxed, but you will not have to pay taxes when you withdraw the money after age 59½. The contribution limits for Roth IRAs are the same as those for traditional IRA accounts ($5,500 per year; $6,500 if you are 50 or older), and the ability to make contributions is subject to an income limit. One advantage to doing your own investing is that you have more flexibility to choose investments compared to many employer-sponsored plans.

If you're self-employed, you have more retirement plan options than those who work for a large company. Perhaps the best option for self-employed individuals is a one-participant 401(k) plan, sometimes referred to as a solo 401(k). The great advantage of this type of plan is that you are allowed to make a contribution of up to $18,500 ($24,500 if you are over 50) as an employee plus an employer contribution of 25 percent of your net income up to a total contribution of $55,000 in 2018.

Another plan for the self-employed is the Simplified Employee Pension, known as a SEP. You can make annual contributions of up to 25 percent of your net income up to a maximum of $55,000.

Now, of course, Social Security will provide some income in retirement (after all, that's why "security" is in the name). But don't be fooled into thinking that this will come close to being enough to live on in retirement. You can think of it as a supplement or a bonus to what your retirement accounts are generating, but it's a mistake to think that this will be a major driver of income in your retirement years.

I'm ready to start putting my money somewhere. What's first?

After you have sorted out your retirement plans at work, you need to think about having a fund for an emergency like a sudden medical expense. Do what dehydrated athletes do: Start with something liquid. That is, in any investment strategy, you have to take a portion of your total investment amount and put that in some kind of liquid account—where you can easily have access to the funds within 24 to 48 hours. This is a percentage of your main investment portfolio—say a 3 to 5 percent minimum of your total investment (or the equivalent of 6 to 9 months of your earned income). This type of account—we call it a liquidity reserve account—doesn't make you much money, but it gives you immediate access (via some kind of online checkbook or debit card that's tied to it).

But what this does is create an additional checkpoint of confidence and comfort— knowing that when life throws you a curveball, you won't swing and miss. In my mind, it is well worth having a portion of your investment portfolio available, even if it won't net you a large return. Knowing that you have that comfort zone essentially allows you to be more diverse and take on additional risks in the rest of your portfolio.

Now what? After I have that liquid reserve?

There's no easy answer to this, because everybody's financial and lifestyle situations are like fingerprints—they're all different. So I like to think of it this way:

For one, this investment portfolio is not your retirement account. That's a long-term goal you're handling with your 401(k)s and other similar programs, which I covered earlier. When you think back to what the entire point of investment is—financial freedom now and in retirement—you understand that deferring your income to later years in formalized programs has to be the basis for any kind of investing that may follow. These other investment accounts will only add to your overall financial picture as you do retire—but more importantly, it gives you freedom and the flexibility to pursue your passions now. Right. Now.

This is the real reason why I'm so concerned about making sure you start with a solid foundation. Life isn't about how many dollars are in that portfolio. It's about your experiences, your memories, your ability to help others, your wisdom you can share with your family, your enjoyment of the people and places in this world. Smart investment techniques allow you the freedom and flexibility to do all of those things. Best of all, you can do them all without even depleting your principal investment—by setting up investment accounts that deliver income above and beyond your professionally earned income. So the first step is in adjusting the mind-set. This investment account is about living life—not about saving it until the end.

Second—and this is a biggie—we always underestimate how much we'll need as we get older. If you thought you could retire on a million bucks, that may not do it these days—not with longer lifespans, more expensive medical care, and the cost of inflation. I can't tell each and every one of you how much you'll need because of all the variables (one reason why a personal wealth advisor is helpful, because he or she can do calculations that would give you a pretty good estimate), but I can tell you that whatever number you have in your head, you probably need to raise it higher. And higher.

One key idea as you consider how to manage your nest egg is to maintain separate savings for the different goals you encounter in life. Each portion of your family portfolio should be developed with a different purpose and goal (that mind map can help you think of your goals in a visual kind of way). So the typical family may have six or ten different investment portfolios—be it with retirement accounts, children's education accounts or personal investment accounts geared toward growth funds (which aren't touched,) or income funds that allow you to derive some money every year.

I want to emphasize right at the start that investing is a long-term sport. Invest your money and forget it. This is known as buy-and-hold investing. If you want action, go to the movies or a basketball or hockey game, but don't react to market ups and downs by jumping in and out of the market, which is called market timing. A study by the Federal Reserve of St. Louis found that buy-and-hold investing outperformed strategies of chasing returns by up to 5 percent a year over the period from 1984 to 2012. Buy-and-hold investors earned up to 40 percent more in cumulative returns over a seven-year period than market timers.

The Cost of Market Timing

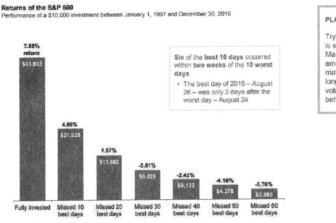

Returns of the S&P 500
Performance of a $10,000 investment between January 1, 1997 and December 30, 2016

Six of the best 10 days occurred within two weeks of the 10 worst days
• The best day of 2015 – August 26 – was only 2 days after the worst day – August 24

PLAN TO STAY INVESTED

Trying to time the market is extremely difficult to do. Market lows often result in emotional decision making. Investing for the long term while managing volatility can result in a better retirement outcome.

On August 24, 2015 the Dow Jones Industrial Average closed down 588 pts. On August 26, 2015 it closed up 609 pts.

This chart is for illustrative purposes only and does not represent the performance of any investment or group of investments.

Source: J.P. Morgan Asset Management analysis using data from Bloomberg. Returns are based on the S&P 500 Total Return Index, an unmanaged, capitalization-weighted index that measures the performance of 500 large capitalization domestic stocks representing all major industries. Past performance is not indicative of future returns. An individual cannot invest directly in an index. Data as of December 30, 2016.

J.P.Morgan
Asset Management

Source: J.P. Morgan Asset Management. Reproduced With Permission

"Given that stock market returns are essentially unpredictable in the short run and move back to their average in the long run, return-chasing behavior can miss the market timing—that is, investors may buy when prices are too high and sell when prices are too low," the study noted.[2]

This brings us to the most important investing decision you will make: asset allocation, or how much goes into each type of investment. What that means is that while it's important to choose individual funds wisely, your portfolio's overall earnings are more determined by the mix of investment types in your portfolio than the individual investments themselves. It's common sense really: your grandmother probably told you it's not wise to put all your eggs in one basket. I know mine did.

You probably know by now that there are several different asset classes you can invest in: equities (stocks or securities that show ownership of a company and are considered more volatile than other investments); bonds (investments in which you loan companies or governments money at a fixed-interest rate); real estate, which can be a property or a real estate fund that invests in things like office buildings or malls; and what's known as "liquid alternative investments," the relatively new kid on the investment block, which includes funds that invest in such things as hedge funds and commodities like copper.

Why not stick with just one type of asset? As I have discussed earlier, markets never follow a smooth upward trajectory. Sometimes, for example, stocks will climb nicely by double digits, while bonds, like the famous tortoise in the Tortoise and the Hare story, earn a constant but dull rate of return. Eventually, however, the stock market will decline—it always does—but those bonds will keep earning that boring but steady interest. When two asset classes, like stocks and bonds, act differently under changing market conditions, they are called uncorrelated. One class tends to move up while the other chugs along or actually declines. By making sure your nest egg is divided into different asset classes, which we call a portfolio allocation strategy, you are much more likely to see consistent returns over time. The more uncorrelated asset classes that you have in your portfolio, the chances of your savings growing steadily are increased.[3]

How can you decide how much of your savings to put into each asset class? Remember our discussion of Irvin's Stomach Ulcer Index on page 29? Your asset allocation will depend a lot on how you answered that question. That's because some asset classes are riskier than others.

In fact, there are two risk considerations that you need to contemplate when making your asset allocation. Your risk tolerance, as I described, is your emotional ability to weather the storms of market swings and sleep soundly. The other type is often called risk capacity: your ability to take a loss without affecting your family's lifestyle. Your risk capacity is determined by a number of factors, such as your present age and the age of your children. If you are 30 years from retirement, you obviously have more risk capacity than if you are retiring in two years' time, when you'll need to start withdrawing your savings.

So every individual needs to adjust their asset allocation according to both their risk tolerance and risk capacity. If I had to pick a generic allocation—one that works for many, many people—it would be this: 60 percent in equities, 35 percent in bonds (which includes the liquid portion of your investment portfolio) and real estate; and 5 percent in liquid alternatives. This is the kind of portfolio that can get you through much of your working life until retirement nears, when you want to start dialing up income and reducing investments in riskier assets. No one wants to start retirement with their portfolio crippled by a market downturn.

Once you have worked out your portfolio allocation, you need to think about what goes into each bucket. Just as owning a number of asset classes reduces risk, it's been shown that returns are improved when you diversify your holdings into several investments in each class, such as equities. In fact, when you own several different stocks, the total risk to your savings is actually less than the risk of owning any single stock.[4] It's simple really: one stock might be an agriculture company and another a bank. If there is a drought, that hurts the company that sells farm produce, but probably not the bank, which will keep on making money. So the portfolio continues to grow. This concept is commonly called diversification.

You could achieve diversification by buying a lot of individual stocks yourself, but there are transaction costs involved and it's hard to keep track of which stocks seem promising. That's why many experts recommend that novice investors use investments called mutual funds or exchange-traded funds, known popularly as ETFs. The share price of ETFs vary throughout the day as the components of their underlying portfolio fluctuate, while the price of mutual funds are reported at the end of each trading day.

Mutual funds come in two primary flavors: they either have an expert or team of experts who pick the stocks in the fund, which is known as a managed fund, or a computer buys all the stocks in a certain category, such as the S&P 500 stock index, which is called a passive fund because no one is making individual investment decisions. Most ETFs are passive.

A number of veteran investors such as Warren Buffett, the CEO of Berkshire Hathaway, believe that passive index funds make the most sense for novice investors saving for things like retirement.[5] One reason is lower costs: mutual funds often charge fees of 1 percent or more of your invested assets annually, while index funds' fees are much lower: an average 0.1 percent. Fees impact your investment, so it's important you understand them.[6]

There are some great active managers who have consistent track records (which is why you need professional help in choosing the right ones.) The higher fees charged by all actively managed mutual funds are supposed to compensate them for earning higher returns, but in reality outperforming the market only happens in a minority of cases. According to Morningstar, the fund ratings service, only one-fifth of large-cap stock mutual funds beat passive index funds over a 10-year period from 2005 to the end of 2014.[7] And don't be swayed by ads that tout last year's stellar performance: that may have been a fluke that is not repeated.

I believe that the do-it-yourselfer should have a strongly diversified asset allocation with a commensurate amount of risk based on the investor's time horizon. Here's my ideal beginning breakdown for discussion (remember, ideal is somewhat arbitrary because of all the variables):

➤ 40-50 percent in domestic equity mutual funds or ETFs

> I seldom recommend individual stocks except for the most sophisticated investors working with a professional wealth advisor because of the much higher degree of attention required to monitor the market for potential downward surprises.

➤ 10-20 percent in low cost international funds or ETFs, including a smaller component to emerging markets

> Despite additional risks and volatility, these investments in international markets can capture important gains not available elsewhere.

➤ 30 percent in fixed-income funds or ETFs (which are an alternative to owning individual bonds)

> You need to be aware that in a rising interest rate environment, there are additional risks in owning bond funds compared with individual bonds. While there is more diversification in a bond fund, you don't own actual bonds but shares in the fund, so there is no chance to get back your entire principal when the bond matures, as you can with individual bonds. So choosing a well-managed bond fund becomes more important.

➤ 10 percent cash/ real estate/ liquid alternatives

When looking at index funds, it may seem like they are all alike because they invest in all the stocks in an index like the S&P or the Russell 2000. But that is not always the case. While index funds like the iShares S&P 500 Index Fund own all 500 companies in the index, the index is weighted by the dollar value of all the shares in the company. Companies with higher share prices get greater weight in the index. That means that emotions, like a fad for tech stocks or oil companies that are out of favor, can influence the performance of the index fund.

A BEGINNER'S MODERATE ASSET ALLOCATION

Real Estate/ Liquid Alternatives 10%

Fixed Income 30%

US Stocks 40%

International Stocks 20%

Joel Greenblatt, an adjunct professor at Columbia Business School, argues that investors are better off putting money in index funds that buy equal amounts of every share. Using the S&P 500 as an example, Greenblatt says index funds that bought equal amounts of stock earned 2 percent more than market cap weighted index funds over a 10-year period.[8]

You can also find index funds for a variety of asset classes and sub-classes, such as equities, global equities and developing world equities; bonds, such as government bonds or corporate bonds.

Once you have made your initial portfolio allocation and invested your savings, you need to determine how you will continue to invest the money you are hopefully saving regularly. I recommend using an investment method called dollar-cost averaging.

Now what is the best schedule to invest your hard earned dollars? Our recommended system is to start as early as possible in an automatic monthly dollar-cost averaging process.

What is dollar-cost averaging, and why is it crucial to the creation of wealth?

Basically it's the technique in which you buy a fixed-dollar amount of a particular investment on a schedule, no matter what the share price, whether it's up or down (you simply buy more shares when it's low and fewer shares when it's high). Here's how it works:

Month	Stock Price	Dollars Invested	Shares Purchased
Month 1	$10.00	$500	50
Month 2	$9.40	$500	53.2
Month 3	$8.80	$500	56.8
Month 4	$9.30	$500	53.8
Month 5	$9.80	$500	51.0
Month 6	$10.50	$500	47.6
TOTAL		**$3,000**	**312.4**

After the six months, at the current stock price of $10.50, the total investment would be worth $3,280, which is a 9.3 percent gain on the $3,000 that was invested. But the stock has only gained 5 percent ($10.50 - $10/$10). This is the beauty of dollar-cost averaging; by making regular purchases and buying stocks both when they are high as well as when they are low, in many cases you can lower your overall cost of investment relative to buying at a given point in time. Also, dollar-cost averaging takes much of the emotion out of investing, as it requires regular, systematic purchases. For those reasons, I highly recommend this as strategy for adding to the investments you already have.

Can I beat the system?

Short answer: NO. If your goal is to get some kind of insider info that will make you millions overnight, well, you have about as much of a chance of doing that as you have successfully walking a tightrope over Niagara Falls. The longer answer, though, is that you can look for things that may not be the current investment fad. For example, financial expert and Wharton professor Jeremy Siegel recommends investing in index funds that are globally diversified. That's based on the belief that emerging markets tend to be undervalued, and you should have them a little more prominently in your own portfolios if you are aiming for maximum growth. Similarly, Siegel supports a concept called "fundamental indexing," which emphasizes looking for stocks that are priced below their peer stocks and below the overall market, because of their potential for growth.

How often should I change up my asset allocation?

Shopping for investments shouldn't be like shopping for shoes. Try this one on, and this one too, how about that pretty little stock in a size 7? No matter what asset allocation you decide on (see pie chart on page 82), wait it out for at least a year. If you try to out-maneuver the market, you'll never find that comfort zone where you're letting your portfolio do the work for you. After an extended period of time (say, a year), it's advisable to take a good look at your allocation and rebalance the portfolio into different asset classes. But be patient. In terms of how you need to think of the approach and time frame of investing, it's a novel, not a text message.

I do suggest taking a look at your asset allocation every year to consider rebalancing to your original percentage portfolio allocations. That percentage shifts as your assets grow and fall, so rebalancing gets you back to your original allocation percentages and strategies. Doing so in a set period (say, one a year) has an advantage: it takes the emotion out of the process, because you're not trying to guess or outsmart the market. You just re-balance when it's time.

That said, there will be some situations that come up that may force you to think about a totally different approach on how you invest. You may need more income, you may need more security, you may need more access to immediate cash. So you should do a risk assessment as described earlier, reevaluating and rebalancing if your life changes in any significant way. These changes could include a change in wealth, a need for more liquid reserves (perhaps a health problem for a family member), reading that your industry is being exported to China, a change in your tax situation, changes in laws, or really any unforeseen circumstance that will change your life. See why those documents are necessary? It gives you a tangible place to go to think about your principles and adjust them as necessary.

Where does inflation fit into all of this?

Glad you asked, since that's a place that a lot of people ignore when it comes to saving and investing—and then being able to spend that money. Fact is, most people underestimate (or fail to even think about) the role that inflation plays. That's partly because inflation has been so low for a couple of decades that it really hasn't affected most people. But inflation has started to creep up again, so it's becoming a more important consideration. Let's say you save $1 million for your retirement and assume that because your portfolio makes 8 percent growth every year, you can earn an income in retirement of $80,000 a year. That same $80,000 you draw every year isn't worth $80,000 in old dollars; it actually decreases in value in terms of what it will buy every year. So there's no accounting for future costs that will rise during retirement. This is one of the reasons why you need to have a balanced investment strategy.

So if you invest only in stocks, it's too risky and you could end up losing a lot of your principal in crucial years when you're drawing income. And if it's too conservative (say, all in bonds), your portfolio won't grow enough to draw income from your base and keep up with inflation. That's why a balanced approach is best—it allows you to draw the benefits of both worlds (you see the rewards of substantial increases in your portfolio when stocks rise) but a safe place to land when the economy takes a turn. In addition, that balance helps you account for any inflation that will happen during the time that you will be drawing from your investments in retirement.

This is one of the reasons why I advocate only sticking to what I call the 4 percent rule: drawing a maximum of 4 percent of your savings each year. Withdrawing only 4 percent of your investments is a traditional approach to ensure that you have money that will last your lifetime. (Note: This 4 percent rule is an accepted formula based on historical trends and real rates of return, not just a random number that some investment advisors decided sounded good.) To be conservative and ensure that your nest egg will be secure, cap your withdrawals at 3 percent per year.

Years of sustainable withdrawals for a portfolio for typical markets
Projected nominal outcomes, 50th percentile

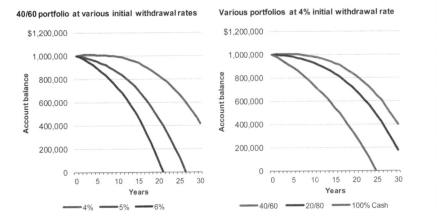

40/60 portfolio at various initial withdrawal rates

Various portfolios at 4% initial withdrawal rate

— 4% — 5% — 6%

— 40/60 — 20/80 — 100% Cash

50th percentile means that 50% of the time you'll have better outcomes. Based on the high percentage of outcomes that tend to be clustered near the median, this may be considered the most likely potential outcome. For the 40/60 portfolio at a 4% withdrawal rate, the real portfolio value at period 30 is $214,164 vs. $417,489 nominal.

These charts are for illustrative purposes only and must not be used, or relied upon, to make investment decisions. Portfolios are described using equity/bond denotation (e.g. a 40/60 portfolio is 40% equities and 60% bonds). Hypothetical portfolios are composed of US Large Cap for equity, US Aggregate Bonds and US Cash for cash, with compound returns projected to be 5.50%, 3.25% and 2.00%, respectively. J.P. Morgan's model is based on J.P. Morgan Asset Management's (JPMAM) proprietary Long-Term Capital Market Assumptions (10–15 years). The resulting projections include only the benchmark return associated with the portfolio and does not include alpha from the underlying product strategies within each asset class. The yearly withdrawal amount is set as a fixed percentage of the initial amount of $1,000,000 and is then inflation adjusted over the period (2.25%). Allocations, assumptions and expected returns are not meant to represent JPMAM performance. Given the complex risk/reward tradeoffs involved, we advise clients to rely on judgment as well as quantitative optimization approaches in setting strategic allocations. References to future returns for either asset allocation strategies or asset classes are not promises or even estimates of actual returns a client portfolio may achieve.

J.P.Morgan
Asset Management

Source: J.P. Morgan Asset Management. Reproduced With Permission

How do I know I need to hire a pro?

Granted, I'm biased because this is my business. But in almost any circumstance, I would advocate to include a professional wealth advisor—so this person (and not you) can worry about the details, the fine print, the tax laws, the tax advantages, the asset protection, and be your voice of reason if and when things get emotional, volatile, or stressful (especially among family members). And once your portfolio starts to grow and grow, it's always a good idea to include a pro. Yes, there are fees involved (I outline them on page 49), but bottom line is that a good advisor will more than pay for himself or herself with the returns they can make that you otherwise wouldn't.

Irvin's Investment Ideology

1. Start investing immediately (and early as possible for offspring).

2. Make it a team sport with your family.

3. Teach family to link personal discipline with courage to stay on a DCA (Dollar Cost Averaging) approach. It works over time to create wealth together if you do not deviate due to the tendency to follow the market volatility.

4. Keep some cash liquid for emergencies.

5. High risk = high reward.

6. Patient, smart, strategic > impulsive, emotional, antsy.

7. Don't save everything. Set aside a budget amount for fun. Enjoy life!

8. Remember: if you lose 50 percent of your money, you need to double the remainder to get back to even.

Traditional Investment Choices	What It Is
Bonds	A type of fixed-income security. You're lending money to a big entity, and they're paying you interest for that loan as they pay it back. Steady.
Stock	You're purchasing a share (or shares) of a company, so in a way, you share the risks and returns as a part owner. Risky, but potentially high returns.
Mutual Fund	Collection of stocks or bonds or other assets, where you pool your money with other investors (supervised by a fund manager).
ETF	Exchange-traded fund holds a number of stocks or bonds and is traded actively like a stock.
Money Market Fund	Like a savings account, but offers a better rate of return with similar liquidity.

Chapter 6
Deal of Fortune

The Savvy Ways to Slash Costs, Save Money, and Negotiate Your Way to More Wealth

We all know the typical times and places when and where we're supposed to get good deals, whether it's garage sales, Black Friday sales, or going-out-of-business-everything-must-go sales. They're alluring propositions, no doubt. Get something that's typically X amount of dollars and pay only a fraction of the cost. In the end, if you do get a good deal, you've won. But here's the issue: not many of us know that you can take a Black Friday approach to so many more goods and services not only the day after you feast on mashed potatoes, but also every day and with virtually every purchase you make. While one of the quintessential game shows of our generation makes a matter-of-fact statement (*The Price is Right*), for many of us, we should turn it into more of a question than a statement: is the price right?

That's something you should ask yourself all the time. Is the price right, and can you find a way to get it at a lower price?

Those should be baseline questions that anybody seeking to improve wealth should ask. Why? Because it's darn expensive to live in today's world. We don't want to pay a lot for cars, or houses, or phones, or TVs, or computers, or massages, or furniture, or the veterinarian, or juice boxes, or the cable bill (oh, what in the world is going on with cable bills these days?), or anything.

As we already know, creating long-term wealth is about increasing our inflow and decreasing our outflow, and being smart about how we manage those two financial pipes going in and out of our bank accounts. Either way, the more we bring in or the more we save means that we create more wealth for ourselves. That's our ultimate goal, one that we keep in mind throughout this whole book.

So the question when it comes to cutting costs and saving money is this: how do we do it? Thankfully, there are lots of ways.

We sometimes think that cost-cutting is all about two ends of the spectrum. On one hand, you have people who try to save fifty cents here, a quarter there, a buck now and again, and over time, those savings add up (think the coupon-clipping generation). And on the other end of the cost spectrum, you have people who try to save money only on the big-ticket purchases—the cars, the homes, the things that are accepted as items that have prices you can negotiate. While both of those extremes are places you can save money and create more wealth for yourself, the truth is that you can do it everywhere in just about anything (or any service) that you need to purchase. This chapter will show you how to just that.

Most importantly, what saving money and negotiating is all about is creating a mindset that gives you license to think about places to save money in all kinds of situations. I don't want you to be obsessed to the point where you're trying to save a penny here and there (because it may not be worth your time), but I do want you to recalibrate how you think.

Example: I recently bought my wife a piece of jewelry from a dealer in a different part of the country. She ended up not liking it, so it was fine for us to return it (because I had arranged a window of time where we could return it). But where did I save money?

Instead of paying $200 to have that jewelry insured by the seller for the cross-country trek, I learned that it would be covered by my homeowner's insurance. So what does that get me? Much more than $200 in savings. It's the savings, which is actually $300 in earned income if you take out the taxes on what it takes to earn $200. But now I get to put that $300 of earned income in a place that will make money. After a few years, that $200 I would have spent on insurance is worth double that, even creeping into four digits. All because I did a little checking around—and had the mindset of not wanting to pay for something I didn't need or want. That's what we're after: creating wealth by creating a new mindset when it comes to costs.

Okay now, are you ready to make some deals?

Your Most Powerful Ally: A Smartphone

If I were writing this book ten years ago instead of now, I'd have entirely different messages. But one of the main ways it would vary is that the scale has tipped more in favor of the consumer. It used to be, if I may generalize a bit, that sales personnel had all the power. They had the product, they had the price, they had the smarts and shrewdness to make a sale, and they could also bank on the fact that you'd be more likely to buy with them than to get in your car, drive across town, and comparison shop. The Internet changed all that, as it gave consumers the power to do some research immediately and on the spot. But having the Internet in the palm of your hands...that *really* tips the scales in your favor.

Nowadays, with a smartphone, you can comparison shop, you can research products, you can find out invoice prices on cars—all within seconds. Having knowledge eliminates nonsense, not to mention saves you dollars and cents.

So step one of any process in making a purchase needs to involve research. Once you know what you want, you need to find out how much it costs, what others are charging for it, if there are any limitations or pitfalls to the product, and even what fellow consumers may say about the product. You gather all of this so you can not only ask relevant and thoughtful questions, but also have ammunition to negotiate a lower price (more on negotiation in the next section).

While you can certainly do all of this research from home, I do recommend that one purchase you make is that of a smartphone if you don't have one. That way, you can simply do in-the-moment research—showing a clerk or manager that competitor A has the same item for a 10 percent lower price. Many stores now having matching programs that allow them to sell you the product at a competitor's price, but they're not going to do it if you don't ask. And you won't ask if you don't know.

Remember, your most important asset is time, so saving time *and* money is your goal. So, let's say that you want/need/drool over a new flat-screen TV. You look around, decide what you want, and then go to big-box store A to take a look. Store A has what you want, but it's $100 more than the price you found at big-box store B. Yes, you could get in your car, drive across town, and go through everything again, but why not just ask for the better price? Saves you money *and* time. Research—and knowledge—allows you to do that.

To that end, I encourage all of my clients to think about ways they can get their time back (which is so important when it comes to improving quality of life). So, for example, many supermarkets now offer delivery-to-your-door shopping. You punch in your list, and they gather the goods and drop them off. Saves you an hour or so every week. If in that hour, you can make more money than the cost of the shopping service, doesn't that make sense?

On the surface, it may seem like you're spending more money to use the service, but the truth is that you have a net gain if you're able to allocate that hour to something that increases your overall wealth (or happiness, for that matter). Especially when you extrapolate that hour every week to fifty-some a year or five-hundred over a decade, that's a serious difference in the amount of money you've earned.

I see it time and time again. So many people waste time talking about creating wealth rather than taking steps to actually do it (whether it's through research or talking to a spouse about priorities). To be effective, you have to take action—and not just wish for better savings or more wealth. It's about carving out time to address your issues—and your desires—head on. And imagine that by saving an hour here and there, you are capturing more quality-of-life time earlier in life (which is really the goal of this entire book).

In all areas of spending money, you can use knowledge to find ways to cut costs, whether it's getting manufacturer coupons sent to your e-mail address or notifications about specials that restaurants are running. If you can make it standard operating procedure to do your research upfront, you'll save big over the long term. Depending on your income and financial status, $10 here or $50 there may not feel like it's worth it to do the research for purchases. But what happens if you do that most of the time? The dollars add up quickly, you get the same product but at a very different price, and that money stays in your pocket—not a corporation's—and compounds in your personal investment portfolios just like my dad taught me. Make every spare dollar sing!

My main point here is that too often I see people using smartphones for things that are very worthwhile—texting, using social networks, taking photos, even taking calls. But we don't use them enough to do this kind of research that can give us information to help us save money in all kinds of purchasing situations. It's not that we don't know the power that the phone has; it's that we don't utilize that power enough.

Why Used Is the New New

Part of the trick with writing about finances is that it's a little bit like writing about health; everybody's situations are a little bit different, just as everybody's bodies are a little bit different. That said, we all still have similar goals—make more money, save more money—no matter what financial bracket we're in. And that means, just like in health, there are fundamental maxims that the majority of people should embrace. The "eat your veggies" equivalent in the finance world may just be this: embrace the phrase "certified pre-owned."

For too long, there's been a stigma about so-called "used" goods. Why would we want to buy anybody else's stuff? Something that somebody else put through the wringer, messed up, soiled, spoiled, and so on? And I get it. There's a certain cache to buying new (after all, there's no such olfactory phenomenon called "the used car smell"). But what does cache really get you, in terms of wealth? Not a whole lot, actually, especially on goods that lose value the minute you purchase them, like cars and a lot of electronic equipment.

So one of the absolutely smartest things you can do to save money and increase wealth is to buy "factory-certified pre-owned." (You also want to look at similar words used for different products, like "refurbished," which is often used for electronics.) What does that mean? Yes, it's used, but it's been restored to be as similar to new as possible. But the product is also backed by the factory and comes with a warranty, so that if it does fail you, you're not the one on the hook for getting it fixed. The manufacturer is on the hook to take care of the costs (with some wear-and-tear exceptions), and that saves you lots of money if something goes wrong. You get something that's almost as good as new for a fraction of the cost. Repeat, *a fraction of the cost.*

So it only makes sense to buy certified pre-owned cars (and for a little extra money, you can usually extend the warranty that it comes with). That alone can save you thousands in the purchase of a new vehicle. Same goes for computers. My wife, for example, was recently in the market for a new computer. She uses it to send e-mail to family members and keep up with the news. She could've bought a new one with lots of power and memory, but why would she need that in order to do basic functions? Instead, she could buy a certified pre-owned computer, which works just fine and does what she needs it to do. She saved hundreds of dollars on that purchase without—here's the key phrase—giving anything up. She didn't lose function. She saved, but still gained.

We should be leery of salespeople who just want to make a pile of money.

You can do the same for tablets, cameras, phones, lots of things. The main thing to keep in mind is that you want to ensure that it has the manufacturer backing, so if something does go wrong, you're not the one who's responsible for it. Also, you can rent expensive tools for special uses or events, like high-end cameras or gowns for that special occasion, and then return them for a fraction of the cost of purchasing them. When you travel, you can rent someone's home through Airbnb or VRBO. Both cut out the middleman's profit and have a more enjoyable residential getaway vacation for a small fraction of the cost.

And also keep in mind the caveat I mentioned: there are people who do need the latest and greatest in some areas. Obviously if you're doing some kind of digital production work, you may need the newest and fastest computer equipment to serve your purposes. But my point is that unless there's a tangible (and cost-related) reason why you need new, why not entertain the alternative? For example, consider an automobile purchase; purchasing a mint condition car from your manufacturer of choice can yield your family a savings of 30 to 50 percent off of the original sticker price by choosing a 2- to-3-year-old certified pre-owned car.

Look Not Just at Today's Price, But Tomorrow's Cost

You've heard the phrase "you've got spend money to make money" because it's a truism for all kinds of businesses, from lemonade stands to high-tech start-ups. But you can also twist that phrase a little bit for another financial truism: "you may have to spend money to save money." Let me tell you what I mean by telling you a little bit more about one client.

Recently, an important client who has had some health issues asked me if he thought it would be worth spending money on a special service offered by the best hospital in the area. That service would give him immediate access to doctors, quick scheduling if issues came up, and more—basically a ticket that gets him to the front of the line. But it cost about $10,000 a year for that service. That's a lot of money. We weighed the options, and he decided to go for it.

What he found was that the service was worth it. He has staff meet him at the hospital to take him where he needs to go (he has some trouble walking). He gets personalized attention at the hospital and from top physician specialists that he needs to see. He gets cell phone numbers of many of his caregivers as well, and they're happy to talk to him whenever he needs them. In fact, my client has said that it's the best money he's ever spent. Did it cost him a lot? Yes, of course. But what he gained has more than paid for the service—not just in terms of money savings, but also in terms of increased time and decreased stress, which, as you know by now, is all part of the wealth equation.

Another good example is in the area of travel insurance. Perhaps you don't need it every time you travel, but spending a few hundred dollars to insure that you can get your money back in the case of an emergency could be well worth the money spent. You may not end up using it (and let's hope you wouldn't), but what if you had spent thousands in non-refundable money and a medical emergency prevented you from going? That few hundred dollars of insurance to get your money back would be well worth it.

Now, I won't use that for small trips that I can reschedule and just pay a small fee to change the airline ticket, but it's absolutely something I would do for bigger trips with greater expenses involved. Sometimes you have to spend money to save some. Sometimes you have to evaluate possible consequences and cost-benefit ratios of particular situations. I'll do the same thing if I'm thinking about making a purchase that I don't know enough about and can't do the research myself; I may pay an expert a small fee to look at my potential purchase. And that person can draw a conclusion whether it's a good deal or not.

Example: I brought in an independent person to evaluate a real estate deal for my office, because it involved commercial real estate and lots of variables that others are more qualified to evaluate. In this situation, the expert could tell me why this particular deal wasn't a good one. I spent money on the service, but I ended up saving it in the long run because it prevented me from making a bad deal that would cost me dearly in the long term. And that leads to a bigger point: while we all have the power to do research (and we should do it as much as possible), sometimes it's actually smarter to bring in a third party who has years of experience in a particular field, because no matter how much research you do, you will not be able to catch up to the experience and wisdom that comes from a qualified expert.

Let's Make a Deal: Negotiation Tricks for Everyone

If you believe movies or TV shows, or any popular portrayal of negotiation, you probably think it's all about winning and losing, sharks and minnows, poker faces and big gambles that get the deal done. While there may be some of that going on in today's world, the reality is that every person has the power to negotiate. That is, everyone has the power—and can have the ability—to get better deals for themselves.

I love talking about negotiation because it's one of my favorite things to do—knowing that I'm helping my clients get the best deal possible, saving them money, and increasing their wealth. (Let that also be a side note. If you have a personal wealth advisor, that person can do a lot of negotiating for you, especially on large purchases and substantial investments.)

Before I go through my tenets and advice on how to best negotiate, there are a few disclaimers. One, not everything is negotiable. If something is not a commodity (that is, a specialty item and not everyone offers it for sale), there's often a fixed price and not a whole lot of wiggle room. Also, on low-priced items, like soap, nobody's negotiating to get a bar of soap a few cents cheaper than the sticker price; and no retailers are entertaining such offers. And two, everything I said in the previous section holds true: You have to do your research. Perhaps the greatest example of that comes to car shopping—simply looking up the invoice price at Kelley Blue Book (kbb.com), Edmunds (Edmunds.com), or CarSense (carsense.com) arms you with information you can use in negotiation. A negotiator without knowledge isn't a negotiator; it's simply someone pleading for a lower price, and that someone usually isn't very successful.

The keys to effective negotiation, as I see it:

Don't treat it like a cut-throat game of winners and losers. Too often, when I see people negotiate, it seems that the process is more about who wins and who loses—in that if you don't leave with the other party completely pummeled, then it wasn't a success. Negotiation is not a game; it's not about trying to best the other person. To be most effective, you have to treat it like this: You're after the best possible price for yourself, but you're not trying to gut the store/clerk/salesperson with a harpoon. My goal in any negotiation isn't to chisel down a salesperson until that person makes nothing on the deal. That's not fair, or right.

My goal is to get a very good value at a very fair price—one that makes me (or my clients) happy. In fact, I even tell people I'm negotiating with this upfront: "I want to be able to smile at the end of this discussion, and I want you to be able to smile as well."

Win–win. Inevitably, at the end of the deal, I'm told that I'm a good negotiator by the seller, which I like, because it's an indication that we both came out with something. That's good for me in terms of saving money and adding value, but it also helps me with long-term relationships, meaning that if I treat the person on the other side of the table fairly, it may lead to other opportunities for our clients down the line.

Negotiate with your brain, not your heart. This is probably the hardest thing for so many of us to get our heads around when it comes to negotiating. You find a piece of jewelry you love, you want that piece of jewelry, you've never seen anything like it anywhere before, you must have that jewelry. That may be exactly how you feel, but you shouldn't let the salesforce know that. Once you let your emotion show, they've got you. And they're trained to capitalize on that. Knowing that you want *that* and only *that* and will accept nothing else means that they don't have to give you any wiggle room whatsoever. I'm not saying this is easy to do, but I can tell you a couple of ways to try to strip the emotion out of it.

One, have a third party do the dealing for you (whether it's a spouse, or friend, or advisor). Automatically, the emotion will be taken away and your side won't appear too eager. Two, go back to what I said a few pages earlier: do your homework. Find other items. Go to other car dealerships. Do your Internet searches. Options give you leverage. Now, if we're dealing with something extraordinary—be it an antique or some collectible that's so rare it's hard to find alternatives—then yes, maybe you won't have much leverage. But that's okay. If that item gives you that emotional satisfaction, then that's not where you're going to do battle. You'll do battle over the other items in your life.

Negotiation isn't only about saving; it's about gaining. Perhaps the number one secret to effective negotiation is this: don't think that a conversation has to only be about slashing the retail price. While that can certainly be part of it, one of your goals in negotiating should be to see what you can get thrown into the deal—that is, extras that typically cost money but the sales people are willing to throw in for free because they're most concerned about getting you to sign on the bigger item because that's where they and the companies make their big money.

Getting some freebies can not only save you money, but also improve your quality of life. This can be for big things or even smaller ones. Buying a TV? Ask for them to throw in a wall-mount or a discount on installation fees. Buying a computer? Ask to see what else they can throw in—an external hard drive, a web cam, a custom keyboard, headphones, or any additional items to sweeten the deal for you!

I'll give you another example. (Remember, I do a lot of negotiating on behalf of my clients, but you can do the same and employ the same principles.) Whenever I negotiate a car, I always tell the dealer that we're not going to sign unless it's written in the contract that the buyer always gets a loaner car and shuttle service or pick-up and delivery for all service visits whenever they are needed for the life of the car. Is that a huge savings in the moment? No, not on the price of the car. But it does save times, stress, and hassle over the course of the life of a car for the family.

Once, when I negotiated for a client's move into in a retirement community, I was able to secure for her a new $9,000 golf cart for the rest of her life, and that included regular maintenance and a parking spot in her garage for her cart. Best of all: if it breaks down, she gets it serviced or a new one—*for the rest of her life*. If that's not a value-added extra, I'm not sure what is. (She's in her seventies, so she could live for many, many years.) That's an incredible service and cost savings for my client, and not that much of an expense for the retirement community, which will be getting her business for conceivably decades. See, we both won, right?

Know the facts about that particular business—and the competitors. This goes back to the basic premise of doing your research. One of the absolute keys for negotiation is being able to identify the supply and demand in any situation, because you get a sense of really who has the most power in a negotiation. If, for example, a retirement community has a 98 percent occupancy rate, I know they're not desperate to sell apartments or townhouses. But what if that occupancy rate is 70 or 80 percent? They have much more incentive to fill the slot and make a deal (throwing in extras, agreeing to no price increases for a certain amount of time, etc.). Related, it helps to know the same facts and figures about competitors. The bottom line is that people negotiate because they know you can go right down the street and buy elsewhere. When they know that—and you're willing to do that—you have much better odds of getting a deal for yourself.

Be ready to walk this way. And by "this way," I mean "out the door." If you're not willing to leave and go somewhere else, there's no negotiation that's going to happen. I remember the story of a friend who got his first job. He was told the salary. And he said (mistakenly, if I may add), "Is that negotiable?" The response from the employer: "Only if you want it to go down." That wasn't a good tactic for a number of reasons. For one, he asked a yes-or-no question that the employer quickly shot down. And two, he wanted that job, so he wasn't willing to walk away and wait for something else. That's the truth whether we're talking electronics, cars, salaries, anything. If you know your options and are willing to explore those options, you have a better chance of both saving money and getting some great extras thrown in.

So if you're shopping for some homemade item that has a unique quality to that seller, you should expect to pay full cost. But in all other cases, there are other sellers who would be happy to sell the product or service to you, which means that just about all sellers should be willing to negotiate. The fact is that ever since we started outsourcing the manufacturing of our products to other countries, prices have gone down, and that gives consumers more and more leverage in the negotiating process. Because the cost is down, there's much more so-called "profit" to work with when negotiating a price.

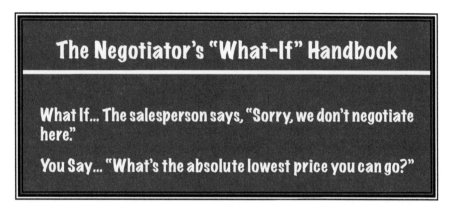

The Negotiator's "What-If" Handbook

What If... The salesperson says, "Sorry, we don't negotiate here."

You Say... "What's the absolute lowest price you can go?"

It's true that some stores don't negotiate, but there are methods that salespeople can use to help you out, like giving you a sales price or other benefits or services.

What If... The salesperson says, "That's the best I can do."

You Say... "When's your next sale?"

For example, I will only buy good-quality suits, but I won't pay everyday prices, so I buy them only when they go on sale at my preferred department store. So part of this process is about impulse control—that you don't need X, Y, or Z right this instant (unless, of course, you do). But if you can train yourself to wait for that item, you'll get it at a much better price (even 40–50 percent off at some department stores) at semi-annual sale time. Or you may even learn that you don't need that item at all. Ideally, you should develop a relationship with a qualified and interested salesperson who can call you in advance of the upcoming sales at your store of choice.

Chapter 7
Owe No!

The Smart Ways to Reduce, Avoid, and Eliminate the Bad Debt in Your Life

One thing I hope you've noticed by now is that I'm not in the business of lecturing. It's not my place to jam my index finger in your shoulders and tell you that you must give up your muffins, make budgets, and save 10 percent of every dollar you earn. Oh yes, I'll tell you they're the smart things to do—and that following sound strategies will pay dividends many times throughout the course of your life.

But I won't lecture, I won't scold, and I won't preach with a you-must-do-this tone. So it shouldn't be a surprise that I'm not going to do any lecturing here. I'm not going to tell you that credit card companies are simply high-interest loan sharks without the knee-cap-breaking steel bars. I'm not going to tell you that running up a credit card bill is just like taking a wad of cash, jamming it down the sink, and turning the garbage disposal on high. And I'm not going to talk down to you if you've put yourself in a position in which you live beyond your means and have learned to rely on plastic as your main means of currency.

No, I won't. Because you already know all those things. You know that credit cards aren't cash and that you pay a dear price for borrowing the bank's money, namely in the form of high interest rates that you have to pay with money that could be better spent elsewhere. In fact, according to the Federal Reserve Bank of New York, Americans have $659 billion in credit card debt (or about $5,000 per borrower), and the average cardholder has four credit cards. That's not even including the amount of student loans we have, which tops more than $1.1 *trillion* (or about $25,000 per borrower). It's an amount that's hard to wrap your head around. The Federal Reserve's Survey of Consumer Finances found that 38 percent of families have credit card debt.

What you may not know—or at least appreciate—is that not all debt is bad. In fact, some debt is good. Some debt will help you get out of your bad debt. If you understand the way interest rates, taxes, and financial strategy all work together, you can use your debt to create strong opportunities to create wealth, so that you can avoid siphoning money from your portfolio and actually add to it. I do think there's a big myth in the minds of many that says you must not owe anything to anyone at any time—that you should be free and clear of owing money to any institution (or some guy nicknamed Bloody-Knuckled Lenny). That myth is just that: a myth, and one that will actually hinder your ability to increase your overall financial success.

The key, really, is to know how to navigate the different options you have for borrowing money so you can maximize your wealth, reduce financial stress, live within your means, and still obtain the things and experiences that you want while planning and securing your future.

Tricky business, no doubt.

So in this chapter, I'm going to outline the principles that will help you understand how to make debt work in your favor, as well as how to take the most advantage of those credit cards.

For starters, I still use the principle that you should keep your living expenses budgeted to the percentages I outlined on page 21. Doing that will ensure that you don't overspend and get yourself into a financial hole that's tough to dig yourself out of. That said, you might be at a starting point where you're already in that hole and need to find the best way out. This chapter will help you do just that.

Know What Constitutes Good Debt

For most purchases in your life—everything ranging from the day-to-day and month-to-month expenses to the holiday gifts and fun stuff you buy—you should budget for them so you can pay for it all within the framework of your monthly income. And if you use a credit card to buy these goods and services (maybe you accumulate points for airlines or hotels, so you have incentive to use a card), your goal should be to pay that balance off in the twenty-five- to twenty-eight-day window that the banks give you before you owe interest.

There are also other expenses that will come up that don't fall into that monthly budget—the infrequent yet significant ones. I'm talking about things like cars, homes, even some educational expenses. Of course, most of us are not in the position to pay those expenses as part of a monthly budget (not talking to you, Mr. Gates!). So you will likely be taking out loans to pay for them, whether they come in the form of mortgages or car loans (or in some cases, people mistakenly even use credit cards to make those purchases).

So how to do you know what's good debt? It all comes down to interest rates and tax advantages. If the interest rate (that is, the "tax" that you have to pay the bank or lender to borrow the money) on that money is lower than the money you can earn by investing it, that's good debt. That is, it makes more sense to borrow someone else's money with a 2 percent interest rate than pay cash for the entire purchase, if you can take the same money and invest it elsewhere and make more than the 2 percent rate you owe after taxes on the investment. Good debt is often connected to a tax advantage, such as a home mortgage debt, which can provide sizable tax deductions when utilized properly.

For example, if you buy a car for $30,000 and can get a loan for a 2 percent interest rate, your monthly payment for forty-eight months (with $2,000 down, say) would be $607.46. At the end of the forty-eight months, you will have spent $31,158.25, including interest, for your car. If you spend $30,000 in cash for the car, you will have saved $1,158.25 over those forty-eight months, so it seems like you saved money because you didn't have to pay interest. But what you're missing out on is the interest or investment return that the $30,000 could have earned you if you had invested it. So let's take that same $30,000, invest it for forty-eight months, and say it earns a conservative 7 percent (depending on where you invested it). The total earning would be $9,323.88. Now subtract those $607.46 monthly payments you'll make over forty-eight months and you still end up making more money in the long run—to the tune of $8,165.63. That's how debt can work in your favor—by allowing you the means to invest in things that appreciate and grow over time with higher rates of return, rather than socking your money in a depreciating asset like that piece of steel we call a car.

Frankly, this is why credit cards are almost always bad options. Their interest rates are so high that you can never catch up, you can't make more than those rates by investing yourself, and you're paying the banks lots of revenue rather than becoming a millionaire.

The other area to consider is that interest paid on certain types of consumer borrowing is tax deductible, meaning that you can write off the money on interest paid on your tax bill. Credit card debt is not tax deductible, so you should never pay any interest to a credit card company—it gets you nothing and only serves to fatten the pockets of the behemoth banks you're borrowing money from. Loans tied to your home, or to securities in your portfolio, are often tax deductible. So at least you get the tax advantage of borrowing that money (reducing your gross earnings, so you have a lower amount that you will be taxed on). Why let the banks have the fun with your money? Keep your money so you can save it, grow it, and enjoy it.

My point: not all debt is bad. In fact, some of it will allow you the power to create even more wealth for yourself in the long run.

Dig Out of Debt with a HELOC

If you've found yourself in a position where your spending has outpaced your income, the first thing to do is stop the excessive spending (it's tough, but you'll have to make a commitment to stop with the extraneous purchases, whether it comes in the form of eating out, or buying purses, or that motorcycle you just had to have but only ride once every two years). The second thing you may want to consider, if you own a home, is to explore a home equity line of credit (HELOC). This type of loan collateralizes your home with a line of credit—meaning that you can pay off your credit cards using the bank's money. The bank, in turn, has the value of your home as collateral in case you default on your payments.

The advantage to you is that the HELOC often has a much lower interest rate than a credit card—currently much lower. Unfortunately, in passing the Tax Cuts and Jobs Act of 2017, Congress decided to remove interest paid on HELOCs as a tax deduction except where the proceeds are used to upgrade the actual residence. But the fact remains that interest rates on HELOCs are much lower than credit cards, so they may still be an attractive option if you have credit card debt. One downside is that, besides having that payment (though lower than a credit card payment), you're borrowing against your house, so you may not have as much equity available if you wanted to sell your home. The other potential disadvantage is that the interest rates do fluctuate, so you can't lock into one rate over the course of the loan; they rise and fall based on changes in interest rates. Another possibility is what is called a securities-based line of credit (SBLOC) or a margin loan, both of which are loans that employ stocks, bonds and mutual funds as collateral. The rules for SBLOCs and margin loans are complicated but may provide investment interest deductibility so you should check with your tax advisor.

Many people find that the HELOC is a good option for buying cars, paying for education, and paying off credit cards, because it allows you to use that money that is in your home to pay off larger purchases. I believe it's one of your very best options to temporarily handle those large or unexpected expenses as well as to help you get out of credit card overload.

Now, that doesn't give you license to go back to spending habits beyond your means, but it can help you hit a reset button periodically. You can build the HELOC payment into your monthly budget, draw up your income/expenses budget, and get a handle on how to live within your means and begin to create the wealth that you want.

Use Debt to Invest in Your Future

Answer this: If you had a pile of cash and could spend that money on some kind of long-term investment, is there something that comes to mind that you've always wanted? I'm not talking about a depreciating thing, like a yacht or a Rolex. I'm thinking about business opportunities that have the potential to pay dividends down the line. Start a business? Possibly spend it on your child's college education? Invest in real estate that you could use as a rental property and a location to retire in? If something comes to mind—and it fits within your family principles and goals—there's nothing wrong with looking at debt options to finance a part of those investments.

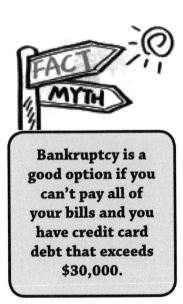

Bankruptcy is a good option if you can't pay all of your bills and you have credit card debt that exceeds $30,000.

One example: I have a client who gets an annual bonus every year (let's say it's in the ballpark of around $40,000). He takes out the aforementioned HELOC to pay for his child's college education, and then he pays back that line of credit once he gets his bonus every year. It's a smart choice because of the low interest rate, and he knows he's getting the cash every year to pay back the line of credit. Another example: You can use a low-interest bank loan or a HELOC to start a business (one that's well researched and not some fly-by-night idea that you don't have a business plan for), because the income and earnings that you can see will more than pay off the loan and help you increase your wealth. Banks typically focus less on what the investment is based on and more on the valuable piece of real estate (your home) tied to the line of credit. So if you don't have the initial outlay in cash to make these investments, it is worth looking into debt options to help get you started. But again, be smart. You need a low interest rate to prevent you from spiraling into a bad debt situation.

Give Yourself the Credit Card Pledge

Credit cards are the sugar of the financial diet. Oh so sweet and convenient, yet if you're not careful, they mess you up real bad. Instead of getting fat and developing heart disease and diabetes, you'll develop horrible credit scores and risk financial ruin because you couldn't resist the savory temptation of that watch you just had to have. The credit card allows us to cave into our impulses (Oh, why not? We love it!), rather than let us think through what actually makes sense when it comes to purchases. So part of learning to deal with spending comes down to some of the principles I referred to on page 21—really thinking through the difference between short-term pleasures and long-term important priorities so you don't create a credit card catastrophe for you and your family.

Just remember that compound interest is wonderful when you're investing. Invest $100 every month and in twenty years, at a 7 percent rate of growth, it can turn to $52,092.67 just by allowing it to grow in a tax deferred account. But what happens when you reverse it? Spend that same $100 every month on some frivolous expense, and with compound interest that you're *paying* rather than *earning*, and that same $100 quickly ends up costing you that same $50,000+ over the same twenty years—and even more if your credit card interest rate is the industry average of 16 percent. That could cost you well over $100,000 on the same $100 a month of frivolous expenses.

Invest $100 every month and in twenty years	7 percent rate of growth, it can turn to $52,092.67 just by allowing it to grow in a tax deferred account

But what happens when you reverse it?

Spend that same $100 every month on some frivolous expense, and with compound interest that you're paying rather than earning, and that same $100 quickly ends up costing you that same $50,000+ over the same twenty years	and even more if your credit card interest rate is the industry average of 16 percent.

That could cost you well over $100,000 on the same $100 a month of frivolous expenses.

Debt, specifically credit card debt, is the number-one killer, alongside stress, of family finances. It doesn't matter whether you make minimum wage, if you're just starting out or have a side job in high school, or if you're a multi-millionaire. In fact, I have clients—ones who make well into the six and seven figures—who have six-figure credit card debt because their families spend beyond their means. You can't out-earn a bad spending habit, no matter how much you make (if you follow sports, you've surely seen many a story of athletes who made millions in their careers but are bankrupt now because their over-spending habits outpaced their earnings). In fact, this is one of the major sources of erosion for families, relationships, and health.

I have a client who makes well into six figures a year, but because of his spouse's spending habits, his debt is so bad his income can't keep up. No matter how much he makes, she spends excessively on silly stuff—clothes, jewelry, etc. And he's considering divorce for this reason alone. If it keeps up, he'll be bankrupt despite the fact that he makes a half a million dollars a year. The truth is, the nouveau rich tend to think that they may be able to sell the excess goods and earn some money back on the goods they purchased, but with the exception of very few items, the value of most goods depreciate so much that they're worth virtually nothing to second-hand buyers, so there's no way to recoup that income when it's spent on frivolous goods.

And that's not even considering the health effects that come from debt. It'll be no surprise that research has found that credit card debt is associated with higher symptoms of anxiety and depression. Some research indicates that debt has an indirect relationship with health as well. Higher levels of debt are associated with people's unwillingness (and financial inability) to seek medical care when they need it.

Tip 1: ***Keep a Max of Two Credit Cards:*** Since you're making a commitment to reduce the spending you do on cards, there's no need to have multiple major cards (Visa, MasterCard, American Express) and then some department-store cards (Macy's, Target, etc.). My recommendation is to keep two major cards, such as American Express (because of the bonuses, upgrades, and perks you get with that one, including hotel credit, free breakfasts at hotels, and things of that nature) and one that is tied into airline or hotel miles or cash back when using the card. In most cases, I'd say you only need two cards. I do think it's smart to have a backup card (be it for fraud purposes if one account gets compromised, or because some establishments don't take Amex).

One of the big fallacies that families believe is that having more credit cards means having more power. All it means is having more risk. The more you have, in fact, the higher likelihood you have of getting denied on other loan options (lenders don't only look at how much debt you have, but also how much debt potential you have—that is, if you have $100,000 worth of credit card availability, they assume that you have the potential of running your cards up that high, making you more of a risk than someone who has, say, a $25,000 credit limit spanning across all your cards). So cut up your extra cards, don't get any new ones (no matter how often they say that you'll save 10–30 percent on your purchases today if you sign up now).

Tip 2: ***Whatever You Do, Don't Make Big Purchases on Credit Cards and Carry a Monthly Balance.*** Have a major credit card in each spouse's name to establish a strong credit record and to keep track of purchases more effectively. I know people who buy cars with their credit cards (to earn frequent flier miles, for example), which would be fine if you paid off the card before the interest kicks in. You're much better off using a HELOC or a traditional auto loan than paying those astronomical interest rates to finance your car. And you have to make a concerted effort to make those payments; banks count on people being disorganized, forgetting to make payments, and just blowing off statements and paying the minimum balance to make their money feel like it's lasting a little longer. This is how banks make their big money. Banks typically charge extraordinarily high interest rates when you borrow their money, but if you invest in traditional bank products like savings accounts or certificates of deposit, they give you little to nothing back when it comes to the interest you are paid.

Tip 3: ***Make More Than Minimum Payments:*** The vicious cycle that is credit card debt goes like this: you use the card, you can't pay off the whole thing, and so you make the minimum payment. But the minimum payment is mostly interest only, so you don't even make a dent in reducing the balance on the actual purchase. And then the balance rises next month, but you want to use the card for more purchases so you only make the minimum payment, and it rises again—because you never actually significantly reduce the actual principal you owe. That's how banks make their money—by you paying them. So if you're not in the position to pay off the entire balance, you have to at least chip away at the principal by paying more than the minimum, or else you'll find yourself in trouble very, very quickly.

Eat Well or Sleep Well?

You've seen this theme from me before in the book, and it applies to credit card principles as well as investments. You have to make the decision between the short-term pleasure of giving into an impulse, and the long-term satisfaction of living smartly and wealthily. This decision is both a lifestyle question and an acceptance-of-risk question. You, as part of a family and as the creator of your wealth, have to ask yourself whether you want to eat well or sleep well. That is, do you want to live in the moment and enjoy the pleasures right in front of you (whether they're food, jewelry, or lattes) at the risk of worrying about your financial future? Or, do you want to sleep well? That is, do you want to make tougher choices when it comes to making purchasing decisions, knowing that you're building your future and that you're reducing your stresses by keeping yourself out of damaging debt?

I can't tell you which path is the best one to take. That's for you to decide, based on your family's desires and values. But I can tell you that the groundwork you lay right here is essentially what your children will learn, the habits they'll pick up, and the things they will model. So if the allure of eating well is tempting to you, ask yourself what you want your children to learn. Gratification of immediate pleasures and purchases, or long-term stability and security? Sleeping well is what leads to true wealth—not just the financial kind, but the kind that brings long-term joy and satisfaction from life.

What if I'm in deep credit card trouble?

It may be smart to get a personal wealth advisor involved in your situation, but if you're going to make the commitment to get out of debt, take these steps:

---

1) Have an honest assessment about all of your bills and expenses. Add them up for a year, put them into specific categories, and then lay it all out, broken down by monthly costs. Then set up your income per month. If you have credit card debt, you may well have a big difference between income and expenses.

2) Make tough choices. Decide what and how you're going to cut. You'll need to make sacrifices, and you will have to make changes in the way you live. But have a family discussion and really talk about what you need and want.

3) Pay the higher-interest loans off first. If you can't do a HELOC, your priority needs to be getting rid of the debt on the cards with the highest rates first and then working your way down card by card. You'll have to pay more than the minimum payment in order to do so. This process may take years, depending on how much free cash flow you can free up from your family paychecks. You can also consider living on one partner's income and using the other partner's salary to pay down any outstanding high interest rate balances (if you are a couple).

Myth. I have never recommended to a client that bankruptcy is a good option. There are other options to get yourself out of debt, like the ones I've outlined here, as well as ones I've previously outlined in terms of budgeting and making hard choices regarding your spending. Bankruptcy may erase your debt, but it will also erase a good credit rating—and your prospects for creating wealth in the near term. You can try negotiating with your lender for forgiveness of the debt balance (or a reduced interest rate) to save your credit rating and hold off bankruptcy, or you may even be able to hire a non-profit debt-reduction or debt-counseling agency, such as the National Foundation for Credit Counseling (NFCC), to help you work out a strategy to avoid going into bankruptcy.

The Psychology of Temptation and Bad Debt

Temptation researchers (often studying the area of food) conclude that the way to fight temptation is to move from a "hot" state to a "cold" state. What does that mean? Well, if you're faced with a dozen cupcakes and you're starving, you're likely to gorge because you're swept away in the emotions and visceral reactions of seeing the cupcake. You're in a "hot," or emotional, state. But if you can walk away when you see the cupcake, drink a lot of water and maybe eat an apple, you've taken the edge off, so that if you then come in contact with the cupcakes, you're no longer "hot," but "cold," and you'll make a decision based on logic, not emotion. So how does that apply to money? Well, you're more likely to make that impulse buy if it's easy to do so (especially now that we have the prevalence of online purchases). So one way to confront temptation is to have a strategy that you rely on (i.e., you institute a family rule that you have to wait twenty-four hours before making an impulse purchase, so you can think it through rather than just browsing and buying).

You can also do things like not carry a credit card with you, except a low-limit one that you need for emergencies. If you make it harder to pay for the item, you'll make it harder to buy the item. That takes you from that hot state to a cold one and ultimately allows you to make smarter decisions and reduce your risk of accumulating personal debt.

Chapter 8
Crying Uncle?

Minimize Your Tax Bill to Keep More Money for Yourself

There are all kinds of uncles—the favorite uncle, the absent uncle, the uncle who always tells stories about how his teachers took the paddle to him if he dared chew gum in history class. But there's one uncle—the big-hatted, finger-pointing man named Sam—who WANTS YOU to pay your taxes (or perhaps even more than your fair share of taxes). Actually, he does more than want it; he requires it. Yep, Sam is the uncle that each and every one of us has to deal with every year and every paycheck for our entire life. And for good reason.

Without taxes, our country doesn't operate—no schools, no services, no defense. Our taxes are what make our government run. Now, we can sit here and debate whether we think our taxes are too high or how we think our country's money should be spent or how the tax brackets are broken down. But that's not what we're here to do. I'm not going to talk politics, and I'm not going to preach about who should pay what and why. I'm talking finance. And our goal here is this: minimizing what we pay the government (legally) so that we can keep more of our money in our own pockets. I love Sam as much as any of our 300-million-strong American family, but that doesn't mean I want to stuff his pockets with more money than he's due.

Let's make this clear: this isn't about scamming the system or fudging numbers. This is about understanding tax laws and guidelines so that you're fulfilling your legal obligation while not mistakenly paying more than you should.

H&R Block often cites research that shows 20 percent of people overpay their taxes by an average of $450 in unclaimed taxed benefits. And a General Accountability Office (GAO) study estimates that close to 1 million taxpayers took a standard deduction when they could have reduced their tax bill by itemizing deductions for mortgage interest and points, as well as state and local income taxes. The GAO estimated that taxpayers could save $473 million by itemizing instead of taking the standard deduction. They further estimated that if charitable contributions and property taxes were also considered, there may be as many as 2.2 million taxpayers not taking advantage of itemized deductions, and that the potential tax savings in this case would be almost $950 million.

Remember, our end goal—saving any money anywhere you can find so you can direct it to investments that make you your millions—is one of the strategies that every successful wealth-builder uses. That goes for cutting back on your Starbucks habit. And that goes for knowing the places you can reduce your tax obligations.

We all know the basics of taxes: You have to pay them at the federal, state, and local level, as well as in other categories, such as states that have sales tax on any items you buy and property taxes if you own a home. We're all legally obligated to pay what's required, and rules vary depending on your state, income level, and a variety of other factors. So this chapter isn't meant to detail every tax law (that would put you to sleep faster than a double-shot of Nyquil™); it's intended to give you the guidelines and strategies for navigating your taxes so you know what to look out for, what to ask, and how to cut the amount you're required to pay the government.

I should also say that certainly one of the strategies you can use is working with your personal wealth advisor and a certified public accountant who is savvy with tax laws, so that you don't need to know every nuance about tax law. But I also realize that especially in the tax arena, there are so many do-it-yourselfers, especially with the huge surge in software and online services that make it simple to plug in your numbers and then file away.

In any case, we can't talk about building your wealth from a global picture until we cover one of the major expenses—the money that comes out of paychecks automatically. Here are some of the things you should look out for when analyzing your financial picture.

Get Militant in Your Record Keeping. This is probably a strategy I should repeat in every chapter. Bottom line is that if your brain, your files, and your home look like an army of ants scattering in different directions, then you're going to have a hard time keeping any of it straight—or taking advantage of potential tax breaks. So if you haven't done so already, you need to make sure your documents, your receipts, and your investment information are all in a secure and well-organized format. You can't claim tax breaks that you can't document, and you can't document your potential tax breaks if your paperwork (or digital files) is either lost in some file-cabinet crack or scribbled on a cocktail napkin.

This will be one of the key components of my 21-Day Wealth Makeover, but you have to get your records in order, if you haven't. Now, this is much easier for the younger generation or those who use an online program or service to file, record, and manage paperwork. And major banks aren't far behind in terms of creating services that will allow you to organize and categorize all of your major financial documents. But it is worth noting that if you don't take advantage of these organizational tools, then you need to make sure you do it on your own.

Take a Little Off the Top. Sure, that's a phrase that many men use with their barbers, but it's actually one of the main keys for minimizing your taxes. Your goal, of course, is to earn as much income as you can. But to reduce taxes, you want to reduce your income. So how do you pursue both goals? Take a little off the top. That is, there are certain expenses you may be able to deduct from your total income, such as mortgage interest, medical expenses, childcare expenses, charitable contributions and business or professional expenses. Flexible spending accounts or health care savings accounts (HSAs) are another popular option offered by many companies in the United States to lower one's taxable income. With these accounts, you can use some of your income before taxes to pay for certain eligible out of pocket medical expenses. That's a huge help, so make sure to take advantage of those plans if they're available. Money contributed to an HSA/FSA is "pre-tax," meaning that it lowers your taxable income by the amount that is contributed each year. When you deduct them from your total income, your reduced income is what you're taxed on, meaning that you'll pay a lower amount of taxes. Some of these are major expenses, of course, and can reduce your tax burden. (All come with limitations, so it's wise to research throughly or employ pros to help with your understanding of these plans and their usefulness to you and your family.)

Say you made $50,000, but contributed $2,500 into a flexible spending account; your employer would only report $47,500 in income to the IRS. Assuming that you were in the 15 percent income tax bracket (and paying 7.65 percent in payroll taxes), you would save $566 in taxes by contributing to the HSA/FSA. (Note: In the case of FSAs, you must use all the money by the end of the plan year or you "lose" that money.)

When it comes to professional expenses, you can deduct expenses associated with your job (such as a home office or a business phone line in your home, and things of that nature). But that area is grayer than a stormy sky, so you really have to be careful in the deductions that you're claiming.

Ideally, you need to be thinking like an entrepreneur (that is, working independently, even if you don't) to determine the things you can do to take full advantage of the proper tax exemptions and deductions. Developing that entrepreneurial spirit gives you a wide array of options for deductions when it comes to tax time. Why is this so important? Because the government is already moving away from the incentives to work for big companies (like defined benefit pension plans that guarantee a set income after retirement), so the burden now falls squarely on you to come up with the plans and tactics that will allow you to develop income for the future and save taxes along the way.

While Social Security increases are modest at best and the average American income level is not keeping up with the cost of inflation, all money managing comes down to the individual—and saving those tax dollars every year becomes that much more vital. So if you don't take responsibility, you'll be in deep, deep trouble, which is why I've emphasized the entrepreneurial spirit throughout the book. It's all about creating more cash flow, whether it's in increased income or in saving dollars in your taxes.

Take Your Pay Later. Well, I don't mean that quite in the way it sounds, that you'll ask Big Boss to give you one large paycheck at the end of every year rather than every two weeks. What I mean is what's referred to as deferred income. That means you earmark some of your yearly income toward accounts that get taxed in the future, not now (i.e., your IRAs and other retirement or deferred compensation accounts). You should be doing this anyway as part of smart saving and investing strategies, but it's also an intelligent tax strategy, because the money you put in these accounts isn't taxed on the income in the year in which you earn it. So in a way, you're deferring that portion of your salary to down the road because you're not using it now and you won't be taxed on it now either. That's the beauty of compounding, which you know about from Chapter 5. It works the same way with your other retirement investments too. Once you get that base going, it grows exponentially. Just for reference, here are the maximum contributions you can make to retirement accounts:[9]

Account Type	2018 Limit (under age 50)	2018 Limit (age 50+)
401(k), 403(b), 457	$18,500	$24,500
IRA, Roth IRA-Catch-up contribution	$5,500	$6,500
SIMPLE IRA	$12,500	$15,500
Defined Contribution	$55,000	$55,000

(Note: If you are an independent business person or self-employed, you may be able to contribute more of your income to a Defined Contribution Plan.)

Use Your Home as Your Shelter. It already serves as your physical shelter, but it's more than just a physical space with a roof and windows and an emotional space with photographs and memories. It's also a fiscal place. That's because within that home, there are lots of ways to ease your tax burden. If you're going to use a portion of your home as a home office, you can deduct a portion of it from your taxes. For example, you can deduct a portion of your property taxes and the interest from mortgage payments from your income, as well as anything associated with a home office (such as the physical space and the cost of any equipment or services specifically and solely used in that office).

And that's not even mentioning the incredible tax break you get by flipping homes, not being taxed on the capital gains proceeds earned from the sale of a home, which I cover in Chapter 10. While I don't advocate using your home to store your money in the literal way (in a closet, under a mattress, or buried in a hole in the backyard), the truth is that your home is a place where you can keep more of your money, save your money, and, by extension, make more money in the process.

Divide It Up. There will be some cases where it will make some sense to divide your income up among family members. What do I mean? You may be able to get tax breaks by making an annual gift of up to $15,000 to your children by using the annual exclusion recognized in the IRS tax code, which is adjusted periodically.[10] In addition, instead of giving money to your child for college, you can pay the college directly (with no gift taxes), not utilizing the annual exclusion, and then you could give another amount to your child for expenses, reaping the tax benefit.

The following scenario really applies to folks where one member makes a significant amount of money more than the other.

New Rules. The Tax Cut and Jobs Act of 2017 made things more complicated tax wise for homeowners, especially those wanting to buy more expensive homes. The law reduces the amount of deductible mortgage debt to $750,000 for new loans, though existing loans of up to $1 million were grandfathered in and homeowners can refinance existing loans of up to $1 million and still deduct the interest. Congress also set a $10,000 cap on deductions for state and local income, sales and property taxes. If you live in a state with high state income tax rates, you may be limited in your ability to deduct property taxes. A number of states are considering alternative tax plans to help their residents deduct local taxes, so you should check with your accountant to see if any options are available to you. While the tax benefits of home ownership are dramatically reduced, I still believe that using the leverage offered by a mortgage can help you save a significant amount of money.

There are some other ways to save under the new tax law. For example, Congress decided to expand tax-deductible 529 plans, which were previously only permissible for paying college tuition, to now include payments for private schooling from kindergarten to grade 12. I explore this option in more depth in Chapter 15 (page 171).

Tools for Doing Your Own Taxes

TurboTax: TurboTax is made by Intuit, the company that created Quicken. It's often cited as being very user friendly, but it may not be the best option if you have a complicated tax situation. It offers both free and paid options based on the complexity of your tax return. https://turbotax.intuit.com/

H&R Block: H&R Block offers a number of physical locations and also provides tax preparation software, with both free and paid options. The software asks you questions about your situation to help you determine your tax liability. http://www.hrblock.com/

TaxAct: TaxAct offers a low-priced paid option for tax preparation as well as a free version. The software offers more options than others for a lower price point, but it's not as personalized as some of the other services available. http://www.taxact.com/

Chapter 9
Live Your Legacy

Plan Your Estate to Protect Your Wealth—and Your Family

Few of us really want to think about happens when we're gone. Yes, we hope that we have somehow left our mark on the world—with our wisdom, our jokes, our caring, our recipes, with a persona that transcends our own world and influences the world of others. We want to live life to remember it, but we also hope that when all is said and done, we're remembered, too. But you know I'm not here to preach about the ways to do *that*; in this chapter, my job is to help you with one very specific aspect of dealing with your wealth and your family's future—planning your estate and making sure all of your paperwork is in order.

When the inevitable end comes, you can ensure that all of this wealth that you spent your lifetime developing lands in the hands that you want. If you don't plan, your estate will wind up in the hands of the state to divvy up; each state has a statute that dictates how the assets are divided if there is no will. I'm confident that's not what any of us want, including the state. Bottom line is that you want to keep as much control as you can so that your wealth can be distributed as you wish.

In case you were wondering, there is a very good reason why I titled the chapter with a "live" rather than "leave." While I do think that one of our innate drives as humans is to leave a legacy for future generations, too few of us realize that this concept doesn't have to be relegated to when we're gone. You should think about it now. To *leave* your legacy, you have to *live* your legacy.

To do that, you have to create opportunities to do so. By building your wealth, you simply have more chances to do the things that you can to improve yourself, your family, and the world. After all, this is the main act. You don't want to get to the end of your life and have regrets about how you spent your time. Wealth gives you the freedom and power to do that.

Here's the best thing about living your legacy and leaving it: It's not that hard.

In fact, this part of wealth planning is actually more straightforward than an angry school principal. There are a couple of things that you need to do, and you just have to carve out a little bit of time to do them.

Unfortunately, too many of us simply ignore the basics. Why? It can cost some money to get these financial and legal directives in order, it does take a little bit of time to make sure everything is arranged properly, and it's simply just not something that many of us want to think about. It's as if we close our eyes and ignore it, somehow we'll magically avoid death.

Well, we all know that the unavoidable things in life are death, taxes, and crazy cat videos, so it only makes sense to deal with it head on. In fact, as part of my 21-Day Wealth Makeover, we'll spend a few parts of it dealing with this very topic—because it's that important. Why would you want to build all of this wealth only to lose control of it in the end? That's right—you don't. So take these steps now to protect your castle, your fortune, and all of your heirs.

Understand the Big Picture. You may be reading this and thinking that, hey, the only assets you have are a car, a computer, a modest savings account, and a 1966 comic book that your pop passed down to you. Or you may be on the other end of the spectrum and have a stable financial situation, many assets in different forms, and own a portfolio of diverse investments. And you may even have assets that you don't think of as assets, such as copyrights or patents, or maybe even some digital assets that have value beyond what you typically think of as being in your "estate."

In any case, the process is the same. If you haven't done so, you need to take inventory of everything you own that has some kind of financial or sentimental value. That, of course, includes all of your financial accounts—ranging from your investment portfolios to retirement portfolios. It also includes your major possessions, whether they are your home or any item with significant value, including jewelry, cars, or a boat. There's a whole category of things that may have some value now or down the line, but you're not quite sure—like antiques, those old comic books, baseball cards, or any other collectibles.

And then there's a list of items that might not have a whole lot of monetary value, but has serious sentimental value for your family—like photos, recipes, new furniture, artwork (translated: things that cousin Joe and cousin Bob might fight over if there's no clear directive for who gets what when you are gone). And now, there's a whole host of digital assets that may have value that you need to think about in terms of ownership when you die—website domains, photos stored online, email accounts, social media accounts, and more.

The reason why you take this inventory is obvious: Before you can plan your estate, you need to have a complete picture of what your estate looks like. Start an inventory, add and subtract as you accumulate and sell from it, and make it a habit to keep a complete picture of your fortune—no matter how big or small. Also realize that there's more to this than just documents and paperwork. Different assets pass in different ways, depending in who gets it (like minors), and you'll need someone to coordinate the passing of those assets.

Take Care of the Non-Negotiables. I know most of us like filling out forms as much as we like cramped airline seats. That doesn't mean you can opt out. To plan your estate—and take responsibility for caring for your family—there are a few forms and documents that you must take care of. A lawyer and/or a financial advisor can help you with them (and you probably need both to properly advise you), but please don't do what you do with the Sunday soup—put it on the back burner.

A will: This is a legal document that details where you want all of your assets to go after taxes and fees (see why you need to keep an inventory of all of them?). The will also outlines who will be in the charge of everything after your death (the executor or personal representative), including who will care for your kids if you have minors. Without this document, the state will divide up your assets. And the last time I checked, the state has no idea which kid most enjoyed mama's antique ring. Of course, you need to include beneficiary designations—that is, who are the people and what are the entities that will be entitled to your assets when you die? You will name primary ones and secondary ones (the secondary ones are in place in case there are no surviving primary ones). Also, you should be aware that your retirement accounts that I spoke of in Chapter 5 have beneficiary designations. These are generally not included in your estate and you should make these designations separately from your will. Special attention should be given to the selection of your executor, especially if you have large or complicated assets. While it might be tempting to designate a spouse or a friend as executor, the job often requires a huge investment of time to gather records and prepare proper accounts. You also want a disinterested party who can make unemotional decisions about such things as when to sell properties. You should also be aware that the executor can be sued by any of the beneficiaries for making mistakes in the administration of the estate, like missed tax deadlines. Don't inflict that on your best friend.

Durable power of attorney: This document allows you to designate a representative (an attorney, spouse or child, for instance) to make decisions on your behalf in case that you can't. Without this, your family will have to go through a court to make any decisions involving finances, a complicated process. A durable power of attorney can be effective immediately or "springing," meaning that it springs into action when an event occurs, such as when you show signs of mental incapacity or you suffer a debilitating stroke.

A living will with healthcare directive: This outlines your medical wishes in case you're incapacitated—what kind of life-saving and life-extending measures you want taken. This, as you can imagine, will help your family avoid some very emotional and difficult decisions and conflicts in the case you're in a delicate medical situation. Related, a medical durable power of attorney allows you to designate a person to carry out the decisions you've outlined in a living will.

Insurance: You need to have life insurance and disability policies to help secure your family's finances in the event of an untimely death or injury, especially if you are the primary income earner. For high-net-worth individuals, I recommend setting up a life insurance trust.[11] In this way, the proceeds of the life insurance policy are not included in your estate, so there are no estate taxes on the payout. When you die, the proceeds can be used to pay the taxes on your estate, leaving more for your beneficiaries. One strategy is to take out a loan to pay the premiums for a large cash value insurance policy in an irrevocable life insurance trust (ILIT), which accumulates value tax free in addition to having a face value payout. The life insurance policy itself is collateral for the loan and the individual has no out-of-pocket expenses because the cash value in the trust pays the premiums for the policy.

Once you have these documents in place, it's then important to decide how you will store them, whether it's with a firm or online or some safety deposit box. In any case, you must tell a neutral and trusted third party how to access them (someone besides your spouse). It may be an adult child, but preferably a family lawyer or personal wealth advisor, who can oversee the documents and the estate when the time comes, to help avoid any emotional, logistical, or family issues that may arise.

That also ensures someone knows how you want your legacy carried on, with no ambiguity and clear directions for how your wishes should be carried out—with all of those choices rooted in your family values that you've outlined and shared with your trusted third party. (I'm certainly biased toward choosing a wealth advisor over a lawyer, because by nature, the advisor is involved in your life regularly throughout many years and understands your goals and values, as opposed to a lawyer, who typically has occasional contact.)

Consider the Extras. As you can imagine, that's only the beginning process for planning an estate. There are so many complex situations—financial ones, familial ones—that many families will need to consider advanced planning tools. This is especially true for individuals with estates valued at more than $11 million.[12] That is the amount exempted from paying estate tax, which was set at 40 percent. While this may seem like a lot, remember that your house is included in your estate and many homes have skyrocketed in value in recent years. If you have more than the exemption amount, your estate will likely have to pay tax, unless you are married. In that case, when one spouse dies, he or she can transfer their assets to the surviving spouse tax free, meaning that married couples can currently shield $20 million plus before they have to worry about paying federal estate taxes, under the new tax law, which runs until the end of 2025. Estate tax planning is especially important when there are different constituencies to consider, such as multiple marriages and children from previous marriages who are potential heirs. Some options that you may want to consider, or talk to a professional about include:

Trusts: These allow you to deal with complex financial situations to protect your assets for your heirs and help pass on your assets with minimal inheritance taxes. I have already mentioned the benefits of establishing an irrevocable life insurance trust (ILIT) to help pay estate taxes for your heirs outside of the estate at little or no cost to you. Trusts can serve many purposes—such as protecting your money from an heir who might blow your fortune on a Las Vegas weekend (because trusts control the income flow based on timelines that you set up). The two main types of trusts are intervivos, or living trusts, which are set up during the life of the grantor (the person who establishes the trust), and testamentary trusts, which are generally part of a will and only come into effect upon an individual's death. And there's a difference between irrevocable trusts and revocable: Revocable allows you to undo your asset transfers from that trust while you're still alive, while irrevocable trusts don't. One of the benefits of trusts is that they don't go through the probate court process, which is what happens when you transfer property using a will. This saves your estate legal fees, time and also keeps the process private, while a will becomes a public document. Many trusts are extremely complicated (they have to be to pass muster with the IRS) so I will include only a summary of their purposes. If you see one that you think could help in your estate planning, I suggest you contact a financial advisor or lawyer trained in estates:

IRA Beneficiary: As mentioned above in this chapter, you should make different beneficiary designations for your tax-advantaged savings accounts like a 401(k). If you have an IRA, it is possible to designate a trust as a beneficiary instead of a person like your son. If you fear a beneficiary is a spendthrift, you name the trust as beneficiary and then have specific amounts paid out of the trust over a period of time. You can also include children from a previous marriage. The problem with a trust as an IRA beneficiary is that it seriously complicates determining when payouts have to occur under IRA rules. You should consult a trust attorney if this route sounds appealing.

Grantor retained annuity trust (GRAT): This type of irrevocable trust is ideal when interest rates are low and you own a depressed asset that you expect to appreciate in coming years, such as a business. You transfer the asset into the GRAT and the trust pays you an annuity payment at a fixed rate. As long as the annuity payment is above a certain "hurdle rate," currently at 2.6 percent[13], you then receive all of the appreciation in the value of your business or other asset which gets passed on to your heirs tax free.

Charitable Remainder Trust: These trusts allow you to transfer assets like stock or a business to a trust for charitable purposes and receive a partial tax deduction, while providing for heirs like children. You designate who you want to be beneficiaries of the trust income for a fixed period of time. That could be you or your children. When the fixed term of the trust expires, the assets then pass to a charity of your choice.[14]

Charitable Lead Remainder Trust: This is a charitable remainder trust in reverse—the income from the assets goes first to a designated charity. After the fixed period, the assets are transferred to the non-charitable beneficiaries, such as your kids.[15]

Qualified Personal Residence Trust, known as a QPRT. This irrevocable trust is designed to hold your primary and secondary residences outside your taxable estate. You are allowed to live in your residence rent free and, at the end of the trust period, the residence will be transferred from the name of the trust to your beneficiaries. If the trust period ends and you want to stay in the residence, you have to pay fair market rent, which further reduces the size of your estate for tax purposes.

Qualified Terminal Interest Property Trust, known as a QTIP. This type of trust is useful to people who have children from a first marriage. It allows you to set up a trust to provide for your spouse while she is still alive. When she dies, the proceeds of the trust are passed to beneficiaries that you choose, such as your children from a first marriage.[16]

Generation Skipping Trust: This type of trust is, just as it sounds, designed to let you leave money tax free to your grandchildren. Why not just leave it to your children? If you have used up your estate tax exemption, your children will have to pay 40 percent estate tax. When they die, your grandchildren will have to pay 40 percent tax, further reducing the estate. The GST also allows you to bypass children who might be going through a messy divorce since the children and their spouses have no claim on the GST.[17] Every person can give up to an estimated $11.2 million—$22.4 million for couples—before a GST tax kicks in.[18]

In addition, there are all kinds of variations and ways you can set up trusts. For example, spendthrift provisions allow you to leave a lump sum to an individual, but only a percentage of it is doled out every year (so if your relative might be likely to spend all of a lump sum payment on retirement in Jamaica, you can set up a trust, so that relative only gets a certain amount of money each year for the life of the trust). That ensures you can provide some long-term financial stability, rather than having all of your earned money go to waste.

Write the Letter. There's no rule that says you have to do it, and if you have all of your paperwork in order, then you'll be covered legally. But one of the things I recommend you do is translate some of the legal-speak that your family will be hearing when they review your will and go over all of the documents. Write them a letter. A personal one. A nice one. Something they'll remember. Yes, include some of the essentials, maybe a few additional directives about contacts for insurance policies and where you hid the family heirloom in the basement. But also include: one last word of wisdom, one last page where you show how much they meant to you, one last thought to leave as your legacy.

SECTION 2

THE NEXT LEVEL

Creative Approaches for Moving Toward Your Millions

Chapter 10
Make (or Break) Yourself at Home

Why Smart Real-Estate Decisions Are the Best Bang for Building Your Bucks

Though we may spend oodles of time in an office or traveling, our home serves as the practical and emotional central nervous system in our lives. It's not only the place to shield us from the elements and store our stuff, but it's also the place where so many magical and meaningful moments may happen. From family dinners to romantic interludes, those moments are so much of what make up the narrative of our lives, and our home serves as the backdrop to many of them.

From a practical standpoint, our homes can also work a little bit like a campfire; they need to be poked and prodded to keep working. But instead of feeding more logs and sticks, we feed them with our cash (anybody remember the movie *The Money Pit*?). So we pour money in to keep it humming. Whether it's the new roof or the broken water heater or just the general upkeep it takes to run a home (not to mention the mortgage payments that we make to live there), there's a reason why household expenses are such a big line on our lifestyle expense budgets. It takes a lot of money to live, and it takes a lot of money to own a home.

Now some will argue that home is just a state of mind—it's where the heart is, right? And while it is, it also has some very practical and financial implications when it comes to creating wealth. Pick the wrong situation and you can lose a lot of money, but pick the right situation and—get this—it is the most valuable and fruitful investment you can make. That's because real estate inevitably appreciates over the long term, and with an amortizing mortgage, you are paying into the principal, essentially keeping the money you've invested and watching it grow as it appreciates.

Even more so, when it comes to younger people just starting out on their wealth-creation journey, your home can be the very best way to create a lot of money in a very short amount of time. We've already seen how the equity in your home (via HELOCs) can help you out of debt or help you use debt to your advantage, but thinking about real estate involves more than just finding an agent and falling in love with a certain house because you like the size of the closets or the bathroom tile with the funky green dots; it's about how you can make this not just an emotional investment, but a financial one as well.

Now, there is one major disadvantage to using real estate as your investment strategy. There's no liquidity. It takes time to buy, sell, and make money, meaning you don't have income coming to you, like you might with other investment strategies. So if you need access to cash fast, then real estate isn't going to provide that. But over the long haul, with a diversified investment approach in other areas, real estate is a wonderful and potentially big-bucks accumulation strategy for you. Here are my guidelines for how to best use real estate to your advantage.

Remove Some of the Emotion from the Home. This seems crazy to say, right? Homes should be emotional. Homes should have meaning. Homes should be about creating memories with the people you love. In the backyard, the kitchen, the bedroom— or even the time Junior threw a baseball through a window (not funny at the time, kind of funny ten years later). But what do I mean by this? I mean that the emotions of your home should revolve around the people more so than the property. Why? Because this allows you, if you're strategic, to create an incredible amount of wealth in a short amount of time. Now, this really applies more to the younger set than those approaching or in retirement, but let me explain how and why.

There's no other mode of investment that allows you to create as much wealth, with such great tax advantages, as does real estate. That is a huge opportunity to build a portfolio and build wealth.

If you are in a situation where you can move every, say, four or five years (Americans are currently moving about every eight years, according to U.S. Census data), the amount of money you can build up in a few moves is extraordinary. But you have to be willing to invest a little time, money, and energy. So let's say you're in your mid-twenties and looking for your first piece of real estate to buy. You take the plunge by buying a fixer-upper. Let's say you research many opportunities, negotiate well, and buy a fixer upper house for $200,000. You put some money (say $30,000) in it to make important, well-thought-out improvements like a kitchen or bathroom areas that elevate it to one of the more desirable homes in the area. Four or five years later—because real estate is one of the few places where we see values traditionally go up over time, rather than tank, with the exception of some down periods or less stable geographic areas in the market—you can sell that house for $300,000. You're now $70,000 ahead, not to mention the equity you have already gained from making payments over those years—and you do not have to pay taxes on the gain. This is so because currently the IRS allows qualified homeowners, who live in their primary residence for a minimum of two years out of the five year period prior to the date of sale, an exclusion up to $250,000 of their gains for single filers or $500,000 for joint filers. What other investment strategy allows you to go tax free on those gains? Right—none.

Now keep playing that scenario out for two or three more house purchases. You can use that $70,000 gain as a down payment on a $350,000 home, put some money into it, and perhaps sell it for $450,000. You make another $70,000 on top of what you already used to pay for it. You can keep doing that, with either more expensive homes or with similarly priced homes, and keep making those types of gains. You are building yourself quite a base of income that you can then invest in the market and make even more money. Because of the potential market increases and the lack of taxes you have to pay on those gains, you're creating a ton of wealth.

Now, there are quite a few disclaimers when it comes to employing this strategy. Typically, you have to have a little bit of cash flow in order to pay down payments and invest in those home improvements that will raise a home's value. You also have to be willing to go through the logistical and time hassles that are involved with purchasing a home and making improvements. Finally, you have to be emotionally willing to move often. That's not for everyone, because the emotional attachment to homes can be so strong, and for those people who think they've found their dream home, they're not willing to move to another place.

So indeed, those are some pretty strong "if" statements. But if you just played that scenario out for a few moves, you can see the kinds of gains you can make. It should be noted that it's not as if you have to move to different cities, townships, or even neighborhoods; you can make those moves and still stay local and retain your social, civic, and educational infrastructures that you prefer.

The last point I'd make here is that you have to do your research to know and understand what the market wants when it comes to resale value. If you can't resell that home when you're ready, then you won't be able to take advantage of the potential wealth you're trying to create. The wealth only comes when you're able to sell and make the money in the increased value without having to pay taxes on it.

So what does that mean practically? It means that you may have to look past what you want and focus on what the majority of others would want. Say you only need a two-bedroom house. Nobody wants a two-bedroom house anymore, so there's no sense in investing your money in one, even if that's all you need. What about school district? Your kids are all grown up so what do you care? You care, because you won't be able to sell to the family of five with three kids in elementary school if you're not in the desirable school district. So you need to think ahead, and balance between your needs and wants, and what you expect the majority of other people to need and want when you're ready to sell it down the line.

Take Your Time. I know I just said that in order to create wealth, you'll be buying and selling every few years. And now I'm telling you that you should take your time. What I mean by that is that you shouldn't really rush into purchases just because you "love" a certain home, or that you could picture yourself living there forever, or that it just feels right. While I don't want to discount those subjective attachments—and I do want your home to reflect you and your values—I don't want you to have those emotional attachments trump doing your homework. We all know the phrase that the three most important words in real estate are location, location, and location, because it's the location, not the actual home, that plays a huge role in prices. The same exact floor plan in the same exact condition can be tens of thousands (and in some cases, hundreds of thousands) of dollars apart in price depending on where they are.

So you need to not only look at what you'll live in, but also where you'll live in terms of neighborhood, desirable school districts, whether the house you're looking at is the priciest in the area (not good) or one of the cheapest (good, so you can build it up and increase value for when you're ready to sell). The way that home price is largely determined is by what are called "comps"—comparable homes that have sold in the area. So, be careful...if you're at the high end of the price list when you're buying, you'll have little room to grow when you try to sell.

Certainly, with so many online resources (such as zillow.com) and the ability to search for information relating to real estate (like info on property taxes and any municipal restrictions or future land planning that could affect sales price), you should be able to gather a more complete picture of what you want.

Now, if your goal is to find a home and stay camped there forever, you may be able to ignore some of these factors, and your goal should be to find the place that will make you the happiest. But if your goal is to create wealth by making sure it has some potentially high real-estate value, then you can't jump into a purchase merely because you like the hardwood floors. Why? Just as there is the potential to make a lot of money on a good real estate deal, you also run the risk of losing a lot of money if you can't sell (i.e., if the value goes down or stays steady, or if it's on the market a long time). Real estate isn't about the here-and-now purchase. It's also about the in-the-future potential as well.

Find the Right Price. How do you know how much you can afford for a house? Good question, since the prices of homes are so large that it often comes off as an abstract number. The way you need to think about it is not in the total price of the home, the sales price. You have to break it down to a monthly payment. And that monthly payment should be no more than 30 percent of your monthly income (remember, building wealth is about living within your means and budgeting). So in order to come up with that figure you'll need to be able to figure out the mortgage payments based on the rate you expect to get and how much of a down payment you'll make, property taxes for the area in which you're living, homeowner's insurance, and a property repair and replacement fund to keep the property in good condition.

To find the taxes, go to http://interactive.taxfoundation.org/propertytax/. According to the Federal Reserve, you can get a ballpark number for insurance by dividing the cost of the home by 1,000 and then multiplying the result by $3.50. And you can figure out monthly payments on online mortgage calculators, such as Bankrate's at http://www.bankrate.com/calculators/mortgages/mortgage-calculator-b.aspx. Plug in various home prices and you'll start to get a sense of what your ideal home price is.

Remember, the key number isn't that sales price; it's making sure that your monthly payment stays right around 30 percent of your income.

Game Your Mortgage. Some of you may be in a position to pay for a home in cash, but most of you will be taking out a mortgage—the loan from the bank that allows you to purchase the home, then pay it off with a currently-low interest rate. Cash buyers still have to pay things like property taxes and homeowner's insurance, so even paying cash doesn't erase expenses, but those using a mortgage will find that these payments (and the associated costs) will make up a significant portion of their monthly budgets. There's a lot of paperwork involved in mortgage and closing on a house, which is why most people get an agent or a lawyer to seal the deal. So it's likely you'll have someone to guide you on the fine print, but here are some things to think about in relation to your mortgage:

➤ *Get one with no pre-payment penalty.* Some mortgage deals will penalize you if you want to pay off your loan earlier than the thirty- or fifteen-year deal that you have. The reason why is that they lose the money they make in interest if you do. If you are in a position to pay it off ahead of time, you should do that, and you need to negotiate upfront to have no penalty associated with that option.

➤ *No points.* Mortgage rates are so low right now that you can get a very good deal on the rate you're paying (the average rate is about 4 percent, but twenty years ago, it was more than 8 percent). What you don't want to pay are "points"—that is, up-front costs based upon the settlement purchase price of the house straight to the bank. Even if you have to pay a slightly higher interest rate, you want little or no points.

➤ *Shop around.* Start with your own bank, but be aware that most banks have specialties. Some banks may specialize in first mortgages, so their long-term rates are good and competitive. Others may specialize in HELOCs, so they don't have much of a business in first mortgages, which means they don't pay much attention to them, have higher interest rates, and don't care whether they get your business for your first mortgage. Don't assume that just because it's your primary bank that you'll get a competitive rate. You must shop around to make sure you're getting a good deal not just in the percentage rate charged, but also other fees that you can negotiate.

➤ *Find a bank or lender that will allow you to make two payments a month.* Even though you'll only be billed once a month, you can cut a year or two off the length of your loan by paying the same amount, just split in half every two weeks. So if you have a $2,000 monthly payment, it makes more financial sense to pay $1,000 on the first of the month and the fifteenth. Why? Doing that means more of your money goes to the principal rather than interest, so you chip away at the total amount that you owe the bank, and you'll thus reduce the length of your loan in the process and pay it off early, leaving you with more wealth at the end of your loan. Do that and everybody wins (except the bank).

➤ *Think about the length of your loan.* You'll likely have a choice between fifteen- and thirty-year amortizing mortgages. Some people will opt for the fifteen-year plan because that means they'll pay off the loan faster. But that also means higher payments and less cash flow for you along the way. So for most of us, unless you have significant cash flow and low debt, you'll want the thirty-year option—for lower monthly payments and so you can chip away at the cost by making two payments a month. Some of this decision also depends in your age, the amount of money you have saved for retirement, and other factors. Most times, though, the thirty-year loan makes the most sense, because as your house appreciates in value, you'll be allowing that value to grow—meaning the real estate will be working for you, by making lower payments at a low interest rate, while your real estate is growing at a higher rate. The other advantage is that if you choose the longer loan, you can always make larger payments along the way and pay it off faster, but if you pick the shorter loan, you'll have larger payments and can't choose to make smaller ones during times when your cash flow may decrease. So you're locked in. The thirty-year mortgage simply gives you flexibility to pay off the loan as you wish, while the fifteen-year choice forces your hand with aggressive payments.

Buy Now. Right now, we're in an era of unusual opportunity. The cost of borrowing money for mortgages is so low that if you can afford to buy a house, now is the time to do so. The median cost of a home, according to Census Bureau data, from the first quarter of 2014 was $265,700. Buying with an interest rate of 3, 4, or 5 percent will save you thousands over the long term, compared to when interest rates get to 6, 7, or 8 percent. Just consider the difference in monthly costs.

A $200,000 mortgage at a 3.5 percent interest rate over thirty years is an $898.08 monthly payment. The same mortgage at a 6 percent interest rate is a $1,199.10 monthly payment. The amount you pay over the life of the mortgage? $323,312.18 compared to $431,676.38. Wow. If that's not a reason to jump in and buy, I'm not sure what is.

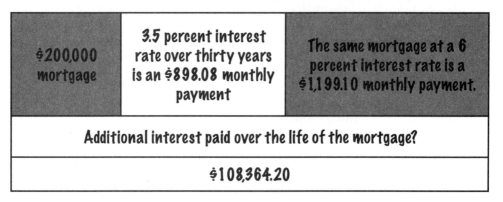

$200,000 mortgage	3.5 percent interest rate over thirty years is an $898.08 monthly payment	The same mortgage at a 6 percent interest rate is a $1,199.10 monthly payment.
Additional interest paid over the life of the mortgage?		
$108,364.20		

Don't Waste Time with an Investment Property. After all I have said about what a killer investment opportunity that real estate is, it would seem to make sense that if you can, you should buy other properties to rent out and make money off them too, right? Probably not, actually. My experience is that those people who make those second-home investments to use as rentals spend so much time and money in general upkeep that it's hard for them to get value from that second home, because they have to pay maintenance people, collect bills from renters, and respond to every request from the renter ("The toilet is clogged again?").

It can be a large headache and financially a wash. Remember one of my main mantras: your time is a key part of your wealth, and if you spend so much time in such endeavors that you can't make money on other areas or you can't enjoy the things that matter in your life, then that doesn't seem to fit in the family and personal values you've created. Another point: the tax breaks you get on your primary home don't typically extend to a vacation home or investment property, so any gains you would make do get taxed, meaning that you're not getting the full potential of wealth gains that you do for your primary home.

There are some exceptions, of course. If you are handy enough to do most of the upkeep (and have the time to do so), it may make some sense to take advantage of the value increase if you can find fixer-uppers that you can rent out, improve, and then sell (it's called flipping). And the other scenario that makes sense is if you can invest in some quantity of rental properties (say, at least five or six). In that case, it may make sense to pay or partner with someone who can handle the repairs, upgrades, and maintenance to improve on your profit making potential.

And then there's a large-enough volume of income from the properties to offset the expenses, and you can see the income as you sell and flip those properties. I'm not against buying properties to rent out; for example, one good option is buying a duplex or triplex and you or one of your offspring living in one of the units. Because you or your children already live on site, it won't be as much of a hassle to take care of needs from the renter, and you can use that rental income to help pay the mortgage. I just think that you'll be more efficient and make the most money either concentrating on your own home or investing in volume. Having one small property usually doesn't prove to be worth it, financially speaking.

Is renting ever a good idea?

Given the fact that I've said that real estate can be the best thing since grilled salmon, I bet you think I'm going to say that you should never rent; that it makes most sense to buy. But that's not the case. Renting can actually be a good idea, especially for people who are in transition or don't know where they want to settle. It makes more sense to rent for six months to a year (and essentially lose that money) than to buy hastily and get into a situation where you can't resell the house because you made a bad decision about location. The money you would lose is much higher than the money you'd lose from renting for a short period of time.

Do I think renting is a good idea over the long term? Typically not, because of all of the wealth and tax advantages received by purchasing a home. But for the short term, in the right situation, it can certainly be the better choice. And you may even consider a lease-to-buy option, which would allow you to rent for a short period, with no obligation, and then that monthly payment could be used toward the purchase of the home if you decide you like it. That's a best-of-both-worlds situation for some potential buyers. Finally, for retirees, renting a home can also be the optimal choice especially for those retirees who want to limit the repair and maintenance costs that come with home ownership.

When you move to a new city that is unfamiliar to you or your family, renting gives you ample opportunity to try out not only the house, but the neighborhood, the school system, and the attractiveness of the area lifestyle-wise before you commit your life and a significant amount of money to that town.

Chapter 11
Extra, Extra!

Alternative Avenues for Making Side Money and Getting Closer to Making Your Millions

When it comes right down to it, this whole financial challenge is really all about the bathtub. While some water (your money) pours in through the faucet (your income), some drains out (your expenses). When it comes to financial management, all of us want the mighty faucet where the water gushes out like Niagara Falls, and we want the drain to be filled with so much gunk that the water feels like it would take forever to drain.

To create real wealth, the inflow must be much stronger than the outflow. But the problem is that the inflow is the toughest to control and the outflow can, well, get out of control. It's *easy* to spend on anything and everything, especially if you're not disciplined and smart about your expenses (like liquid Drano if we're not careful). It's not so easy to amp up the income. Most people get their income from employment and investment income, and that's about it. It's not as if you can magically wave a wand and tell your employers you want a 50 percent raise to offset the drain of tuition or other expenses. So that's why much of our life is about finding that balance of the bathtub—so the water levels stay high and steady and we're never left in an ankle-deep tub wondering how the heck we're going to fill it back up again.

I've addressed the drain and the faucet, and how to balance the two, in other chapters. This chapter is specifically about how to power up your faucet so you can increase the rate at which the water pours in. How can you be creative in the ways you increase your income and your wealth? How can you increase your family's net cash flow? How can you get your tub to overflow?

While that's the last thing we'd want in our homes, the overflowing tub is exactly what we want in our financial lives—lots of money coming in with the bare minimum going out. When it comes right down to it, that's the scenario where you can play with the rubber duckies of life, enjoying everything around you rather than worrying that you have no place to play.

Now, will these situations drastically change your income? Probably not. Think about what a little extra income can do for you and your future. An extra $500 or $1,000 per month could help bulk up your investment portfolios and get you to the success that you dreamed of years earlier. Yes, we'd all love if we could just double our salaries, but it doesn't work that way unless you're an NBA free agent or newly Oscar-nominated actress. That's why us ordinary folks should seek alternative avenues to boost our incomes.

The bottom-line question you can ask yourself to increase your income: what do you have that others want?

That can come in the form of goods, services, wisdom, property, or anything. (About 18 percent of Americans have a side business that is not their primary income source.) So if you'd like to find ways to add a little extra income in your life, consider the possibilities.

Change How You View Yourself. We're in a different world than we were a generation ago. New technology means new opportunities, and we (no matter your age) need to get out of the nine-to-five punch-a-timeclock mentality. Even if that's your main job, that doesn't mean it has to be your only source of income. So the first step, really, has to be changing your mind-set.

Instead of thinking about your "job," you should think about your "unique skill set." And then the next logical questions are: who wants to use that skill set, and who would be willing to pay for that skill set? The answer is that there are likely many people. Today, it's easier than ever to get side gigs that can supplement your income, such as through websites like Elance.com or Guru.com, where people buy and sell services. With our digital culture, it's easier to work remotely (and flexibly) and get jobs done on your off hours. In fact, this is how I've recently made several hires for specific projects or tasks.

If I need a small project done on my office and I don't have someone with that skill set to do it, it makes no sense for me to pay a full-time salary for a one-time project. So I outsource the project (after I collect credentials and conduct interviews in the same way I would hire for a traditional job). That person makes money from the project, and I get the service taken care of. It's a win–win for both of us. So the point is that there are more and more opportunities to increase your income through your skill sets on your own timetable, not just your job.

Sell Your Stuff. The old-fashioned way to clean out your rooms, attics, and garages is via the good old yard sale. You haul your stuff to the curb, slap a one-dollar sticker on an old TV and there you go—you clean out your house and make a few bucks. Therein lies the problem: it's usually only a few bucks. Nothing wrong with that, but it's not as if you'll make back the money you originally spent on the goods you sell, and a once-a-year garage sale is hardly change-your-life kind of money.

Luckily, the Internet isn't just a nice time waster for Facebook-addicted folks; it's also ripe with opportunities to pump up revenue in ways that the old-fashioned yard sale can't. Certainly, the classic site eBay is the avenue that most people think about, but there are other possibilities as well, ranging from sites that serve as central hubs to sell clothes (at better values than consignment shops), to commodity-specific sites focused on a particular kind of item (like specific kinds of sporting goods, for example). The advantage of those sites over eBay is that shoppers are very focused on what they want or need, so you have motivated shoppers who may be willing to spend a little more than what you would expect to get from a garage sale (and even general classified sites like Craigslist).

Now, all of those sites work really well for goods that you want to sell, and it goes without saying that the rarer your commodity, the higher the price you can ask (classic supply-and-demand principles at work here). So when you extend that principle a little further, you can even command a little more money.

Example: If you have art skills or crafts prowess, you can create items for not a lot of cost. What makes them valuable is their uniqueness. And with the rise of sites like Etsy. com, you can create your own marketplace to sell your goods. These avenues may even provide a good opportunity to involve your whole family, where you and your kids make some unique items using household items (bracelets out of bottle caps, anyone?). In those cases, you do two things that will contribute to your wealth: earn some extra income, and teach your family a bit about the entrepreneurial spirit (and processes).

That's not even mentioning the quality time—and the memories—that you create at the same time. In fact, I know some people who buy up a load of stuff from the dollar store and then resell it online for much higher price, and I know another individual living in New York City, who has made a living buying used high-end designer items (especially women's shoes) that she finds at thrift stores for next to nothing and then turning around and reselling them online for quite a profit.

While there are certainly people who have made their careers out of buying and selling from sites like this, it's just one way to think about how you can increase your cash flow. What do you have in your home that you no longer want or need? Consider donating those goods to charity, or you might find a place to sell them. Now, considering the depreciating value of most things, you can assume your rate or return won't be that high, but it's better than leaving the treadmill-turned-storage-bin in the corner of the garage.

Sell Your Space. Now this option isn't for everyone, but hey, this chapter is all about creative ways to think about increasing your income. Why not consider renting out a spare room or your entire home while you're away? Especially if you live in an area that people like to visit, you can make all kinds of money by renting out that space through sites like Airbnb.com. I recommend that site for people looking to save money when they travel, because the cost of renting out rooms or homes is cheaper than staying at many hotels. But the flip side also applies. You can make money you would otherwise never make because you may never have considered being the landlord in this type of travel situation. (Note: Be sure to follow up on your safety checks before you go.)

What's great about this site is that it's not just for luxurious rooms on isolated islands. It's for all kinds of places where people want to stay, from full houses to small apartments in a destination on your "must go" list. So think about various opportunities you might have depending on where you live. Maybe you don't live in a highly touristy area. But what if a major soccer tournament comes to your town every July? Maybe there's a fall festival of hot air balloons that attracts thousands of people to your city? Or maybe you live in a college town where alumni come back for football games? In any of those cases, you could make some extra cash by renting out your space to people looking to save money by not booking through traditional hotels.

Market Your Services. The whole concept of business transactions doesn't have to stop and start with the regular job. Yes, you get paid for the services you perform for your company. That's the agreement. You do x, employer pays you y. But why not add in a z as well? That is, when you're not working, are there opportunities to make a little cash on the side for services you perform (provided it doesn't mean there's a conflict of interest with your regular job)? It could be as simple as some menial tasks (some sites specialize in listing jobs like running errands, driving people places, and other simple tasks—you get paid for your time and the completion of the service).

It may sound odd to suggest because most of us think that babysitting is the niche market owned by preteens, but there are some sites looking for childcare providers of all ages. If you have the time, you can make some decent money caring for children a few nights a week or on the weekends. Of course, the place where you have the most opportunity is in specialty areas of service. Whatever it is that you do for a living, can you find a way to help others and/or outsource your talents in similar areas?

I have a pilot friend who is part of a charity organization that flies patients in his own plane who can't afford flights to various hospitals across the country. While he doesn't get paid per se (except for the expenses of fuel), he is getting paid, in a way, because he enjoys the flying; he's saving the money he would normally spend joyriding on the weekend, therefore getting the best of both worlds—enjoying his life and being able to earmark money he would have spent on gas to enjoy a different hobby (thus, making it in a form of extra income).

The point is that there are plenty of people who would rather spend some money to hire someone to do a job like writing articles rather than take their own time to either do the job or learn how to do it. We all have the same twenty-four hours, so it's really about how to leverage those twenty-four hours to the best of your ability. So if it makes sense for you to invest your services in the time that's involved in the task, it could provide a solid area to increase your income.

Sell Your Kidney. Well, just kidding on that one. Sort of. I'm not saying it's for everyone, but people do make some money offering up their bodies in the name of science. Sometimes that comes in the form of being involved in clinical trials or experiments (it helps if you live in or near a college town). There's also a rich market for those who want to be an egg or sperm donor. Again, this isn't about a moral judgment or me suggesting that you can or should become a millionaire by being a regular customer at the sperm bank, but I do point it out to repeat what this is all about: if you have a skill or service that somebody else wants, there's usually a market for that. The higher the need, the more you will make.

Sell Your Smarts. Now I'm not suggesting you go and rent out your brain for sixteen-year-olds who are taking the SAT. But I am suggesting that one of your most valuable commodities is actually not what you're storing in your attic, but what you're storing in your noggin. Your accumulated wisdom is something that has real value in the same way that your services do. Yes, maybe you're imparting your knowledge to others in your regular job, but there may be some arenas where you can do even more.

For example, if you have the time and inclination, you could sign up to be a tutor to help kids who are looking for extra help in certain subjects like math, science, or history. Perhaps the most exciting area is the one involving virtual consulting; that is, you serve the role of consultant to individuals or businesses looking for expertise for a finite amount of time (or project based). Consultants are great for businesses because they save money in the long term (no need to hire a full-time employee to simply address one issue), and the consultant makes out because he or she can have multiple projects at once and do the work in a shortened or temporary time frame.

I might add that this is one of the best areas to introduce to your kids. We tend to think that a consultant has to be someone in retirement age that has forty years of experience in a certain field. But these days, consultants can come in all forms. How many seventeen-year-olds do you know who have more tech savvy and smarts than people triple their age? Lots, I bet. So why can't these teens serve the role that was previously reserved for the older generation? They can. And they can make a lot of money on the side doing so.

Chapter 12
Think Outside the Stocks

Alternative Investment Strategies to Make You Money—if You're Willing to Take a Chance

As a society, we tend to value creativity only in those fields where it's most evident. You know, we love to see creativity in our artists, our writers, and our musicians. We'll even acknowledge that other fields also require practitioners to use their right brain as well as their left—like architects, athletes, and teachers. But when it comes to those fields where there are more numbers than nuances, we tend to write those people off as quantoids, rather than folks who can use creativity to do their jobs better.

So a knee-jerk reaction may be to think that engineers, accountants, and statisticians aren't the artsy type, when the reality is the exact opposite. Almost every person in every line of work uses his or her creative side to solve problems, come up with new ideas, and create opportunities.

The same is true for wealth advisors and for you as an investor. It's not all about percentages, multiplication, graphs, and charts. It's about *thinking*. It's about thinking and strategizing and figuring out creative ways you can maximize your money. Some of it comes down to big-picture principles. How do you want to run your life? That is, do you need to declutter your physical surroundings to declutter your mind to make better decisions? Do you need to hire a part-time bookkeeper to help you handle mundane details of your business so you can concentrate on your own unique abilities and maximize your time so you can make money? How can you take assets or talents you have and turn them into wealth? There are lots of ways for you to think creatively about maximizing your finances and giving yourself more time and freedom.

Throughout the book, you have and will continue to learn about my base principles and strategies. And I do think you'll find that there are plenty of creative approaches throughout (e.g., the mind map found on page 39 is one of the ways to unlock your own preconceived notions about life). This chapter, though, is really about maximizing your creativity when it comes to investments. I covered the basic tenets of investments in Chapter 5, as I took you through asset allocation and the like. All of that will provide a baseline for what you should do when investing your money.

This chapter is about taking those strategies one step further—thinking about new and creative ways to build the asset base you deserve and create the life you want. One caveat: this chapter is really for people who have some financial stability and sufficient liquid reserves. With high reward often comes high risk, so some of these strategies won't always pay off. If you don't have your basics covered, then you shouldn't necessarily be making risky or volatile investments or going beyond the foundation principles I've outlined.

But if you do have a little nest egg, some stability in your job, liquid reserves, and a strong and diversified portfolio, and you are well on you way to building your retirement, then you can afford to take some chances at building even more wealth. As always, this may be a case when you want to involve a wealth advisor to help take you through your evaluation and the steps. I outline these to help give you new ideas, to help you think outside the box, and to give you the opportunity to grow to heights you may have never imagined.

Take a Shot at Your Great Idea. You probably know all about the newfangled ways that people fund their ideas and projects. They go to sites like kickstarter.com, pitch their idea to the masses, and then people kick in a few dollars (or more) to give them the capital to create an app, start a restaurant, write a book, whatever their entrepreneurial idea may be. (In return, people usually get something for their investment, maybe a credit or some kind of prize.)

I'm not suggesting that you be the one to fund the project, but how about you take a chance on your great idea? You can raise the initial capital through these crowd-funding sites, develop your idea, and then take it to market. This kind of path allows you to follow your dreams and perhaps even make it big, because there's so little investment on your end because the masses are the ones who are helping you build that initial capital.

Go Vintage. These days—even in an age when phones talk, 3D printers push the envelope of high-tech manufacturing, and cars are almost ready to fly—there's a great market for all things retro. We love the past. We love history. We love the way it feels to look back at things that have value *because* they're old. I can't tell you what to like, but if you have a hankering for vintage cars, baseball cards, wines, or art, there's a chance that others do too. So one way to create investment income is to put some of your money into these retro-type goods. Chances are good that somewhere down the line you can sell them and make your money back in spades (provided you don't want to keep it because you love that 1968 Camaro Z/28 too much). There are so many wonderful examples of things you can sell, such as furniture, antique jewelry, paperweights, sterling silver flasks, and so on. The key here is that you have to do your research to make sure you understand the market and that you're getting proper quality.

Chapter 13
The Urge to Splurge

How to Find the Balance between Crossing Stuff Off Your Bucket List and Not Blowing Your Wealth

Splurging too often on almost anything is usually a recipe for trouble. Splurge on ice cream sundaes, and you'll wind up with a whole host of health problems, not to mention clothes four sizes larger than you have now. Splurge on tequila, and you'll wind up wrecking your liver and quite possibly waking up in a gutter. The same is true for your money. If you go gangbusters, buying everything you think you want every time you think you want it, you're going to end up in the gutter for other reasons. That's because you're eventually going to outspend your income, live beyond your means, and be unable to pay for your basic necessities.

If you read just about any financial advice about treating yourself to life's indulgences, you get the picture: no can do. That is, cut what you don't need and focus on what you need. Ask yourself tough questions about what is necessary and what is luxury, and make decisions about how to live below your means and about saving first before spending. Where people get into trouble (I know from my dealing with some clients in this very situation) is they want and want and want, and some think they deserve it. They feel their income levels can keep up. But here's the thing: no matter what your income, most of us can't keep up with overindulging, impulse buying, and frivolous expenses that seem to satisfy us in the short term at the expense (literally) of our long-term well-being. We aren't entitled to successful lives; we have to earn them just like the rest of the world.

Here, however, is where I want to twist things around like a Chubby Checker fan. I want you to indulge. I want you to use your wealth to enjoy life. I want you to follow your

149

passions. And, if a $300 pair of shoes gives you such rich and deep life satisfaction, then buy the $300 pair of shoes.

The catch is (there's always a catch, right?) that you must manage the indulgences, you must prioritize your purchases, and you must be able to assess the difference between what you are deeply passionate about and what you *think* you are (I'm guessing it's not the $300 pair of shoes when it really comes down to it).

I could fill an entire book telling you that if you want to be the millionaire you think you deserve to be (and the one that you can be at an early age), you must save, save, save, invest, invest, invest—and not deviate from this process. You will do that, and you need to do that. But I will also tell you that real wealth isn't always about the number at the end of your portfolio; it's about how rich and satisfying your life is.

So you shouldn't feel handcuffed by your goal to save and invest. In a way, it's a little bit like going on a diet. Yes, you could eat fish and vegetables for every meal, but once in a while, you need to let loose a little. For me, I like to indulge on frozen yogurt with berries or fresh fruit from time to time. That's the key phrase: "from time to time." If you splurge in your diet all the time, you'll compromise your health. Do it with your money, and you'll compromise your wealth. But the occasional dive into a bowl of chocolate—literally and metaphorically—isn't what does the damage.

You should feel free to use the money you've earned to cross things off your bucket list, to make memories with your family, and to do the incredible things that life has to offer. And that's exactly what I do. I make sensible choices when it comes to everyday expenses, not wasting money on store-bought lattes and taking full advantage of sales and specials when I buy commodities like suits or cars. But I also don't scrimp when it comes to making sure my family and I are living the lives we want. So we take trips together, we spend time at the shore in the summer, and we're building memories in the process.

For example, on my fiftieth birthday, my family and I traveled to Germany, where we bought my wife a car that she'd always wanted (it's actually a better deal when you travel to buy this car, because of the incentives that the manufacturer offers). We rented a beautiful apartment with breathtaking views of the Matterhorn in the Alps. I even fulfilled one of my lifelong dreams of skiing in the Alps. It was a trip that I will remember for the rest of my life—and one my family will remember too. So I don't have one regret about spending money on that trip, because I don't do those things all the time and the money spent was well worth it because of the dividends it paid in terms of family connection.

But it's not just about trips and travel. You can find ways to reach the same goals of splurging and creating memories for your family. One tradition our family has is that every year, during the week before Halloween, we host a pumpkin-carving party. It's actually a contest in which thirty or forty people come over and carve pumpkins. We cater it, and we hire a world-class classical guitarist to play the background music and set the stage for some fun conversation and a good old-fashioned pumpkin carving competition with great prizes! It's a special day for my family and friends, and it doesn't cost all that much money, just the cost of food and hiring the musician. In a yearly budget, it's just pennies. Those are the kinds of things that have no monetary value—but they're the ones that last a lifetime. The point is, it doesn't have to be the Alps or pumpkins that you do. But it should be something that's meaningful to you and your family. That, in my opinion, is the most strategic way to splurge.

When you're trying to figure out how to balance between living within your means and spending on life's luxuries, my biggest recommendation is to really prioritize (as a family) what's important to you. While I can't give you the answer that works for you and your family, I do think the most value comes from when you choose experiences, memories, and stories over stereos, jewelry, and four-digit bottles of wine.

After all, what is the point of developing wealth if you can't spend it in some of your prime years? This chapter is about how to find that sweet spot between establishing and developing a plan for financial security and also making sure that, well, you live a little (maybe a lot!) too.

Be Impatient. One of the goals of this book is helping you reach your financial goals some five or more years earlier than you might typically be able to do, and if you follow my strategies, you can make that happen. That said, I don't want you to think that the sped-up time frame means you need to morph into penny-pinching mode, waiting to live your life until you reach all of your financial goals. I do admire people who decide to live it up in retirement—those people who travel or really do it up once they reach a certain age and have financial stability. There's nothing wrong with following that path, if that's what you want to do.

But I have a slightly different point of view about the way you should approach doing the things you really want in life: do it now. Don't wait until you're sixty-five or seventy. Why? You're very likely in the prime of your life—body-wise and brain-wise. And heck, we know all too well that you can never know what your fate may be, and there's no guarantee that you'll even make it to that sixty-five- or seventy-year-old benchmark with a sound mind and body.

For example, my dad died at eighty-seven years old, and in hindsight, I felt he died too early. I wish I knew he was going to go downhill fast. If I had, I would have tried to maximize even more of the experiences he had with his children and grandchildren when he was in his sixties and seventies. I don't want to pepper you with "carpe diem" pleas, but that's exactly what you need to do. You need to be smart about your money, but you also should not have a "wait until tomorrow" approach to doing the things you've always dreamed of. You can do it now, you should do it now, and you'll be happier if you do it now. Don't settle for the status quo. Explore, dream, make plans, and follow through (within your budget).

Get Tangible. You know that bucket list that's been swirling around in your head? You know, the one that says you want to take a safari in Africa, drink wine in Napa, spend a month one summer at the beach, or learn how to play piano, guitar, or a ukulele? Write it down. All of it. I don't care if it feels more outlandish than a poodle in a purple dress. Put it on the list. Better yet, make it a family affair and have everyone get together to talk about their bucket-list items. When you get them all in one list, discuss each item—why you want to do it, what it means to you, and when you'd like to do it. Whether your list is four things or four hundred, your next step is a crucial one: prioritize them.

Now you don't have to rank them from one to ninety-nine, but you should group them in different categories based on a timeline: what you want to do tomorrow, next year, within the next five years, and long term. This timeline gives you a sense of prioritization so you and your family can agree on common goals.

Remember, having those common goals and values is what helps you plan and strategize financially. But I will also say this: as the breadwinners in your family, you as parents should take the lead and even feel comfortable mandating those goals. Why? Your time is limited and your kids will have their own lives to fill their own bucket lists. So if you want an active vacation of sightseeing and your kids would rather be at the beach, it's okay to take the lead. One, they'll appreciate that they've seen the world (even if that appreciation comes some years later), and two, as the parent you have earned the right to take control of the family ship. Every decision doesn't have to be a one. You do it because life throws lots of curveballs your way and you don't want to wait to fulfill your own dreams.

I will also say that you should be as specific as possible when writing down your lists. Don't just say you want to travel; say you want to go to see the Northern Lights in Iceland. Don't just say that it's important to buy a motorcycle; say you want a Harley-Davidson Superlow 1200T. Being tangible doesn't lock you into that destination per se (it's not as if you're signing a contract), but it does help you start to plan and figure out what it will cost to help you live life large—right now.

Have a Search Party. Now that you have your list, you and members of your family have your job, which is to do your research. Find out how much your bucket-list items will cost you (that smartphone is about to become very handy in the "search party process"). How much are violin lessons per month? How much is a trip for four to Antarctica? How much for that backyard hot tub? You don't need to have exact numbers (after all, costs do change over time), but you should have ballpark numbers so you can start planning how you'll pay for them. You can even split the tasks or pay your kids an hourly rate to do the initial research—that's a win–win situation in lots of ways (see my chapter on teaching children about wealth). This also helps kids get excited about these splurge items (if they're not initially), maybe even to the point where they want to see if they can contribute to the planning (or paying!) for a tiny slice of the trip too.

Your main goal: when you have that priority list of your top five or ten things on your collective bucket list, you can now place the price tag next to each item. This gives you the power to take care of the next steps when it comes to actually being able to afford these items: calculating the costs and making the first one or two goals on your list a reality.

Work the Pluses and Minuses. Now that you have the approximate costs of your bucket-list items, you can come up with a financial strategy to make your dreams a reality. And it all just comes down to very simple accounting. You have to work in these variable costs of your wishes into fixed costs of your monthly or yearly budget, whether it's going without certain things or shaving a little from what you're going to earmark for investments. You simply have to make the numbers balance. Now I would certainly recommend that you don't compromise your future retirement or monthly dollar-cost averaging budgets. However, where you could shave costs is from your other expenses.

Can you find areas to cut that you can then divert to your most important bucket-list line item? That's what will ensure that you not only have money for your dream expenditures, but that you also don't sacrifice any of your long-term security to get there. But see how this works? If you just say that you're going to put the Porsche on a credit card, then that's how you'll keep the monkey on your back—unable to keep up with payments, then finding yourself in a heck of a mess. Spending on seemingly frivolous things is different from spending frivolously. If you budget right and plan strategically, it doesn't matter what you spend your money on—if it makes you happy and doesn't sacrifice your long-term wealth.

And really, this is all about establishing priorities and values. I have clients who live in a modest house (in need of some repairs), but they pay for private school so that their three children can pursue their musical talents. Sue and John don't have much disposable income, but their kids sing in the Philadelphia Boys and Girls Choir and they've traveled to places like Italy and Australia to sing in churches and amazing venues around the world. Sue and John don't complain; they've made a decision about what their financial priorities are. Some people would call the investment they've made a splurge, and that's okay because they make other financial sacrifices based on what they've established as priorities in their lives—and the kids are experiencing something that very few children get to experience. That's often something you can't put a price tag on.

Create the Recess Account. Admittedly, trying to budget for bucket-list items above and beyond your regular entertainment items can be daunting. And it might take a long time to build those safari funds if you're just squirreling away a hundred dollars a month. So another option for you is to create an entirely different account—one that has nothing to do with your portfolios or your regular budget, where you're using income to pay bills, save for retirement, and invest. This play account is solely for the big bucket-list items (that you and your family agree on).

That allows you to create a budget within a separate account (i.e., if it has $20,000 in it, then you agree that $5,000 will be spent on a trip, $2,000 on the pet llama, and so on). Now this situation could work best for people who have extra sources of income, be it in annual bonuses or side businesses (see Chapter 11). I do like this option because when you agree that all of your above-and-beyond fun money is coming from one account, you're less likely to risk dipping into your monthly account to pay for things you shouldn't be spending money on. Again, the key here is that you have to mutually agree on what priorities are and how much you're all willing to spend on them. Then, with all the online options at your fingertips, stretch your recess account by using your smartphone or computer to shop around for all commodity type purchases.

Repeat This Mantra Three Times. Indulge is not the same thing as impulse. Indulge is not the same thing as impulse. Indulge is not the same thing as impulse.

I want you to indulge in the finer things in life, and the definition of "finer things" is all up to you. What I don't want you to do is do is make decisions by impulse. Impulse spending—giving into immediate and short-term temptations that don't really provide soul-satisfying happiness—is the exact thing that gets you into trouble. Spending on a whim on things that seem like they're important but really aren't (that diesel-powered blender, perhaps?) is the reason why so many Americans are in debt. And when you see that difference—between indulge and impulse—you can create the kind of wealth I'm talking about. That's the wealth that exists not only in your portfolio, but in your heart as well. If you follow the steps I outlined here—create the list, prioritize the list, design the plan, and make the budget—then you've taken away the power of the impulse buy while still getting exactly what you want out of life.

SECTION 3

FINANCIAL FOCUS

Managing Life's Special Wealth-Building and
Wealth-Threatening Circumstances

Chapter 14
Child's Pay

Make It Easy for Your Kids to Make Lots of Money

With the exception of a small percentage of children who learn about money at an early age, most kids have a fairly limited view about what money is, how it works, and why—despite the number of times you've told them—it simply does not grow on the oak tree in the front yard. After all, maybe they learned about cash via Monopoly money, where the stakes are low and your paycheck comes when you roll the dice and Advance to GO. Or maybe they learned that money was a piece of plastic in mommy or daddy's wallet with no idea about what a credit card meant. Or maybe they just thought of money as the coins they found in the couch, the dollar they get for doing chores, or that fifty-dollar bill grandma slips into a birthday card every year.

There's also a good chance that kids grow up on either side of the extremes. Either their parents are very frugal, so kids learn to never spend money, or their buy-anything parents show their kids that they can afford whatever they want. As is the case with any extreme, both have their downsides—that is, kids don't really learn what money is, or more importantly how to create wealth. They don't learn how to think about their financial future and the outcomes they desire until they're well out of the house and on their own.

The truth is, you have a great opportunity to teach your kids about wealth, to instill good habits, and to reinforce your own family values by teaching them about what money really is—and how it should be treated. And that's something that, no matter how many times you get out of jail for free, Monopoly can never do.

I'm lucky in that my parents taught me the value of money early on. In fact, one of my earliest memories was receiving several silver dollars as gifts from my father. I treasured them, and I still have them. I learned that not only were they valuable because they were worth more than the face value of the coin, but there was also an emotional attachment since they were from my father.

So this chapter is really for anyone who has kids—no matter their age—to help you navigate the often tricky waters of introducing your kids to money in a meaningful way. The reason it can feel awkward is because many of us were taught that finances were private—and they are. But sometimes we mistake privacy for secrecy. Just because our kids don't have to know the amount of money in our bank accounts or what our salaries are, that doesn't mean they should be shielded from financial principles—the major one being that money is more than just an earn-it-spend-it proposition.

One of the reasons it's so important is because kids, quite frankly, won't get this education unless it comes from you. According to information gathered by the Council for Economic Education, while 90 percent of people believe that financial education should be offered in schools, only 19 states require that a personal finance course be offered (and that doesn't necessarily mean that everyone takes it). Simply put, many children will not learn basic financial fundamentals unless parents do the teaching. If parents don't take a leadership role, their kids will grow up without a clue about the proper techniques and strategies to follow.

As I have done with my three kids, I would encourage you to integrate some financial lessons into your already full parenting plate. Yes, I know there's so much to cover. You're dealing with trying to teach your kids to be good students and good citizens, to share toys and drive safely, and so many other lessons. But I can assure you that the habits aren't hard to establish, and the payoff is great. It will give them the foundation for being smart custodians of their own fortune—starting it, growing it, cultivating it as they become adults. If we as parents view one of our jobs as being the protectors of our children, this early financial education is certainly one very good (and often ignored) way to do it.

Ultimately what you're trying to do is teach your kids that money, if used properly, is a tool they can use to open up opportunities for themselves.

With wealth, they will have more freedom to seek what they want in life. Of course, that's a difficult concept to explain to a child (especially a young one whose main focus might be trying to convince you to buy the new Barbie or Nerf toy). But the way you do it is not by using phrases like "leverage opportunity;" it's by using very small, relatable tactics that teach them lessons about how money works.

Though different ages require different strategies, it's never too late to start, even if your children are nearing their flight from the home quarters. These are my guidelines for teaching them the financial lessons that will stay with them—and their families—for their whole life.

Ages and Stages

Age	Money Lessons
Toddler	Teach values of coins, play "store" with fake money, talk and show other people working, talk about "needs" and "wants"
Under-7	Compare prices of items you need at the grocery store and have them do the same with toys or things they want; start with three jars for saving, spending, and charity
Preteens	Discuss savings, compound interest (by showing how much money they can make), the danger of credit cards; show them bills
Teens	Discuss taxes, expenses, college costs, budgeting, dollar cost averaging, sample bank statements, and even retirement accounts

Use the Rule of Thirds. Certainly, part of the trick to teaching your kids anything, whether it be manners or why they should always root for your hometown team, is establishing those habits early on. For almost all of these strategies, the earlier you start, the better shot you'll have of the lesson sticking (early, being about seven years old, since that's the approximate age that they can grasp basic money concepts). That said, the very first habit you should instill is that any income your children receive—from gifts, allowances, jobs, whatever—should be divided into thirds. This is how I did it for my children:

➤ 1/3 to save for something long term (like that car in ten years)

➤ 1/3 to give to others (be it a church or charity or those in need—in an area that's of particular interest to the child).

➤ 1/3 for fun (to spend as they wish)

I do these ratios for a couple of reasons. For one, that second category is extremely important in teaching kids that there's a bigger world around them—one that involves more than just them. That's an important family value my wife and I have, and we think it helps teach kids to be kind, compassionate, well-meaning adults. And two, I like to establish early on that they can start budgeting between what they want right this instant and what they might want in the future. It teaches them how to balance short-term and long-term thinking.

This actually gets them ready for the idea that later on, they're going to have to pay taxes to Uncle Sam (at state, local, and federal levels)—not that taxes and charity are the same thing. But it still reinforces the concept that some of "their" money can go elsewhere. Most importantly, though, it helps delay gratification. That is, it's not healthy for kids to always get what they want when they want it; they have to work and save for what they want. And when they do, the item has more value. That's a concept that we can reinforce with this rule of thirds.

I like the Rule of Thirds allocation because it's simple math for even young minds to learn. You can create three different buckets, cans, or piggy banks to make it a a fun weekly process. The key point to kickstart their learning is that you make those three categories the family value that becomes the standard by which all of their money travels. They will accept it, learn from it, and thank you for it (especially when they turn sixteen and have a bigger nest egg!).

Remember the No. 1 Rule of Parenting. Make them eat the broccoli? Always read to them at night? Never tie their shoes together because you think it would be funny? While yes, those things are all important, the rule that trumps all rules might just be "your child will model your behavior." If you model spend-thrift behavior, your child will likely mirror those habits, as they will with saving, spending, giving to charity, and any other financial habits you have and they can see. As the saying goes, you have to walk the walk, not just talk the talk. And if you want your child to grow up with good habits, you have to own it and really work at it. It's not enough to just hope everything will work out. You have to behave in the way you want your kids to model. Then as they get older, you can talk about it and be explicitly clear about these concepts, which they will start to relate to as they become more and more aware of the value of wealth.

So no matter what you say, they will follow what you do and how you act. No matter what kind of ideal financial world you want to create for them, it won't mean a thing if you spend frivolously yourself. If you create the rule of thirds for your kids, then you should explain how that works in your household too; you don't have to give the specifics, but you should show them that money is something to value and that you work very hard for it. Don't make light decisions on how to spend it, and and let them donate it to causes that you and your family think are important. Those lessons—even if the kids seem too young—are essential and you should start early, because they see *everything* you do.

"Show Me the Money" Is More than Just a Means to Buy Videos Games. Part of this comes from establishing the flow of their money to charity as I described above. But I also think that part of teaching about money is instilling the worldly view that there are other people around them in different financial situations—and there are some people who are in great need. So what I want to show my kids is that when we think about our own wealth, we can also spend some time thinking about how we can contribute to the greater good.

So let's say my daughter decides she wants to spend money on new clothes. We go through her closet and find clothes she doesn't want anymore that she can donate, not only to make room for the new clothes, but also to show that there's still value in what we have and that others may benefit from it. This applies to toys, games, books, and anything that others in need could use. It's a lesson on charity and helping others, yes, but it's also a lesson on valuing what you have.

Give Them the Gift of Ownership. Oh, the birthday gifts, Christmas gifts, Hanukah gifts, Easter gifts. They want the truck, the jewelry, the toys, the animals (stuffed or live), the games, the balls, the dolls, the trampoline. They want what's fun. All parents will likely agree that there is a certain joy watching a child open a gift that he or she really wanted; we love the way their eyes and mouths open and the pure innocence that enjoys whatever is under the wrapping paper. Wonderful moments indeed. While I don't want to take that joy away from them (or you), I do want you to consider less commercial gifts and substitute another kind of gift that you can give your children—a piece of the pie. Not in the grandmother's-apple-pie kind of way, but in the you-own-some-of-the-company kind of way.

That's right, I want you to consider giving your child one or several shares of stock in a company that he or she really likes. For example, my kids have stock in Disney, General Mills (because my son loves Green Giant frozen peas), and Kraft (because my daughter loves Kraft macaroni and cheese). I even told my daughter that I was giving her a share in Kraft mac-and-cheese. That's not accurate, of course, because you can't buy a stock in one single food item, but I did it on purpose because that's how she relates to it—and that makes it more meaningful. Simultaneously, I deposited the real share of Kraft in her custodial account. If we as parents can create those connections with the things our children love, the ideas that we want to teach them become real, become relatable, and become the foundation for the habits and values they will have as they grow up.

I bought my children stocks as gifts for a few reasons. One, it gives them their first lesson in the way the market works. We can watch it together, look at the numbers, talk about the growth, and they can see their money earn (or lose) value over time. I observed my daughter as she accompanied my wife and I to the supermarket. We selected a box of her Kraft mac-and-cheese off the shelf and placed it in our shopping cart. You should have seen the excitement in her eyes knowing that a piece of the company she owned was going into our shopping cart. Because it's in a company that children like, they're interested and they can relate to it, it's not some abstract conversation about the market.

Two, I do this because it's a better long-term investment than the traditional way we used to invest our children's money—in banks. Traditionally, we'd put money in a savings account, it would earn some interest, and they'd make a little money on the original investment. But that's no longer a realistic option since banks currently pay you so little interest. So this lesson in investments teaches how money can grow.

Three, I like that it teaches them about how companies work—that public companies are owned by shareholders who can have a say in the way the company works. Unfortunately, most elementary and high schools in America today do not teach a personal finance or investment course. The responsibility to jumpstart your children's financial learning process and curiosity about saving and investing rests squarely on your shoulders as parents or grandparents. Your very young kids may not fully grasp these concepts, but as they get older, your regular financial interactions will show them a bit of how the corporate world works. You will, in effect, bring them your own version of a personal finance course complete with financial benefits that they will enjoy as they take over the reins of their own financial future later in life.

Finally, I like this technique because these ongoing gifts have long-term benefits, not just financially but also educationally. A toy or doll is wonderful for many reasons (namely because of the emotional attachment it provides between parent and child in the way the coins my father gave me did). But the gift of stocks—or even better, shares of many different stocks over the course of an entire childhood—is something that can grow with them for a long time. That has both a tangible and emotional benefit for the kids. With my older children, they've learned how the stock market works and are now making decisions about their own investments. That's something that few high school kids do, but the experience they got as children provided them the foundation to do this on their own. Incidentally, it has bolstered their self confidence in an essential area to better take advantage of financial opportunities later in their adult life.

Even better, this gifting technique is perfect for relatives to participate in because it can provide meaningful conversations and connections between your child and, say, his or her grandparents. For example, if the stock is in a company with which they share a common bond (like, Disney, if you all took a trip there together, or maybe even Microsoft if they all enjoyed playing Xbox together) then they will have more in common to discuss in future family gatherings. I really believe that this is more than just a gift of a share of a public company. It's really a gift of inspiration—to help your kids think, dream, learn, and develop their own sense of wealth and life satisfaction. They will also observe (assuming I have selected strong growth companies) significant appreciation over their adolescent and young adult years, which will translate into appreciation due to the magic of compounding over time.

> **Question: Should I pay my kids for getting good grades on report cards?**

Answer: I say yes, if the child needs a little extra motivation (or may have trouble focusing). And the reason is that because kids have very little opportunity to make money at a young age, they need to have some sort of foundation to start saving and teach them money lessons. So this is one technique to do that. The amount, of course, depends on your own wealth, but if you divide it properly with spending, saving, and charity, then it's not as if they're getting a frivolous $20 to spend on whatever they want.

Many people disagree with this, and I can see why. The thought is that parents should expect kids to do well in school. They want their kids to enjoy learning and not do their work just because they're going to get a bonus for doing well. But to me, the important point isn't that you're paying for the grade; it's the lessons with what you do after that.

Don't Buy Them Everything. This may sound like a no-brainer. Of course you're not going to spend money on frivolous items just because your child wants a surfboard or roller skates or the latest and greatest in sparkly thingamadoodles. But it's actually a lot trickier than it sounds. What happens when they want a piece of candy in the checkout aisle or that ninety-nine-cent toy in the clearance bin?

It's easy to say, "Sure, you've been good. Why not? It's only a couple of dollars." But the lessons you teach them early will still hold true as they get older—and the little-ticket items become big-ticket items. After all, when it comes to money, patience really is a virtue, especially as we learn not to indulge in those immediate-gratification items. So early on, you and your partner should decide what the essential items are, be they clothes, books, or anything else. Those are the things that you provide as parents. But you also should try to think of things that belong in the nonessential category—things like that candy bar.

If you don't keep candy in the house because you don't believe it's healthy, but you do think your kids can have those kinds of sweets every once in a while, that's the perfect kind of item to start teaching them about money. Say, "If this is something you want, then you can take from your piggy bank to buy it." This forces your child, even at an age of seven or eight—to start thinking about the value of money. That ninety-nine cents may not seem like a lot to you, but it sure is to a child when they only have five bucks to spend.

Now, perhaps the most difficult part of this is that the line between essential and nonessential blurs a bit as they get older. Take sports equipment. Where does that fall? Perhaps you want them to participate in sports because of the values that they can instill (my daughter, for example, has gained a world of knowledge from the values and skills she learned by competing in lacrosse). But what happens if your child is just trying out a sport? How much equipment should you have to buy? Those are the things you as a family need to decide.

For us, lacrosse was an important investment because of the values she has

> **Question: How do I help my child find and prepare for his or her first real job??**
>
> **Answer:** Besides having documents in order (such as a resume of school activities and tax forms), you should network to see what places might be looking for a kid for part-time work (besides taking the usual routes of Craigslist, classified, and job posting on websites and in stores). Perhaps the greatest thing you can do is help prepare kids with a mock interview of questions that might be asked and help them with your connections to find initial temporary jobs.

learned while competing—the values of hard work, diligence, and committing oneself individually and to a group activity. It helps give her a sense of identity and self-confidence (traits that will undoubtedly help her as she gets older), and those are the things that we, as parents, want to invest in because the benefits will come back in spades. And that, I believe, is one of the reasons why parents do choose to invest in those extracurricular activities.

So what about the smartphone that all of their friends have? Kids often need a phone these days to communicate with parents when they're separated, but is a smartphone necessary for a nine-year-old? I have never believed that my children need that kind of luxury at a young age, even though their friends may have them (mainly because of the monumental distractions from society and family that they can cause). Our solution: our youngest child has a regular phone and can borrow my smartphone when she wants to play games or use apps; that way, the time is limited and she can still enjoy the device without being obsessed about it.

We don't view the smartphone as an essential (though many selfie-obsessed kids would argue otherwise!), and we've told our daughter that she'll get one when we believe it's the appropriate time. And our solution—allowing her to pop on Instagram or whatever she likes a few times a day—has worked. She can still indulge a little, but not obsess to the point where her nose would be stuck in the phone all day long. So we've done three things—instill the values we want her to have about the importance of personal interactions (rather than technological ones), found a way to save some money for a few years, and taught her that valuable lesson about delayed gratification.

The answer, in these cases, differs for every family, and it's why you have to articulate those family values that I talked about at the beginning of the book. I can't make *your* list of what's essential and nonessential; the point is that you should make your own list so your kids have clear boundaries and can start thinking about this part of wealth: deciding what you want, what you need, and how to make those choices about buying what you want depending on how much money you have.

Give Them Opportunities to Earn. We all know that kids, even at a young age, will be integrated into the mix of doing household chores. Whether it's taking out the garbage, clearing the table, or bringing the laundry from room to room, all children will have more everyday chores as they get older—not only to help out, but also to instill the habits that it takes work to run a household. And everybody should contribute to that process. There are certain things everyone must do without the expectation of receiving anything in return.

That said, you can't teach kids about money unless they have a little of their own. After all, it is important that they have fun and enjoy the pleasure of buying what they want, whether it's candy, a stuffed animal, a video game, headphones, whatever. You do need to give them the opportunity to experience that pleasure, and you can help them do that (and value their purchases more) by showing them how they can make their own money.

Before they're of legal working age, it's difficult for them to earn any money short of collecting for birthdays or setting up lemonade stands. So I've always believed that we should give our kids the opportunity to make money—and that's how they learn to treat it with respect (following the rule of thirds I outlined above). So especially as they get older, you should think of ways that they can earn money (and potentially save you some in the process). Maybe it's spreading the mulch, moving some boxes, or even doing some computer research work as they get older.

This work-for-pay system can work well in families because it's a win–win for both sides. The kids get to earn some cash, and you get more help around the house and potentially save money by not having to hire professionals to do tasks that your kids could do. I believe you should treat these jobs as professionally as you can—outline the expectations and the rate, and offer supervision and guidance as necessary. Heck, you can even write them their paychecks on Fridays if you want. Treating it professionally helps instill a good work ethic and makes expectations clear—habits that will carry over to their first and (hopefully) all jobs.

Send Them Into the Neighborhood. When your kids get to be preteen age, they will be ready to take their talents outside the house. Be it by babysitting, yard work, dog walking, pet sitting, carrying groceries for older neighbors, or maybe even some tech talent, your kids can start to make some money. Besides the fact that these jobs pay pretty well per hour (and the money won't come out of your own pocket), your kids will help save money for the neighbors for the same reason: kids are cheaper than the pros.

I also really like this method because it will force your kids to go out of their comfort zone of working for their own parents, teaching them a different kind or responsibility and also giving them lifelong skills such as confidence (and even marketing, as perhaps they try to drum up their own work with fliers or whatnot). Our goal here is to help them develop strong work habits as well as start growing that nest egg. And remember, when it's all divided into thirds, the savings will add up.

Don't underestimate the power of their tech talents, especially compared to those of your generation. There will be things that your kids can do with a computer, phone, tablet, or other gadget that we might not even be able to dream of doing. All it takes is a little networking to find out what your neighbors might need, and your kid could make a nice little chunk of change by helping out with some of those areas.

Whether it's uploading videos to YouTube or creating a website, your child might be able to offer high-quality services for a fraction of the professional price. You can help your child use his or her talents to think creatively about ways to earn money. And as they get older, they may even find professional ways to use those tech talents; some firms hire younger folks after-hours to help with IT support. What a great entry into the real world—solving real-world issues with the flexibility of being able to work after school.

Don't Buy Them a Car Outright. Oh, the car. For the kids, it's the symbol of freedom. For the parents, it's the source of worry. But you take away those two aspects of what driving means and just make it about the money for our purposes. Then at some point, you'll probably have to make a decision about what wheels the kids get. Do they get to borrow yours? Do they get a car of their own?

Here's my recommendation. Even if you have the means, do not buy them the car and just hand it over. This will be the greatest expense of a kid's early life, and this is one of the reasons why you set up the rule of thirds to begin with—to give them that pot of money that could be put toward a car as they get older. The chances of them taking care of the car responsibly greatly increases if they're involved in the financing of it.

Now does that mean you can't help them out? Of course not. But you can set up some kind of system, be it that the child pays half and you loan the other half. Or you can do something like I did. I bought a car (that I deemed as safe and appropriate) and set up a system where my son would pay for expenses, such as gas, and then have the option to buy the car when he moves out of the house if he cared for it well. So while I paid the initial expense to get him going as a sixteen-year-old, if he wanted to keep that car when he moved out, he would have had to save enough money to buy it at the depreciated value—and be able to pay the expenses. That kind of partnership, I think, is an important one for helping establish financial responsibility.

Think Partnership. Just as I described in the case above, splitting expenses can be an excellent system for how you treat some expenses in your household, both at an early age and as kids grow older. This certainly could apply to college expenses. Perhaps you make a deal where you pay for the tuition, but they must cover living expenses, which would encourage them to get a job, save, etc. (More on college in Chapter 15.)

It could also apply to texting and data plans with phones, the costs of which have soared with the speed of rocket boosters. Does your child get a free ride on your phone plan? Perhaps, but maybe you make a deal where your child has to pay a certain amount per month if he or she wants unlimited data (all those Instagram and Snapchat photos and other videos can add up!).

It doesn't have to break their bank, but again, this helps teach them about bills and reinforces that all the money they earn should not go just toward fun stuff. This is one of the key values I've tried to instill in our kids—that it's not all about money earned and money spent. Remember, the point isn't for you to take a couple of bucks off your phone bill every month by having your kids pay some; it's to teach them the true value of using, saving, and investing money.

Get the Whole Family Involved. Finally, this may be the most important strategy of all when it comes to creating wealth for your children. Have grandparents, aunts, uncles, and extended family members all contribute to your children's wealth. They can do it in a number of ways. Does every single birthday gift from a relative need to be a toy? Of course not. If they ask, you could politely suggest the idea for a share of stock or a contribution to a college fund. It may not be very "birthday friendly" for a five-year-old, but it's something that will help them immensely, and they will value and appreciate it as they get older.

But it doesn't have to be just a financial contribution; it can be a "life lesson" contribution as well. I remember my uncle talking about investments all the time, and those lessons have stuck with me. If you have extended family members who are financially savvy, there's no reason to discourage them from teaching your kids little lessons along the way. This is often a wonderful role for grandparents to play, because they don't come off as lecturing, disciplining, or enforcing rules; they're simply sharing their wisdom and passing it down.

My father, for instance, had a one-word saying that he passed along to me and my own children. He explained it this way: If I had a flag flying over my house, it would say "today" on it, because tomorrow may never come. Today is the day to take action! In other words, make every day about making important decisive steps, like to save, because today really is about preparing yourself for tomorrow. That's a lesson—a simple, poignant one—that has stuck with me for half a century. And now it's one that will stick with my children too.

Chapter 15
Your Tuition Mission

Tackling One of the Biggest Expenses Parents Will Face: College Education

Let me say this upfront: I know college isn't for every kid. In today's world especially, there are plenty of opportunities for children to pursue after high school that don't involve two-year degrees, four-year degrees, or graduate school. There are places like trade schools and specialty schools. There are entrepreneurial opportunities, there are careers that don't require college degrees, and there's life on the road with the band made up of a group of long-bearded fellas living out of a 1987 minivan. Your children's paths after high school is up to you and them to decide.

Some form of college does tend to be the path that many kids take. The kids want it as the next logical step in their career, and they know there are many educational, professional, and social networking opportunities that await. It's the place where we often see our kids truly morph and develop from the tykes we remember to the tycoons they have the opportunity of becoming. So it's no surprise that many of us choose the college path, whether it's a big school or small school, no matter what the major or the location. It's often the place where our children's eyes open to the world of new people, new ideas, and new ways of thinking about their own careers.

Along with those possibilities comes a price tag that will make your wallet whimper. According to the College Board, the average yearly cost for a four-year college education at a state school is about $9,000 for in-state students and $$22,000 for out-of-state students, while the average cost for a private education is about $30,000. And that's not even including room and board, which often costs upwards of $10,000 a year.

Multiply those numbers by the standard four years (and in some cases, longer than that), and multiply that by the number of kids you have, and then factor in that annual fees have traditionally risen about 5 or 6 percent a year over the last ten to twenty years. The final total for what you have to pay for a college education can feel like a wowzillion dollars. (One research study projected the annual costs of a private college, including room and board, to be around $130,000 a year in the year 2029–2030; public may be around $45,000 to $60,000 for tuition alone.)

While there are some families fortunate enough to have the cash to fund education without a worry, many people aren't in that position and need to find strategies to do so. Like every area of wealth, the earlier you start saving and planning for these kinds of experiences, the more likely you are to build the wealth to minimize the stress and maximize your ability to pay these costs. But I am also a realist and know that no matter how early we start, these college-related expenses are just too high for many families to handle. This chapter will help you come up with the tactics—and funds—to make sure your children can have the educational opportunities they want after high school.

With two kids in or having graduated college and a third who I fully expect to do the same, as well as hundreds of clients, I do have extensive experience with navigating the world of college tuition. I believe that with some savvy strategy, you can help defray the

> **What's the best investment I can make to help my child get into the college he or she wants?**
>
> **Answer:** Well, certainly this isn't a simple question because so much goes into the admissions process, from grades to test scores to extracurricular activities. And finding the right match—what college your child wants and what college wants your child—can be a dating game of sorts. Ultimately, I would invest our time and some money into visiting the colleges with our child that he/she is most passionate about. Remember to include both "reach schools" and "safety schools" in the mix.

costs and teach your kids some valuable lessons before they even step foot in their first college class.

Make a Deal With Your Kids. I think you know by now that one of the primary responsibilities that parents have is not to just create wealth for their own family, but also to teach their children about how to do it for themselves so they're instilled with good money and investing habits throughout their lives.

So I believe the first rule of paying for a college education is that you involve your kids in the financial plan. No, it's not about making them worry about how you're going to pay for college, but it's about getting them involved in one piece of the puzzle.

Example: For my son's college education, one of the arrangements we have is that he will have a living expense budget (that's above and beyond the tuition and related costs). This is a necessary part of any college-payment tactic because, like it or not, this is when our kids start "living" and need money for the high-dollar tuition bills as well as for managing their lives every day. So in that budget, what we've arranged is that anything he saves from that budget at the end of the year is his to keep.

I do this for a number of reasons. One, it teaches him to be smart about the money and only use it for what he really needs (or really, really wants), as I've already outlined in this book. Two, it makes him start thinking about his own wealth-creation strategies for when he moves beyond college. Three, it creates a situation where the money he earns himself can supplement his budget and he can *really* make his own wealth grow even during his college years. (In his case, he's attending a co-op university, so he'll be earning money from his job, but it also works for any situation in which a student gets a part-time job during school or over the summer.)

Finally, I do believe that these kinds of "keep the extra money" incentives work. Let's say he really wants to spend money on a new guitar, a new car, or a spring break trip with his buddies. He gets to control that income by making smart decisions about what he uses his money for every day. This way, he can create his own budget—x amount for food, x amount for entertainment, x amount for related college expenses, x amount to save so that he can spend it on whatever big-ticket item he has his eyes on.

Rather than just saying, "Oh, we're going to pay for your expenses," we've given him some guidelines to follow so he can transition from being provided for to being the one who's starting to do his own providing (granted, he's had a good base of experience saving and thinking about wealth creation, because we've used many of the strategies I just outlined for teaching kids early about finances).

The bigger point, though, is this is the kind of system you should be creating with your college-bound children. Make one of their lessons one that doesn't have to do with any class they'll take. Teach them the value of thinking about money as an adult. So no matter how you'll be paying for college (or perhaps how they'll be paying for a hunk of it themselves), you want to think through a way that they can contribute to their own wealth creation, which may be crazy to hear when college costs are so high. When you think about it, this is your last shot to really play a role and influence them on their skills and habits, and it's their first shot at taking what they've learned into their new world—before they get to the real world.

> **Ponderable Question: What's the best way to teach my kids about helping others?**
>
> **Answer:** The best way is to make them divide their "earnings" so that a portion must go to donations to those in need. But here's another great idea: once children in our extended family reach the age of twelve, they no longer receive gifts from aunts and uncles for their birthdays or holidays. Instead, each aunt and uncle gives their nieces and nephews $100 that they must use to donate to a charity group that means something to them. Each child must first get in front of the entire family and explain why they chose that particular cause.
>
> The dollar amount isn't as important as is the process of teaching your kids about how to think about helping others. One nice benefit is that the aunts and uncles give the money in the name of the children, so the children are the ones who receive the thank-you notes from the organizations, which helps them feel even better about the gift they have made.

The Mom & Dad Children's Savings Plan. To jump start the concept of tax deferred savings in a pension plan form, I introduce the concept of a real world 401K or 403B plan by using our own family matching program. As you may recall, a tax deferred savings plan provides deferral of taxes owed on earned taxable income within an account. We want a strong work ethic for our kids and we offer a matching program that mirrors what they will experience in a real 1099/ W-2 issuing job. In our family, for every dollar they earn (at jobs in which they get a 1099/ W-2, not babysitting or pet-sitting type of jobs), I match fifty cents on the dollar for every dollar they put into a Roth IRA. In a way, I'm almost paying them to work, but I think that it's essential that they take responsibility for creating their own wealth as early as possible. Additionally, they learned about financial commitments and the need to stay invested for the long term as these retirement funds must not be used prior to age 59 1/2.

Besides the very practical reason to do so (to help bolster their retirement nest), I also think the process has a very strong personal effect. I'm sending the message that we care about our children, that we have confidence in their abilities to earn and save, and that I believe in the power of family partnerships. And those are lessons that they can take with them, no matter their interests or careers. This matching program incidentally mirrors what our kids may experience in their future pension plans that their future employer offers.

Just like in the real working world, I insist they make their own investment choices and get used to enjoying the growth of their money plus the parent-matching funds. They also get to experience the joy of success (appreciation and income) or the agony of defeat (losses) if they make poor choices or trade too often. In my view, this matching/investing in a Roth IRA for our children not only mirrors a real adult-life responsibility/challenge, but also allows them to experience mistakes (losses) while the dollars involved are small.

Start Packing It Away. As is the case with just about any financial issue we encounter, the earlier you start saving, the better your outcome. If you look at the budget we outlined on page 42, then you already know that I suggest taking some money from your monthly income and marking it specifically for college costs. Start the process as soon as your kids are born and you'll have a nice little pile of money to pay the costs of college. The programs you may want to consider are the Uniform Gift to Minors Act (UGMA), the Uniform Transfer to Minors Act (UTMA), trust accounts and state 529 plans. UGMA and UTMA are custodial accounts that allow minors to own securities or other assets without a formal trust, but income is subject to the kiddie tax. Be aware, having these accounts could hurt your child's chances of qualifying for financial aid because these accounts are considered assets of the student.[19]

There are several different kinds, including a prepaid plan in which you pay today's tuition rates for credit toward a future tuition (and thus save money because of the rising costs that could happen between now and when your children go to college). Then there are 529 investment plans that allow you (and others, including grandparents) to make contributions to an account that's used for educational costs.

Both strategies work and have tax benefits, but rules and guidelines do vary by state, so it is smart to work with a professional wealth advisor to discuss your options and which work best for you. It should be noted that these 529 plans do have some disadvantages. States can change the rules and guidelines at any time, and some states require that the 529 be used for colleges only in that state, and you will owe taxes on the money if the funds aren't used in a way that's not outlined by the plan. But for many people, 529 plans do work well. As I mentioned in Chapter 8, Congress created a new wrinkle in 529 plans to allow parents and grandparents to pay private school tuition up to $10,000 a year tax free before college. There is no minimum time requirement, so you could theoretically deposit the money in August and withdraw it in September to pay a tuition bill. What's more, any money left over, which has grown tax free from the time you invested in the 529 account, can be used for all college expenses without the $10,000 limit.[20] It should also be noted that while these are state plans, some private schools have created their own version of a 529.

Don't Stress Out. I know there are plenty of things that scare you about college: the safety of your children, whether they will find their way or get lost in the shuffle, how well they'll manage themselves without having their parents be their back-up alarm clock for the 8:00 a.m. exam, or remind them to do their laundry. It's a wonderful time for kids, but it can be an angst-ridden time for parents.

The hefty price tag doesn't help matters. I know I used a sort of a scare tactic when I added up the potential costs of college a few pages ago, and on the surface, it looks like you could buy a yacht for what it costs to fund a college education. I don't, however, want you to go crazy thinking about the big number at the end. Why? Because that's not an absolute number.

There are so many opportunities for loans, aid, grants, and scholarships to help bridge what you have saved to what you need, that it's possible to pay for college in a number of different ways. Some of them will mean that you or your children will be saddled with some debt after they graduate, but the bottom line is that I don't want you to panic about the bottom line. With about twenty million people enrolled in college either full time or part time, the College Board estimates that the average full-time college student receives about $15,000 in aid a year (that includes both grants and loans). It can be done, no matter what you've saved. That doesn't mean it will be easy, but it does mean that it's not impossible.

Don't Break Your Own Bank. Much of life is about managing the temptations around us, whether they come in the form of financial ones ("I'd really love that hot tub for my porch!") to nutritional ones ("I'd really love that hot dog for my belly!"). As is the case with all temptations, we talk ourselves into choosing one option that will make us feel better in the short term at the expense of what might happen in the long term. When it comes to paying for college, here's the temptation you must avoid: using your retirement savings to pay for college.

If you have built up any kind of wealth in your retirement account, you may feel tempted to use a portion of that to help defray the costs of college, but it's the wrong move. Why? Because you and your kids have much more ability to pay for college expenses (right now and as loan payoffs) than you do to make money up in retirement.

So don't even think that's available to you to use for college. Besides being heavily taxed if you withdraw it, you'll lose all of that good foundation you have spent years building up. Education, we would certainly argue, is one of the most important things you will ever spend money on. But don't even think about touching your retirement to pay for it. There are better options to help you manage the costs.

Apply, Apply, Apply. It's no secret that there's money to use to help pay the costs of college, whether it comes in the form of loans (which you have to repay, though at lower interest rates) or merit scholarships and financial aid (which you don't). But you don't get them if you sit back and wait for somebody to knock on the door with a check made out to your college of choice. You must apply, and you must be assertive about it. Look for the standard places to apply for financial aid and loans, but once you have your college choices narrowed down, also look for specific scholarships that are offered within that university, college, or even major. It is absolutely worth scheduling a meeting with the school's financial aid office to talk about specific plans and programs that may apply to you. Federal loans typically offer more advantages than private loans, because you don't have to pay them back when you are in school or unemployed, and they have fixed rates, while private loans can have variable rates.

That said, if there's one thing I would recommend you invest in, it is this: tutoring for the writing of a college admissions essay and prepping for important tests like the SAT or ACT. Often, with all things being equals (like grades), admissions officers have to determine which student is slightly more qualified or unique and appealing than another. That splitting of the hairs comes down to the admission essay and the test scores. Which essay stands out more? Which shows more potential, personality, character? It's part of the subjective process of college acceptance, but it can give your child the edge in close calls.

I would invest the few bucks (prices vary widely depending on the individual) it can cost to get a prep course or private tutoring including multiple practice SAT/ACT tests to make sure that your children test to the best of their abilities. It would be useful for your children to create a compelling and engaging essay about themselves to help stack their admissions applications to college more in their favor.

Chapter 16
What Gives?

Sometimes, Creating Wealth Isn't Always about What You Make, but about What You Pass On to Others

By now, you know the main mantra of the book. It's what I've been telling my clients for the thirty years I've been in the business of helping people create wealth and the life that they want: Keep as much of your own money as you can, and let it do the work for you so your money can grow like Rip Van Winkle's beard. Slow and steady.

I fear that I've let that message roll over you like a series of waves that keep on coming. Save 10 percent to let that money grow. Use HELOCs for a line of credit rather than a bank credit card to avoid high interest rates. Negotiate the price of just about everything so more money stays in your pocket and less lines the pocket of Mr. Car Dealer or Uncle Sam.

Yet now it's time for me to make a friendly amendment. Sometimes you *should* be giving your money away. I know, I know. If this book is about building your own castle of cash, then why in the world would I spend any time talking about donations and charitable giving?

For one, I believe it's our moral duty in society to help others who need it, and that we should spend some of the wealth we've created to assist those people and make the world we live in a better place. And two, I do think that charitable donations, in a very big and very real way, contribute to our own wealth, because of how I define that word.

Wealth isn't just about investment portfolios, 401(k)s, and the fact that you might have a bunch of hundred dollar bills hidden in a cookie jar buried in the back yard in case of emergency (you don't, do you?). Wealth is about having enough money to take care of yourself, your family, and your future—to build the life you want. It's also about achieving all kinds of life satisfactions, one of which comes in the form of knowing that you helped change people's lives for the better. So, yes, we should spend some time talking about the savvy ways to donate, to make sure you are maximizing your good deeds.

Plan for It Like Any Other Expense. I don't want to sound as cold as a Popsicle when I say this, because charity is often very emotional and, in many cases, you should be making decisions with your heart. But making financial decisions with only your heart is like driving with your toes on the steering wheel; it's not the right body part for the job. So the first order of business when you're making, fine-tuning, or reorganizing your lifestyle expense overview is creating a line item for charity.

Decide how much you can give away, and budget for it. (Remember, this is what I advise you to teach your kids early on: one-third of what a child receives via gifts, odd jobs, and the like should go to charity, so they learn the importance and value of helping others, and to help them understand that this should be part of their own budgets as they grow older.) Yes, you may need to sacrifice some dinners out or the tricked-out cable package, but if you plan what you can afford and budget it in, you'll be sure to make a smart and sound decision, rather than a) overextending yourself by giving to everyone who asks, or b) not doing your part by not giving at all.

According to the Chronicle of Philanthropy, the average American gives 4.7 percent of his or her income to charity (for a median contribution of $2,564), and I certainly wouldn't tell you how much you can or should be able to afford. Certain religious organizations request gifts (upwards of 10 percent of an annual income in some cases). If you do choose to do that much with a religious or any kind of group, you must be especially sure to budget that amount because of the high percentage allocated for charity.

Choose Passionately. I can't sit here and tell you that you should donate to educational institutions, healthcare groups, or nonprofits that specialize in a certain population of disadvantaged people. What I can tell you is that you'll live a much richer life—metaphorically speaking—if you let your passions drive your decisions when it comes to who you're going to donate to. (I know I just said you can't leave charity decisions to your heart, but that only comes to how much you budget for them. When you decide who you want to give to, your heart should indeed take the wheel.)

I would also recommend that you make it a family decision. Talk about what organizations and groups could benefit from your help. You can even have each of your children come to dinner with three suggestions for kinds of groups they think the family should help. Maybe there's a classmate who suffers from a rare disease and there's an organization that's raising money to support research to find a cure for it. Maybe there's a group that assists those with a particular ailment that a grandparent died from. Or maybe your kids were really moved by seeing homeless people in a certain area of your town and they want to help people in similar situations.

My point is get everyone involved. It's not that you want to make it a game or trivialize anyone's situation, but what you want to do is make it a meaningful experience and decision for your whole family.

Check 'Em Out. As is the case with many things I've covered in this book, I'm all about the research, whether you do it online, on your smartphone, or even at the old-fashioned library (yes, they still exist!). Donating to charity is no exception.

To make sure your money is not being wasted (or worse, stolen by scam artists), you'll want to do research on the group or groups you're planning to donate to and learn their nonprofit status, what donations are used for, and if there are any claims against that organization for misappropriations of funds. You should check websites like www. charitynavigator.org to help you evaluate charities. This will help you determine what percentage of each dollar you contribute goes to helping the needy, what percentage goes to administrative costs, and will give you insights as to how they operate. Just a quick search will reveal a lot, but don't hesitate to call local representatives from that group and ask the tough questions either. That conversation will likely give you a very good idea whether the group is authentic and genuine or not.

Lastly, you do want to make sure that no matter who you are giving to, that they allow you to get tax breaks; that means they need to be a bona fide 501(c)(3) nonprofit organization. The IRS website (www.irs.gov) outlines what categories you can give to and get tax deductions.

Reduction through Deduction. If this whole chapter sounds too touchy-feely with me saying that you ought to give because it's our obligation to each other, then take comfort that there's also one very practical reason why you should: giving to a qualified charity allows most taxpayers to deduct that gift from their income so that they don't have to pay taxes on it. Depending on your income and the percentage of money you give away, that can be a significant saving of money—money that you can then use and turn into your own wealth.

For example, let's say your gross household income is $200,000. If you are in a 33 percent federal tax bracket, you would pay $3,300 in taxes on $10,000 of additional income. Now let's say you give that $10,000 to charity (5 percent of your income). You'll now be taxed on only $190,000 of income and would thus save $3,300, which means that the $10,000 charitable contribution only costs $6,700 on an after-tax basis. Your tax bracket, of course, changes depending on your household income and your other deductions or tax credits, so the percentage of taxes you pay decreases with a smaller household income.

Now be sure that you receive receipts directly from the charity, track them carefully, and make notes of all charitable donations you make, because the IRS needs more than just a copy of your canceled checks to allow those payments to count as deductions.

Consider an Internal Gift. Not charity, but each U.S. taxpayer can currently gift $14,000 ($28,000 for a married couple) to anyone they choose under the "annual exclusion" rules and not pay any gift tax. Since the government allows you to give $14,000 annually to anyone including family members (double that if you're giving with your spouse), you can help your grown family members to get them started on their journey in life. This path is an excellent choice for some, especially grandparents who'd like to contribute to a grandchild's education (e.g., via a 529 plan). So you get to skip paying the gift taxes, and they won't get taxed on the income either. It can be a win–win for both parties. You can also assist family members with college bills provided that the institutions are paid directly, as opposed to you giving the money to the family member and having them paying the bill. However, it must be noted that this gift exclusion only applies to paying school tuition to qualified educational institutions, i.e., colleges, universities, vocational schools, or postsecondary schools that participate in student aid provided by the U.S. Department of Education.

Redefine Your Notion of Charity. A few times throughout the book, I've strayed off the topic of wealth creation. For example, when I spent a whole chapter telling you how much I like salads with avocado and walnuts. It was about having good health, but also because I believe health is tied to wealth. The same is true when it comes to charity. I'm going to stray off the path of coins and cash again for just a moment to say that I do believe charity is about more than just writing a check and feeling good that you did something to help your fellow man. Your donations of time and energy—as an individual and a family—can have as much of an impact on other people as does money. So if you're not in a situation to give money to others (and even if you are), you can donate time. One of the things I'm most proud of when it comes to raising my children is how much time and thought my kids give to helping others.

Let me explain. For years, I would participate in a program with my Quaker Meeting in which we would make sandwiches for the needy. One man would deliver the meals to homeless people at St. Vincent's Catholic Church in Germantown, Pennsylvania, through a program in our area called Face to Face. I enjoyed doing it and was happy to volunteer my time.

About five years ago, it hit me: I wanted to see the faces and look into the eyes of the people I was helping. I wanted to see that what we were doing was making a difference. So I took my son down to deliver the sandwiches. I realized what a wonderful experience it was for both of us to see the faces of the people who were so thankful for our donations. That's when I got the idea that as a church, we should start a multi-generational program.

In the new program, we would go out individually, order the supplies, make the sandwiches, and deliver them to the church. I volunteered to head up the program, and I ended up volunteering to donate $300 to $400 a month for the supplies on a monthly basis. We get between fifteen and thirty people (half of them children) to volunteer one Sunday each month throughout the year. The thanks we get—in the forms of smiling faces and words of appreciation—make it all worth it! The way I see it, I win in at least four different ways.

One, I get a tax deduction for the money I spend on the program. Two, I get the satisfaction of encouraging an intergenerational approach to community service and helping bring together families to do good together. Three, we feed a lot of hungry people. And four, I get so much satisfaction knowing that I—and my children—put in sweat equity that has a lot of value in making the world a better place. Does this have a direct correlation to making your investments grow? Some would say no, not really, at least in the traditional definition of investment. I say definitely yes. If you consider investment to include investing in your family and passing on your values, your dividends will be off the charts.

Chapter 17
Who Cares?

GOT IT?

YESSSSS!!

WANT SOME MUFFIN?

When You're Dealing with Aging Parents, the Answer to that Question is Quite Often You

You've heard enough about the sandwich generation to know that the phrase isn't referring to a turkey on rye. You know it has to do with the predicament that many adults are finding themselves in, taking on the financial and emotional burden and responsibility of not only caring for their own kids and themselves, but caring for their aging parents as well. This can be an incredible strain on family relationships when you must make tough decisions and deal with the stresses that come from your parents' declining health and potentially eroding wealth.

Let's not discount that with increasing life spans, we're also talking about "kids" in their seventies taking care of parents in their nineties. That's a double-whammy. Not only are they dealing with their parents' very fragile health, but they may also be experiencing a lot of health problems themselves.

Fortunately, quite a few aging folks have handled the eventuality of needing increasing levels of care as they get older. For example, they have arranged sufficient assets and arrangements, such as long-term care insurance or purchased local life care programs at home to be prepared ahead of time. If that's the case, you should be thankful. While you may have to deal with the mental strain that comes with health problems, at least you won't have the added burden of figuring out how your parents are going to pay for their care.

Sadly, that's not the case for most of us. Statistics from the Family Caregiver Alliance show that 43.5 million Americans provide unpaid-for care for adults over the age of fifty.

And some studies show that family members lose more than $300,000 in wages and benefits caring for family members, totaling an astonishing loss of $33.6 billion per year in productivity. If your parents aren't in a state of bad health or old age right now, I would advise you to help them get all of their affairs in order (see Chapter 9, or even buy them a copy of this book).

This chapter is specifically set up for people whose parents may be on the cusp of some financial and health issues. We also can't discount the mental stress that comes with caring for older family members—how to deal with not knowing what's going to happen next, the various levels of support from siblings, and the pressure to want to do what's best for your parents, even if it means adding conflict to the family.

As someone who has grappled with these issues both personally and professionally, I do have some perspective on what works best. It's not just from a financial perspective, but also from one of trying to preserve your sanity and your relationships.

Communicate, Communicate, Communicate. I know that the conversation may be about as comfortable as sitting on a family of porcupines, but it has to be done, especially when your parents are in a healthy state of mind and preferably when they're in good health body-wise too.

Typically when my clients reach their late sixties or early seventies, I encourage them to have a frank discussion with their kids about their finances, their inheritance and charitable intentions, their wishes if their physical health starts to fail, and all of the other things they want to hash out now before physical and mental capacities are compromised. It also may be a good idea to bring in a third party, such as a wealth advisor, to help prompt and coordinate these discussions and resolve any conflicts. They should talk about their wishes as they get older, their financial state, what their plans are, and—as much as I hate to say it—what they want to do if their health situation turns sour. You are the caregiver as well, and you may not always be able to uphold their wishes. After all, most people want to stay in their own homes, but that's not always the best or realistic option.

The point is, you need to at least start talking so that the conversations are easier when the situations aren't. And it also may give you some time to take care of any financial necessities, such as increased insurance or long-term care, and have open discussions about how they want to make and keep memories while they're still young. I suggest bringing in other members of the family—your siblings, for example, or whomever you consider to be in your inner circle. It doesn't have to feel like an intervention or a confrontation, just an exploratory and productive conversation about the future. It's also worth noting that you don't have the conversation just to have the conversation. You have to be an attentive listener, really considering needs, desires, and wishes, even if they don't align with your own.

Check the Docs. Not the doctors, but the documents. Your greatest power in uneasy and unpredictable situations is being able to fall back on legally binding paperwork so there's no question as to wishes and desires, and there's no in-fighting among the kids or other people who are trying to decide what's best for your parents. Sooner rather than later, you want to ensure that your parents have the essential pieces of paperwork in order. Those include wills, living wills, health care power of attorney and health directives, durable power of attorney, revocable and irrevocable trusts, and any documents dealing with property or ownership of material goods of any importance. In conversation with your parents, try to make them aware that these documents are drawn up to preserve their wishes. Having your T's crossed doesn't make tough situations any easier to stomach emotionally, but it does eliminate some of the heart-wrenching decisions that can pop up. And like just about everything we've talked about in this book, you want to have everything in working order *before* you need it.

Plan for Backup. This may be too late of an option for some of you, but if your parents are roughly sixty-five or seventy, you still have time to purchase long-term care insurance or a long-term care rider on their life insurance policy. What this does is allow you to pay a monthly premium that will cover costs that are customary with nursing homes, hospital care, or in-home care if your parents have any health trouble. The premiums may rise as they age, but it's often cheaper than the astronomical cost of nursing homes today. The U.S. Department of Health and Human Services estimates a semi-private room in a nursing home to be about $6,300 per month, with a private room costing around $7,000 per month or more.

While we're at it, you might as well think of long-term care insurance for yourself to buy peace of mind. By going through this with your parents, you will take a huge burden off yourself and your own kids. Long-term-care insurance or a life insurance policy with a long-term care rider to benefit the person insured (or future generations) is one of the things that you should seriously consider working into your own budget.

Don't Do Too Much Too Fast. Let's take a step back for a second and think about the central question here: what are the goals of you and your parents? Your first answer is likely to provide your parents with the best possible care with the lowest possible financial burden. But there's another factor that you shouldn't just toss out like a banana peel: how do you want your parents to feel? I don't think any of us want our parents to feel lonely or tossed out like some piece of biological cargo that gets placed in some storage facility.

They want dignity. And we want them to keep it. We want them to get as much satisfaction out of the lives that they have left.

So how do we achieve that? It's not easy, I know, and in some health circumstances, it may not even be possible. You can make big improvements by focusing on small changes. We can't know how delicate and fragile this situation is until we actually live it ourselves, but what we can do is soften the blow. That's why taking preventive steps, such as carving out time for focused discussions and organizing documentation, can be so helpful. They represent gradual change and an acceptance of what may come next. If you can, offering them options like facilities that have different levels of care (55+ communities to full-on nursing facilities) can be advantageous. It allows your family members to gradually move into living situations where they may need more and more care without major upheaval. While you may be in a rush to get things settled and move on with your life, I believe your goal should be to take it easy so your parents can continue to get the most out of theirs.

Know Your Resources. In terms of finances, besides the basics of long-term insurance and basic health insurance, the two big ones you'll need to know the difference between are Medicare and Medicaid.

Medicare covers a percentage of most healthcare costs, but not nursing facilities. Medicaid does assist with housing costs for older people with health problems, but only once their income and assets have almost run out. Medicaid is available to people with an income less than 133 percent of the federal poverty level. Medicare does provide some short-term benefits following hospitalization for illness or surgery, and some Medigap policies will help with copayments for Medicare-eligible nursing care. (Veterans with long-term care needs can also receive benefits.)

Another option may be a life insurance policy with an accelerated death benefit, which allows the person to receive some benefits while still living (it's deducted from the end amount that beneficiaries would receive). The reality is that many parents, especially of this generation, didn't expect to outlive their retirement savings. That doesn't mean you should expect that cushion, but it does mean that there are some options if your parents' savings can't cover their costs.

Assess Options. If given the choice, many aging people are going to say that they want to stay in their own homes, even if their physical or mental health makes it unsafe for them to do so. And yes, we wouldn't mind that either, because that's what's easiest and where they're comfortable, and that's what would make everyone happy. But we also know that's not always reality. Sometimes, our parents need help.

We are increasingly seeing a very large increase in people who quit their jobs to care for aging parents. That's largely because caring for the elderly is a huge expense. The central question here is whether or not you know the spectrum of options. Certainly your financial situation will partly determine which way you go—and which is best for your parents. This is why talking early on is so important, to get some sense of what would make your parents comfortable if they do need to move from their home. Can they afford in-home care? Is that what they would prefer? Or should they move into a retirement community that has some services but not full-on medical care? Or a facility that has various levels of care? Or a full-on nursing home with memory care?

If they need full-time nursing care, the average stay in a nursing home is 835 days, meaning that folks are only living a little more than two years once they go into a nursing home. Finances, health status, and other factors will help make that determination, but as someone who has helped many clients figure out this very question, I can tell you that you'll always be in a better situation the earlier you start assessing your options, rather than waiting until you're desperate for an answer.

Beware of Scammers. It's no secret that the elderly have long been victims of financial scammers—people who try to get their money or other assets because they're either too naïve, too scared to say no, or simply too optimistic to see through the games that scammers play. Scammers can come in all forms, from the straight-up thugs who rob homes, to salesmen slime who ask for money to invest in a "sure thing."

If you're in this situation, I know your plate is already stacked higher than a Thanksgiving Day meal, but you have to be on alert for these people who will try to drain your parents of their savings. When you hear that $1.6 billion is lost to fraud annually, according to the Federal Trade Commission, you know this is serious business. The FBI estimates that Internet scams account for about $240 million in losses annually.

Take Care of Yourself. I don't want to sound colder than a bucket of ice, but you need to step back and make sure you're caring for yourself. You cannot drain your own stamina, physical health, or retirement account; you'll only put yourself and your own kids in a bad situation. You can't stop thinking about your own budgets and goals. You have to work within your own means to do what you can for your parents and ensure you are still working toward creating your own wealth. This is also why pre-planning is so important. It allows you to help your parents with everything from long-term care insurance or other ways to finance their future. Even though you're doing the most unselfish thing in the world by caring for your parents, you need to make sure your own future needs are not ignored.

Chapter 18
Don't Stop

Who Says You Can't Redefine What Retirement Means?

I'm just going to say it: "retirement" is a four-letter word. No, I'm not mathematically challenged. No, I'm not disparaging the notion that retirement is one of the things that so many of us are working toward—that time in our lives when we can decompress from the stress and pressures of work, knowing that we've done the right thing and saved for this exact moment. And no, I'm not disrespecting those who can't wait for the moment that work stops and channel-surfing begins.

I'm a very strong believer that when you retire and become an inactive couch potato, you have signed your own death warrant. Without day-to-day challenges, your body and mind begin to wither. You don't nurture yourself. You are on the fast track to an early grave.

What I am suggesting, though, is that when you reach this age and when you're thinking about retirement, I want you to forget about that "re-" word and use another one: "reinvent."

This is the time in your life when you should redefine what it means to retire from your career. This is the time when you reinvent what your life is about. This is not the time when you kick back for two decades, but when you push forward—to pursue your passions and enjoy (or perhaps even increase) your wealth. Retirement is a great gift, but all of the blessings and problems that occur in retirement are the results of one's own actions or inactions. This is where planning is essential.

I get it. There are lots of reasons why people want to retire in the traditional sense. They're tired of the hours, the stress, the boss, the rat race. And at the same time, they have a bucket list of things they want to do without the constraints of a forty-hour-a-week job. With freedom, they want to be able to knock things off that list, without having a fire-breathing boss yipping at them every hour of the day.

Those are all good reasons, and I get them. But my assertion is that retirement doesn't have to be an all-or-nothing proposition where you work or don't work. There are ways to get the best of both worlds—the stimulation and benefit of staying engaged in some way in some career, while also having the freedom and joy that comes from the traditional notion of retirement.

In Chapter 5, I already covered the ways you should plan for retirement and how you can figure out the amount you'll need in your investment accounts for you to live comfortably for the rest of your life. (Keep in mind that could well equate to another twenty, thirty, or even more years beyond the average age of retirement.) So, yes, we can't even begin a discussion of what to do with your new life if you haven't taken care of your lifestyle needs.

Assuming you have that locked down and have yourself in good financial shape with your investment income and retirement plans, that's when you can think about redefining what life is like in your sixties, seventies, and beyond. I will tell you that from experience with many, many clients in this exact position, retirement is a time when you can and should feel very rich—not only with how much money you've saved, but also with the new life you're about to lead.

Here, my tactics for how I'd encourage you to think about the next chapter. Remember, the home stretch of life doesn't mean that you have to spend every single second at home.

Keep on Going (with Some Adjustments). Granted, I know there are plenty of people who hate their jobs. Don't like the boss, tired of the same old routine, feel underappreciated, on and on. And perhaps one of the carrots waiting for you at the retirement finish line is that you no longer have to put up with the Grumpmeister as your direct supervisor. But I also know from dealing with so many people as clients, there are many of us who absolutely love what we do.

I love my clients and coworkers, and we feel more like a family, which provides a deeper level of relationship naturally. We love the challenge of work, the connection with people, the mental stimulation, the decorum, the sense of purpose, and all of the things that are mental jumper cables to our brain. If you fall into that category, then here's the question:

why stop? Keep on working, keep on doing, keep on stretching your mind and living what you're passionate about. That said, you now may be able to play "let's make a deal" with the people you work with and for.

Example: If you've solidified your retirement accounts, fine-tuned your cash flow (i.e., paid down your mortgage, helped your children find their way in the world, paid off student loans), and feel quite independent, you might ask to cut back to three days a week at a reduced salary. And with you having Medicare and Medigap coverage, your company will not only save in salary dollars, but also the extraordinary amount it has to pay for health insurance for you. The other bonus is that working longer allows you to save a little less during your working years. As my favorite professor Dr. Richard Marston says, if you postpone your retirement to seventy (as opposed to, say, sixty), your depletion of savings could dramatically decrease (meaning you can spend more during the balance of your life).

So this is a win–win. You keep doing what you love, you get to continue adding to your wealth by having some sort of salary you didn't think you would keep, and your company gets to keep your expertise on staff for a fraction of the cost. Remember, this is all about reinvention. A part-time gig at your formerly full-time place can give you the best of both worlds—the flexibility and freedom that comes from retirement and the high amount of mental stimulation that comes from working.

Start a Second Career. What person in his or her right mind would start a new career at age sixty-two or older? You. Many people are living well into their mid-eighties with sharp minds and agile bodies, so that's more than twenty years that you could pour into a new career. Maybe it's a modest one, maybe it's one that has nothing to do with your current skill set, or maybe it's something you've always wanted to do but never could afford.

Whatever it is, now may be the perfect time, with the added bonus of supplementing your post-retirement income. Of course, there are some areas that are off-limits (those Olympic bobsled dreams are probably over). But why not try something else? For example, some of my clients have pursued second careers in such fields as starting a new business, teaching, consulting, lecturing, and customer service, or even writing or teaching on a virtual basis from their home office.

There have been reports of retirees who have a desire to help people and keep a decent income starting second careers in nursing. Or maybe you could even take a chance by starting a family business with one of your kids—that old-fashioned ice cream shop (or newfangled fro-yo shop) on the corner of Main Street, as is the dream of one of our technologically savvy client couples.

Retirement can actually be the perfect time to become an entrepreneur; it's when there's less risk involved (assuming your retirement accounts are stable and your major family expenses of education and debt are paid off), and it could be the perfect chance to bond with your family at a stage in life when you're both mature and you have lots of experience and wisdom to offer your kids. (In our generation and culture, we rarely go back to live with our parents when we reach middle age, unless there's a health problem. But many countries do have the tradition of multiple generations living together. There's a collective wisdom and unity that happens when those groups are together. And it's the kind of magic that can happen when multiple generations go in a business together. The older generation can provide the wisdom and funding, while the younger ones provide the energy.)

Leverage Your Wisdom. Another popular option for the retirement set: use all those decades of experience and expertise to help others, without the binding nature of a full-time job. By starting a consultant business (either formally or informally), you'll be able to set your own hours, work as much or as little as you want, and have some additional income while keeping your mind young and fresh.

Take the case of my friend, Charles Hummel, who is now in his eighties and has now spent more than twenty-three years in reinvention after a thirty-six-year career. He took advantage of an early retirement plan from the Winterthur Museum in Delaware, where he worked, but he decided not to have a "rocking chair retirement," because he believed that having an active approach to retirement would contribute to good health physically and mentally. So he's stayed active in his profession by keeping involved with people and volunteering at the museum.

"I found it important to give something back," he told me. "We all have special skills, experiences, or interests that can be put to positive use. In my case, I could only make modest annual financial contributions to the museum, but that hasn't deterred me from mentoring, teaching, serving on various boards of trustees and advisory committees of other institutions, and lecturing as a way to continue making use of my experiences and knowledge, while occasionally contributing modest sums to my retirement income."

Pursue the Passion. Okay, so I know I made a joke about channel-surfing a few pages back, but I see it way too often. People enter retirement and assume that their day should be filled with breakfast, a nap, a few hours of staring at the news channel only to complain about the said news channel, another nap, a cocktail, an evening game show, then off to bed. Yes, after forty-some years working, you might deserve a double nap from time to time. But please don't whittle away the balance of your life doing *nothing*.

Retirement should be about pursuing your passion in earnest, whether it's spending time with your grandchildren, traveling and reconnecting with long-lost friends, working on your golf game, or whatever it is that jazzes you and keeps you young and spritely. I think this really stems from two fundamental questions: What's your purpose? What do you want to accomplish in this world?

That's something that goes deeper than just spending time with grandchildren; it goes to imparting your wisdom and experience to those who want it, or volunteering to help people who need your help. (By the way, one of my secrets is that I always try to make friends and spend time with people much younger than myself. It's one of my career secrets to build success, since I'm never going to retire fully. Think about it and realize...just the sheer energy of being around people younger than you empowers you.)

Now, this option isn't about adding to your bottom line because I'm not suggesting that spending four days a week on the greens will allow you to make the Senior PGA Tour, but remember how I define wealth: it's not all about the number in the bank account. It's about spending all those years putting yourself in a position to have the freedom to bathe and splash and have a ball in that proverbial fountain of youth. As my father always said, "They're going to take me out with my boots on." I humbly suggest that's the way you think about life too.

Chapter 19
Flying (Back to) the Coop

Navigating the Rough Waters of Helping Out Your Grown-Up Kids

You know a surefire way to send parents into a tizzy? Have them try to list every single thing they've spent money on for their kids. From the diapers to the daycare. From the toys to the tuition. From the Air Jordans to the hair accessories to the birthday gifts to the summer-camp costs to all the rest, it takes a lot of money to raise a child. Current estimates from a U.S. Department of Agriculture report called *Expenditures on Children by Families* illustrate that, for the typical middle-income family, it takes $300,000 to raise one child for the first eighteen years of life.

That number can certainly skyrocket for upper-class families, between the costs of tuition for private school and other expenditures—and then add in the cost of college. It's not unrealistic for each child to cost close to the neighborhood of a million dollars or more. It's not that we mind all that much, of course. There are few joys in life like raising children and watching them grow up. But if we were to see all of the costs in one itemized bill, our jaws would drop and our mouths would open so far that we could slurp dinner crumbs right off the floor.

Do you really want to throw parents into a DEFCON 5 tizzy? Let them hear these words: "Mom, Dad. I'm moving back in."

Here you are, thinking you're in the clear, and a child—maybe in a bind, maybe just going through a period of indecision or misdirection, or maybe because that's simply what's easier—wants a little more time with that roof over his or her head. And that's not even mentioning everything that child thinks comes with that roof—the food, the laundry service, sleeping until 2 p.m., the free cable and Internet, and on and on. All the amenities of living at home with none of the rules ("I'm twenty-three! You can't tell me what to do!").

If only it were that easy—for your kid and for you. When it comes to creating wealth, protecting your wealth, and teaching your children about the responsibilities of life, this is actually one of the trickiest areas to navigate. After all, you love your kids and want to support them and help them. None us want to see our kids going through rough patches, whether it's their fault or not. But we also know deep down that we're not lending them any support to manage their lives in the long term if we acquiesce and give them a free ride in the short term.

I hate to give you a fist-pounding warning, but I will say this: If you don't help your child fly the coop by using the strategies I outline in Chapter 14, then you do risk bankrupting your entire family—you in the present, and your children as they grow up. They need the appropriate skills to make them marketable, but they also need to be taught sound financial principles for how to deal with money when they start earning it (or, at least, trying to earn it). When you factor in the enormity of student loans (they outpace credit card debt), then you know that your kids can be in an especially tough spot as they prepare to go in the real world. Making the right strategies is more than necessary; it's rather urgent, in fact.

The most commonly held vision for my clients has to do with this very subject. They want to be successful enough to fund a college degree for their children and then enjoy that satisfaction that comes from doing so, especially when that degree is complete.

I know every situation is different, and there are very good reasons why adult children may want to move in with their parents. In fact, it's so common that a Pew Research Study found that about 48 percent of people ages forty to fifty-nine have given financial help to grown children. So my message here isn't for you to put a moat around your home and ban your kids from knocking at the door with a few suitcases in hand. The goal here is to help get your kids back on their feet and teach them lessons in financial responsibility, while protecting the family's wealth at the same time.

These are my strategies if you're dealing with children who either want to stay longer than they should or want to move back after they've been gone for some time.

Talk Big Picture. Okay, so let's say your kid presents you with this question: "While I'm looking for a job—you know, the market is really, really bad—is it okay if I move back into my old room?" Initially, your heart may warm up like a microwaved slice of pizza. After all, he's your kid and you'd love more time with him. And yes, it's wonderful if you feel that way, and I'm happy that maybe you can eke out a few more games of Scrabble, a few more dinners, and a few more of those precious moments that you thought were gone for good.

As is the case with many concepts in the book, however, you can't allow your emotions to dictate decisions. Why? Spoiling your child—at eight or twenty-eight—does him no good. You won't help prepare him for the rigors, demands, and craziness that come with adulthood if you coddle him financially while he's living with you. So in the immediate aftermath, you ask this question: "What are your goals?"

It doesn't matter whether it's going to school or getting a job or both, but there needs to be articulated professional goals ("What are you going to do with your life?") and next-in-life goals ("What are you doing to get there?"). Even if your kid doesn't know what he wants to do, he needs to have a goal for trying to figure it out. Why? Because with goals come accountability. With accountability comes maturity. And with maturity comes some semblance of taking financial responsibility. Once those goals are in place, that's when you help your child with the next phase—a plan ("What are the steps you're going to take to reach those lifestyle goals?").

If you're providing either the shelter or the assistance, you have every right to ask these questions and expect good answers. After all, what this really comes down to is parents helping their children—not with the wallet, but with the frame of mind it takes to get going and get started in life. That's *your* goal here, right? Get them out of the house, and get them going in the right direction.

Don't Fear the Ultimatum. In some cases, what works best is establishing a period in which you're willing to help. A realistic timeline may be six months. As long as you give the expectations, you can enforce them and use those six months to help him get on his feet, offering suggestions about how to cut costs of living (like sharing an apartment with roommates).

I know using the word "ultimatum" sounds negative, but in the long run, you're actually helping your child by establishing clear timelines and rules. Obviously the trick here is that you have to be willing to enforce the boundary that you set, and that's something you have to ask for yourself: what will happen if you reach that six-month mark and there's been no progress? I hope it doesn't come to that, because if you employ the other principles here (by being a helper, not the evil enforcer), you can avoid that deadline day so that he'll be on his own before that.

I have one couple as a client who had a good sense of what they spent in their lives, but not how to make their money last. Their real problem was they wanted to help their adult kids all the time. I had to look them square in the eye and say that wasn't going to work (they were going to run out of their assets and have nothing to live on in retirement). In many ways, they needed to do the same thing with their own kids.

Come Up with a Financial Deal. Of course, the reason why kids want to move back to live with Mom and Dad is likely not because you make a killer lasagna. It's because the cost of living is either significantly decreased or nonexistent when they think they can have amenities like food and cable for nothing. That's where parents with returning kids make their biggest mistake: they allow that to happen. You won't teach financial responsibility if the only expenses your adult kids have is paying $10.99 a month for their Netflix subscription and $5 for their fancy cup of coffee at Starbucks. You must establish the framework right from the start in terms of what your child is going to be responsible for. Of course, maybe you cut him a deal on rent (after all, he may be in an unemployed bind of some sort). Don't forget you can now claim a $500 tax credit for a non-child dependent over 17, whether it's your 27-year-old son or aged father.[21]

While I won't tell you what percentage you should charge for rent or other expenses, the bottom line is that you should charge *something*. That will force your child to look at expenses, search for jobs, get back on his feet, and prepare for the realities that await. I personally would recommend doing a small monthly expense for rent and a percentage of other bills to give a taste of what's coming when your children are out on their own. That doesn't mean you have to jam your kids up with ungodly costs, but you should make them earn some of their keep.

And in some cases, I would even recommend drawing up a family-friendly contract to show the seriousness that you expect. Believe me, your kids are not going to want this, but they do need it. The greater good is that you're teaching them that there's no such thing as a free slice of lasagna out in the world. And even greater is the education you're giving them. Even if it takes six months to a year for them to become financially independent, that time when you're setting expectations and teaching more financial principles will be money well spent as you prepare them for what's ahead on their own journey.

Manage Expectations. If you've established some guidelines for how your kids are going to contribute financially, you're now ready to do the same in other areas. Maybe their cash flow really is lower than a river bed in the middle of a drought. In addition to paying rent and other expenses, you can think of other ways to make up for expenses. How could they save you money in other areas (like yard work or handiwork or grocery shopping or helping with computer-related tasks)? You should also outline your expectations for house rules. After all, while you're still the parent, you're technically not really fulfilling the caregiver role anymore, so your kids may think that anything goes with drinking and socializing in your home.

If there are areas that are hot-button issues for you, you are well within your right to outline them upfront. That technically has nothing to do with your finances, but it has everything to do with setting up a system that allows you to be clear about any things that could turn into major conflicts down the road.

You can't underestimate the change in family dynamics that happens when an adult child moves back in and changes the vibe of those still there. The new habits (after perhaps four years away at college) may interfere with what goes on day to day. The point isn't to say that there will be inevitable conflict, but that it behooves everyone to understand the house rules and that you have to work through potential tensions and conflict with honest communication and expectations.

Rethink Your Role. One of the best things I ever read about parents assuming the role of caretaker for grown-up children after they thought their nest was empty was that you have to redefine that role, in that you should think of yourself as less of a manager and more of a consultant. I thought that was a wonderful way to think about your relationship. While you can establish rules, you don't micro-manage every little step, decision, or action. Instead, you consult, you assist, you morph into an advisory role rather than a supervisory role. That really does provide the foundation for you to help your children in ways other than just providing financial assistance.

You Are Not a Malfunctioning Slot Machine that Empties Coins Indefinitely. If you're in a good spot financially, it may be tempting to slip your child a twenty here, a twenty there. But if you want to teach your kid to create his own wealth (and protect your own), the International Bank of Momma and Papa cannot be open 24/7. That's why those expectations you set forth early on are so important.

If you feel like you have to lend money to help your child out of a jam, perhaps you set up some kind of loan with interest. Or you set parameters. Maybe you will assist in reducing credit card debt, with the understanding that you will only do it one time. Some situations can be so complex that it often does make sense to bring in a personal wealth advisor to be an objective third party to help sort out issues and talk about decisions that are best for both you and your child. It also allows you to stay away from internal family and emotional issues that may arise in resolving these conflicts.

Use that Two-Letter Word. When our kids are toddlers, one of our favorite words is "No." *No, you cannot have a twelfth cupcake. No, you cannot put your thumb in an electrical socket. No, I'd really rather you did not do a somersault down the stairs and see if you can land in a perfect headstand. No, no, no, no.* And you do it because you know the long game is what you're playing. "No" teaches boundaries. "No" protects them from harm.

The same holds true here. You don't need to say yes to every request. It's okay to say no and explain why and talk about other options. *No, I'm not buying a new computer for you; you'll need to save up for it and you can use ours when you need it. No, you can't have a twenty to go out drinking with your buddies. No, you may not turn the guest room into a doggie day care for Great Danes; I admire the entrepreneurial spirit, but let's think of more realistic options.* It may feel harder to do as they grow older, because your children feel more like friends than children, but "no" has the same goal as it did when your kids were toddlers. It establishes boundaries, keeps them safe, and teaches them how to take responsibility for their actions.

Be Smart. Parent to parent, I know the sacrifices you have made—to give your children what they want, what they need, and to have the opportunities that will allow them to grow up to be good people. In return, we get the satisfaction knowing that we did a good job in teaching our kids to be contributors in the world and to the families of their own that they may have. For many of us, we have spent the better part of two or more decades putting our children's needs ahead of our own. That's just part of the job.

If you have to enter this part of your life that perhaps you didn't expect, I want to assure you that it's okay to put your own needs first. While you will help, guide, and assist your grown-up children who are in need or a bit misdirected, you will do them a bigger favor if you don't do what you did when they first tried to cross the street: hold their hand. So part of the trick of navigating this situation is finding that sweet spot between total care and abject neglect. It's not easy and every situation is a bit different, but I do think that besides the strategies I've outlined here, it's important to keep in mind that by taking care of your own needs, you're actually teaching them how to do the same thing for themselves. You're teaching them to be independent. That's smart, not selfish.

Chapter 20
Disaster Relief

When the Going Gets Tough, the Tough Get Some Help

In sports, desperation is being down by three home runs with two outs in the bottom of the ninth. In love, desperation is searching Match.com on February thirteenth. In movies, desperation is hanging from a helicopter with one pinkie. We all know what desperation means, no matter the genre. You've got no shot, no answers, no hope. And, even if we don't spend much our lives in desperate situations, we can imagine how it feels: like being lost in a national forest at sundown. We want out, but we can't find the way out.

Now, when it comes to financial desperation, we can joke all we want about grand slams and Herculean pinkies, but the reality is that this is serious business—the kind of trouble that puts families in financial ruin, destroying their lives with little hope for bouncing back.

In my multiple decades in this business and my experience with many clients, I've seen it first hand: financial conflict ruins marriages—and lives. In a 2014 Harris Poll, 44 percent of Americans described their financial stress as either high or extremely high.

Chances are good that if you're reading this book and are interested in building real wealth, you aren't in this situation, or even close to it. And if you're practicing the principles I've outlined throughout the book, then you certainly won't be anywhere close to feeling the financial desperation that many people experience. But I am going to outline the warning signs so, in case you're on a downward path, you can avoid it. I won't spend a lot of time covering this topic. But I will review the basics in case you do feel as if you're at risk of losing control of your finances.

So what do I mean by "hardship"? No, hardship isn't that your cable bill went up—again. Hardship isn't that you have to decide between the hundred-dollar shoes and the two-hundred-dollar shoes. Hardship isn't even the fact that you haven't gotten a raise in a few years or that your investments are only making 6 percent instead of 10.

Hardship is that you are dangerously close to exhausting all of your financial resources, blowing all of your savings, struggling to pay your bills, destroying your credit rating, and searching for shelter. In simple English, it means that your lifestyle expenses continue to far exceed your earned income. One of the first things I ask my prospective clients is, "Do you live above your means, beneath your means, or at your means?"

If the answer is "way above" their means, that's trouble (unless they have many zeroes attached to their name), and frankly, I'm not interested in that person as a client. No matter what happens, no matter what rate of return we can achieve, the situation is going to be a failure. It's not a question of "if"; it's a question of "when."

Now, to be fair, these financially desperate situations can come about for all kinds of reasons, whether it's an unforeseen circumstance (like a health emergency that drains your portfolio, or a loss of a job) or a lack of attention to financial affairs. No matter the reason, the result is still the same: you're living in desperate times—and very often, it comes at your own hands.

As I said, I hope this doesn't apply to you or your loved ones, but here are the most vital strategies for pulling yourself out of the mess if indeed it happens to you.

Change the Batteries in Your Smoke Alarm. You know the rule. Every time your clock springs ahead or falls back an hour, you change the batteries in your smoke detector. You do it so your batteries never run out and the smoke alarm never fails you in the event of a real emergency. It's like an insurance policy on an insurance policy.

So what does that have to do with financial ruin? You need to check your batteries. That is, you need to recognize the warning signs that come with the descent from financial stability to financial ruin. Ignoring the signs is like forgetting to change the batteries. So the best way to avoid ruin is to recognize those signs before the fire starts; that way you can address issues before they become *too* desperate.

So what are they? There's a good chance you're putting your family at major risk if you consistently take cash advances out on your credit cards, if you consistently make only the minimum payments on your credit cards, if you miss payments (or are late) for bills of any kind (which will trigger a late fee and more interest), if you're unaware of your total debt, or if you consistently dip into your savings to pay monthly bills. Of course, the extent to which you do any of them is what will determine how deep the trouble is. But if your financial habits include any of the above situations, your first steps are recognizing them and then reviewing strategies throughout this book for how to get yourself out of those habits (see Chapter 7, on reducing your debt, for example).

Cut, Cut, Cut. Now that you've acknowledged you're swimming with the sharks, it's time to get yourself up into a lifeboat. The first opportunity you have to get yourself into a safer situation is to cut expenses. Your job, first and foremost, is to reduce what you spend your money on—and even open your eyes to new possibilities for ways you can cut. If you're a two-car family, for example, can you figure out how to get by with just one? You'll not only save money in payments, but you'll earn a little money from the sale of the car and reduce associated costs (maintenance, gas, insurance).

Is it your ideal situation? Maybe not. But carpooling, using public transportation, or utilizing a city's Zipcar program may save you money in the long run and help you get back your feet. Also consider using Uber, Lyft, or other ridesharing services to reduce your out of pocket costs in the place of the second car. You may need to wake up earlier or allow more time for travel, but you will save some money along the way. Tough times require tough decisions—and to get comfortable, you're going to have to move out of your comfort zone. You'll also want to use strategies that I've outlined throughout the book, such as consolidating your personal debt with a home equity line of credit, if you own a home.

This may be the time for you to dip into your liquid reserves account to help get you back on your feet. Remember, you must remain diligent in your strategy to always refill that emergency bucket over time so it will be there for you in financially difficult times. I still would advise against pulling from any retirement accounts, because your money grows tax deferred or tax free and pension accounts should be one of the last spots you take from.

Don't Be Too Proud to Ask for Help. We all know how an embarrassed puppy acts. Little Bluto runs to the corner, hides his head, and hopes his owner won't see that he just gnawed on pop's favorite loafer. When people get into some kind of financial trouble, their instinct is to act like Bluto—run for the corner and hope nobody will know, nobody will see, nobody will judge.

That's the worst thing you can do. Your number-one tactic if you're missing payments and running out of money is to contact a few different folks. You should start with

Consumer Credit Counseling Service agencies, which are non-profit organizations that provide counseling for families who need financial help. Counselors with basic money-management and debt-consolidation experience can help you look at your specific situation and help you figure out a plan for digging yourself up and out of the hole.

Second, contact your bank if necessary and ask for the hardship specialist, who can provide similar counseling and advising services. Lastly, I would call all of the places where you have necessary monthly bills (like gas and utilities) to explain exactly how and why your finances have changed. Try to work out some kind of alternative payment plan to give you some relief. There's also one other group I would try: your family. It may seem obvious, but if your family is in a position to help (and you have a good relationship where they'd be willing), a loan with a low interest rate from family might be the way to go.

One way to do it is by drawing up a contract where the money you're loaned is deducted from any inheritance you may get down the line. In any case, if you are able to borrow from family, I would have a legal document drawn up so that the lending parties, such as your parents, are protected and will be comforted in knowing what the terms of the loan are.

Don't Take Bankruptcy Lightly. If you're in an extremely tight spot—like a crisis-type tight spot—then you've probably had to ask yourself this question: what's the end game? As in, will I end up on the street? What if I can't save myself before it's too late?

There are companies that negotiate with your creditors on your behalf for you to pay a settlement rather than the full amount you owe. These do come with some risks and often costs, in that they can take a long time to have debt actually settled. Some require payments for three years before they'll settle, to ensure that they'll make their money. There is no guarantee that you'll actually have your debt settled by one of these companies, but it might be a last resort before you consider filing for bankruptcy. As you can imagine, this is serious. It's not a willy-nilly decision that you should make just because you think it's the answer to freeing yourself from your debtors.

While it's true that bankruptcy will eliminate your debt and give you a clean slate, it also comes with consequences, namely in the form of bad credit. It will stay on your credit report for seven to ten years depending on the type of bankruptcy that you declare, meaning it may be hard to buy a home once you do get back on your feet. There are two types of bankruptcy available. Chapter 13 allows you to keep property, such as a house or a car, as long as you can make good on payments you've defaulted on (you'd have a series of years to make good). Chapter 7 means that all of your assets may be turned over to the people you owe money to, including your home. Both kinds of bankruptcy can buy you some time to get on your feet, because they may stop foreclosures on your home or utility cutoffs.

Chapter 21
In a Scam Jam

Don't Lose Your Wealth by Becoming the Victim of Financial Fraud

The way I like to operate is pretty simple: treat people with honesty, kindness, and in good faith, and those same things come back to you over and over. When you give goodness, you get goodness. Is this trampoline of behavior a failsafe philosophy? Of course not. I'm not naïve enough to think that just because you pepper your peers with politeness that everyone will do the same.

Especially now that we're in the age of hyper-fast and hyper-advanced technological methods of interacting and doing business, the reality is that there are many ways that scammers and thieves will try to get at what's not theirs. Past eras may have seen pirates and pickpockets, thieves and thugs who would muscle their way in to find the treasure and take it for their own.

Today's villains will still find ways to take your passport and credit cards, but now also include cyber-sneaks that you may never see. They come at you from behind the scenes—or, rather, behind the screens—to scam their victims out of money. They try to get at your fortune by stealing identities, stealing passwords, stealing account numbers, stealing whatever they can to get access to their victims' accounts. They infiltrate the system, withdraw the money or use the credit, and leave their victims flailing with frustration and panic that their accounts have been broken into and depleted.

Some of the scams may be overt (who hasn't received an e-mail telling them that $5 million will be placed in their account if only they would be so kind to pass along their bank account number?). And some may be covert (such as getting a credit card number and using it to make purchases before you even know that someone has taken your number). It's one of the scary parts about managing your money and trying to build your wealth in today's society. With the greater ease and access that technology provides, it also raises the risk.

Since you've spent a lot of time, energy, money, and sweat figuring out how to build your wealth, the last thing any of us want is to have it taken away, especially by criminals who make their living by wanting a piece of yours.

While there are mechanisms in place to help protect you if you're the victim of fraud, identity theft, or other financial scams, that doesn't mean that you can't lose some of your money in the process. Perhaps more importantly, even if you can protect or regain your assets, your stress levels and the time used to fight fraud can leave you reeling—and also chipping away at your wealth indirectly. For example, being the victim of credit card fraud when you're traveling can impede your self-confidence and be a royal pain the rear end especially when you are on a tight travel schedule.

I hope none of you have to deal with financial fraud during your life, but with 17.6 million Americans a year having been the victim of identity theft alone, you should be prepared—and take steps to protect yourself. (This is also another advantage of having a personal wealth advisor on your team; your advisor can help you navigate these issues if they do arise.) In this chapter, I'll briefly outline the steps you must take to prevent it and what you should do if you are a victim.

It's worth mentioning at the outset that a good practice for everyone is to stay vigilant by periodically checking your credit reports, by making sure no unfamiliar withdrawals are coming from your accounts, and by checking to make sure there's no unusual activity, so you can catch any potential problems before they get too serious.

When you're in a family situation in which three or four people may have access to certain accounts, you may assume that that your teenage son or daughter used that card at the mall. The reality could be that the purchase was made by someone you don't know. I'm not recommending you run a police state with every purchase, but you do need to stay aware of any activity that is happening with your accounts for this very reason. Also worth mentioning: don't give your kids your own card. Many banks will give you a different card tied to your account if that's what you choose to do.

Your goal is to prevent fraud before it happens in cases when you can. It's to protect your family's wealth and to help them develop the skills necessary.

Steps To Prevent Fraud

Control the Chaos. Bills, documents, account numbers, websites, files, statements, e-mails, on and on. These days, you have documentation, paper trails, and electronic trails for all of the things that make up your financial picture. How you organize them (manually, electronically, in a file, under your bed, all over your desk) is largely up to you and your organizational personality. I can tell you that the more organized you are, the less likely you are to let some kind of security breech happen (and more likely to nip it in the bud if it does happen).

So if you are organized, congrats! If not, take a half of a day and get everything in order. (See the tools I recommend starting on page 40), or take a class. Many local community colleges offer some kind of class that helps you get started in organizing your finances. You'll likely need some kind of hybrid system of both paper files and electronic files that you keep as secure as possible to avoid any tampering.

Don't accept excuses—from yourself, even—that you can't get organized. There are far too many choices now to allow disorganization to permeate your life. (Bonus: If you can demonstrate to your kids that you are organized, you'll also be a good role model for them to learn from in their formative years.) Keep a copy of your credit cards, IDs, and other important documents in a safe place. Copies facilitate the cancellation/replacement process mightily.

Throw Some Change-Ups. Your account is only as strong as your password. So get into the habit of changing your passwords often, using passwords that aren't easy to figure out. The best ones involve numbers, lowercase letters, and uppercase letters, and don't easily make up a real word. You can use password-helping programs to help store your passwords securely so you don't have to try to remember every iteration for every account. You can also enlist (at a cost) the help of identity and credit card protection services such as LifeLock to give you and your family additional security.

Know Your Nos. While there may be some scenarios that you can't avoid (because your accounts were hacked or your account numbers were stolen off machines), there are steps you can take to reduce your chances of becoming a victim of fraud.

➤ Don't wire money unless you are absolutely sure who the recipient is. In cases of fraud, it's very difficult to recover wired money because it's treated as cash and not protected by financial institutions.

➤ Don't give money to groups associated with disasters unless it's an established charity (typically a 501(c)(3) organization, which is duly registered as an authentic charity, such as the Red Cross). It's sad to say, but in times of disaster, scammers can prey on the emotions of people, set up fake accounts, and take money that's intended to go toward victims and their families.

➤ Don't click on the e-mail link. You already know about phishing schemes (fake e-mails that appear as if they're being sent from credible accounts). Anytime you get an e-mail that appears to be from a vendor you work with, it's best not to click any link that's included, but rather copy and paste the link in a browser (this will prevent them from accessing secure info). Even better as a first step: don't look at the name that appears in the senders e-mail, but the actual e-mail address from where it's coming. For example, a scammer could set up an account posing as a bank representative. You should know that something is fishy if you see an e-mail address like "bankofmerica@iamahugescamartist.com" that looks close to one you are familiar with but not exactly the same.

Look at the Fine Print. Contrary to popular belief, scammers don't usually start off with the thousand-dollar computer purchase with a stolen credit card. They usually start with a small item to "test the waters" and see if they're going to be able to get away with a purchase.

While many banks have fraud departments that are trained to detect unusual activity on your card or account, it's not a bad idea for you to jump into your account and look at all purchases to make sure they're coming from you. Not only should you read monthly statements, but I suggest you also monitor online activity as well, so you can do so more frequently than once a month. I review every line item on every single bill, to make sure it's legitimate and there are no errors.

Get Shredded. Though we often don't think of our paper documents being the source of theft anymore since so much activity is online, many thieves still use paper as the source of information that they can use to steal account info or open up new accounts in your name. Even if you think you're in a respectable neighborhood where people aren't picking through trash, the fact is that you're better off shredding all documents with any personal info—names, address, and of course account information after an appropriate retention period.

IMMEDIATE STEPS TO TAKE IF YOU'RE A VICTIM

The moment you realize that your account or accounts have been compromised, you feel an equal mix of panic, anger, and worry. Not only do you feel violated, but you also want to make sure your assets are protected. Luckily, in many circumstances, your money is protected by the applicable financial institution so it can be recovered. (One big caveat: You have to report it early. If you delay reporting fraudulent activity, you may be responsible for the money taken.) If you do notice that your accounts have been compromised, take the following steps:

➤ Let your financial institution know immediately, and follow their directions on what to do about that particular account. If it's a credit card, they will cancel it immediately and send you a new one with a new number (make sure that any online automatic payments tied to that credit card are redirected).

➤ Place a "fraud alert" on your credit file with the three main companies that handle credit reports—Equifax, Experian, and TransUnion. This will make sure that legitimate folks who need to access your credit know that your accounts have been compromised, and that you're not responsible for the misdoings on any particular account.

➤ Freeze your credit. That means that no new accounts can be opened in your name. That way, if someone has stolen your info and tried to open a credit card of some type, the lenders will deny that account when they see that a freeze has been placed on any new accounts.

➤ Get a copy of your credit reports (from one or more of those three companies) so you can inspect them for any suspicious activity and have any activity you're not responsible for wiped off your credit report so it's not held against you when you are applying for credit, such as mortgages or car loans.

➤ If your info has been used in various ways (true identity theft rather than just one card being used, for example), you'll want to file an identity-theft report with the police.

Chapter 22
Time's Up

Playing Catch-Up for Retirement Is Possible

We all know how sugarcoating works. A parent douses broccoli with melted cheese in hopes that the vegetable will taste a little bit better. A boss gives you praise for a good effort before sending you back to the drawing board. The cop asks how you're enjoying the beautiful weather before slapping you with a ticket for going 79 mph in a 55 zone. The spoonful of sugar, they say, helps the medicine go down.

You know what? I don't like too much sugar. So I'm just going to give it to you straight.

If you've gotten a late start when it comes to saving for retirement, you can't simply snap your fingers, wave a magic wallet, and expect to make up for lost time. Simple truth is that the biggest asset when it comes to saving for retirement isn't the actual asset, but rather time. Time is what makes even modest retirement contributions grow like a blade of grass in a Florida thunderstorm. Time is what turns one hundred dollars a month into millions. Time is what gives you financial security. So if you're in your twenties (or even younger!) and stumble across this chapter, then give yourself a pat on the back for vowing to treat your retirement accounts with the seriousness they deserve. But if you're, say, in your fifties and semi-panicked (or fully panicked, for that matter) about how you're going to live in retirement, then yes, there is reason to worry a bit, because you've lost that valuable asset of time.

The reality is that good habits and strategies can't do what years and decades of steady contributions can do. So if you hear the clock ticking or see the sands of the hourglass draining, you have every right to blurt out an expletive or two and wonder what the heck your next play should be. Do you fold? Do you bet everything you have? Well, none of the above is the right answer. Your retirement strategy isn't a poker table or Powerball, and you need to play it smart—even if you're behind where you want to be, or where you should be for someone your age.

Does that mean you're destined to sleep on park benches and bus stations if you haven't saved as much as you would have liked? Of course not. There are ways you can make up ground to give you some income, some stability, and a financial cushion when you reach retirement. While you may be behind the eight ball, that doesn't mean your life has to be smacked into the corner pocket.

As is the case with just about every financial matter I cover in this book, it's virtually impossible to generalize about this topic without knowing your specifics—your health issues, your income, your current retirement balances, your age, how long you want to work, your risk parameters, your time horizon, and all of the other factors that play a role in how you can make up for lost time. This may also be a good place for a mind map, to connect your family values with your assets with any health-related issues so you can get what you want out of life (see page 39). This is why a wealth advisor can be especially helpful—to drag you through those seemingly complex but necessary questions to lay out your priorities and ensure that you don't miss the connections.

Remember, as I said in Chapter 5, most people advise that the way you calculate how much you need in retirement is to take 4 percent of the principal in your retirement account—and that's the annual "salary" you would live on. So if you saved a million dollars, your annual income would be $40,000. That should give you some pause about how much you need to save if you want to have a much higher income during retirement.

Now, even though every situation is different, there are some guiding principles that will help steer you while you're trying to catch up. These are mine:

Change Your Mindset. Before you get into the nitty-gritty of how you're going to speed up your savings for retirement, the first thing you have to change isn't a percentage point or a dollar amount. It's your mind-set. You have to realize that you may indeed have to change your lifestyle to make up ground.

With a smaller amount of productive earning years ahead of you, this is the time where you may have to make some changes you wouldn't have considered when you were younger. I'll give you an example. I work with a married couple who spends a month each year at a beach home they own. They don't rent it out, choosing to just enjoy it for that period of vacation. They love it. It's an important part of what their family does and who their family is.

You know what else they do? Spend about $68,000 a year in order to have that home. So when the subject of retirement came up and we discussed that they needed to make up some ground, we put the house on the table. They didn't want to sell at first, but I said, "Look, you can still spend a month at the beach, but why own the home to do so?" Eventually they agreed to sell the home. With the proceeds from the sale, they are still able to enjoy their time at the beach—with extra money in their pockets that they can invest and grow.

Conservatively, if the net proceeds from the house sale earn 4 percent, they're making a lot more than they were when they spent it on the beach house. And if it makes 6 or 8 percent, then, wow, they're making lots of money by just occasionally renting at the beach, rather than spending the money to own the home. Best of all, it didn't really change their lifestyle all *that* much; it just meant the house they stayed in wasn't theirs per se. That example shows what you need to do. Make some changes to make some money. You may have to alter some long-standing traditions, but when you're trying to make up significant ground, that's what you have to do.

Buckle Down. We all want to make sure we have money available over the long haul. You've taken a good first step by acknowledging that you need to start contributing to retirement accounts. In Chapter 5, I outlined the basic principles for saving for retirement. These still apply to latecomers as well. The first order of business is to take care of all the basics.

Namely, that means you have to make sure you're contributing as much as you can to your 401(k) plan—the current maximum contribution is $18,500 annually—and that you're taking advantage of any employer-matching programs that your place of business offers. Many companies offer half of what you contribute in the form of a match. If you contribute 6 percent of your income, your employer will may add in another 3 percent, giving you a sizable 9 percent going to your retirement portfolio. You maybe be able to contribute an additional $5,500 a year to a nondeductible IRA, which maybe able to roll into a Roth IRA so that even more money is earmarked for those to-be-used-later funds. This is especially important today because for the most part, 401(k) plans (or 403(b) plans for nonprofits) have replaced traditional defined pension plans. Therefore, the responsibility to invest them properly rests on your shoulders.

Back Off on the Risk. If your time frame to save for retirement is short, then be thoughtful about the level of risk exposure you can accept. Often, the markets are volatile over the short run. The riskier your investment, the higher your potential rewards—and risk always has a way of balancing out if you give it enough time. The challenge for latecomers is that they don't have the luxury of time. It is easy to be tempted to invest in riskier assets to make quick money. But the reality is that because you don't have time as your financial airbag to protect you from catastrophe, you do not want much risk. You want to invest in safe and steady areas that will provide safe and steady income with some appreciation.

Even if your risk tolerance is high (remember the Irvin Stomach Ulcer Index test?), this is not the time for rolling the dice on the majority of your assets that will produce income marked for retirement. (If for some reason, you do find yourself with extra money to play around with, such as a small inheritance, you could take some of it and put in riskier investments, but do not put entire accounts in risky areas.) Simply, if you're within sight of your retirement, you can't afford to be too heavily invested in high-risk and volatile market-based investments.

Scrutinize the Budget. When you're in a situation in which you feel like you're at the back of the pack trying to work your way to the front, it does take some doing to get there. One way to claw your way closer and closer to where you want to be is to examine your expenses. What can you sacrifice now so you have more security in the future? Can you lower your cable bill? Do without dinners out on the town (remember coffee, lattes, and muffins)? Scale back on vacations?

Unless you're living extremely modestly, it's my experience that most families can not only find *some* areas to cut, but also find *many* areas to cut and rethink the family priorities to save money. Might be a good time for a family powwow, where you can decide for a closer-to-home vacation than the Vail ski trip.

Now that you're serious about catching up, take a good look at your lifestyle priorities and make decisions on what to choose. It may hurt a bit at first, but it's a little bit like putting an ice pack on your body or alcohol on an open wound. Stings at first and then you hardly notice it after a while. These good decisions will give your family a much better future.

Don't Panic in a Bad Market. When people are maybe ten or twenty years from retirement—a time when they can really see the ocean waves or the golf course right around the corner—they have a tendency to get very jittery about how this is going to all unfold. If your account feels like it has too few zeroes in it, then that panicky feeling gets even worse—to the point where you start making bad decisions.

One of the bad decisions I see is that when the market turns sour, people get nervous and withdraw, rather than riding out the volatility of the storm at hand. Even if you're fifteen years away from retirement, that's enough time to allow your well-allocated portfolios to bounce back after a rough market, and you'll end up losing more of your family portfolio value by constantly trying to time the market by getting in and out. Even when the finish line is around the corner, patience is like a Labrador retriever—your ally forever.

Be Creative about Ways to Earn Extra Income. If you're in a position where you can't make extra income above and beyond your everyday salary (via a second job or bonuses, for example), you may have to find alternative ways to get some extra cash flow to help bolster your tax deferred retirement accounts. For one, you can consolidate your retirement accounts, helping you reduce any fees associated with multiple accounts (and thus allotting those fees for actual retirement).

Keep On Going. If you haven't read Chapter 18, do not pass go and immediately go back read this pivotal chapter. There's nothing—*nothing*—that says you have to retire at a certain age or at a certain time in your life There's a million (well, at least eight or nine) different ways for you to think about retirement, many of which allow you to continue to earn income even when your day job is done.

So, yes, you may feel like you're in a dire situation because you haven't saved enough for retirement. I'm not going to lie to you and tell you that you can order up a cool three million bucks in the next ten years. While I don't want you to feel desperate, you must reimagine what retirement should be as long as you can keep your health (see Chapter 4). There's no financial reason why you can't keep enjoying the riches (financially, mentally, emotionally, and spiritually) that come from working and earning an income well into your sixties, seventies, and beyond.

Chapter 23
Sweet Dreams

A Financial Windfall Won't Be Worth a Thing if You Don't Take Care of It Properly

Let's take a moment to talk about the American dream—you know, the one where we find our passion, put in honest days of work, build our nests, and live a happy and secure life with our loved ones. That's how most of us are going at it every day: we're plugging away with Energizer-Bunny-type tenacity and creating our own fortunes. Some of us are farther along than others. Of course, the definition of fortune is different for every person and family, depending on your jobs, background, and so many other factors. But if we take a step back and ask ourselves about our preferred way to build wealth, many of us—deep down—wouldn't mind if the narrative took a turn and went a little something like this:

We win the Powerball, buy four homes and a yacht, quit the job, receive daily massages followed by cucumbers-over-our-eyes naps, dine with wine, and then fall asleep to the sweet sounds of the South Pacific (the real one, not one on a white-noise app). Living the life.

Only problem: you have more of a chance of doing a one-fingered handstand than you do of winning the 3-bajillion-dollar Powerball.

So the reality is that very, very few of us will receive the change-your-life-forever lump sum of money—the kind of money that dreams and Hollywood scripts are made out of. But—and this is an important "but"—there are quite a few of us who will experience some form of windfall in our life. A windfall could be defined as an unexpected amount of money above and beyond what you normally earn in your employment, investments, or other budgeted earnings. So a windfall could be in the amount of a few thousand dollars, or even in the seven-figure variety.

A windfall can come in the form of such things as an inheritance, a smaller lottery win, an insurance settlement, a work bonus, or another gift of some kind. In addition, your point of view on the magnitude of a windfall also depends on your stage in life. For a college student, $5,000 may feel like a million bucks, but for someone else, that might feel like a mortgage payment.

While your eyes may open, your jaw may drop, and your wallet may fatten if such a windfall comes your way, you can't treat that cash flow like fun money that you toss around like it's nothing. Do you want to chug or sip? That is the question.

That's why it's important to talk to your partner to really communicate about what's the smartest strategy. If one person has a tendency to go out and spend, you may need the other person to step in with the voice of reason so you can plan, save, and spend wisely.

This exact situation came up with clients of mine. The family, whose parents made about $50,000 a year each, had gotten a windfall through a work settlement. They really wanted to spend their windfall on a down payment for a beach home, but after talking through options, we agreed that a better use of some of that money was a renovation of their bathrooms as they were in dire need of upgrade. A few years later, with smart investments and some patience, we were able to go ahead and use some of the windfall for that down payment. They got what they wanted, but they were patient about it.

So if you're fortunate enough to be on the receiving end of some kind of oh-wow gift of money, make sure you follow these guidelines so you're not tempted to blow the whole thing on some toys that sound whiz-bang fun today but won't do much for you tomorrow.

Step off the Gas. I get it. You're notified that you're going to be getting a chunk of change that you didn't expect, and your instinct is to act like you're Oprah giving gifts to the studio audience ("Cars, jewels, hot tubs for everyone!"). Yes, it can be exciting to come into some money, though sometimes it doesn't always come under happy circumstances, as is the case with inheritance.

The number-one rule for dealing with any type of windfall is that you cannot accelerate into shopping sprees, elaborate trips, and other spend-it-all habits. You need to slow down. Be patient. What I advise is that you take a minimum of six months (perhaps longer) before making any big decisions about how you want to spend or invest—and see how life changes for you and your family. That way, you're not acting out of impulse, but rather out of strategic decision making that you do with your entire familial and professional teams. Slow and steady always wins the wealth race, and even in times like this, the same holds true. Take a deep breath (one that lasts half a year minimum), and then assess your financial priorities.

There's one exception to the six-month rule: If your newfound wealth allows you to pay off your credit card debt, do it. You'll save money over the long term by not paying those high interest rates and ones that have no tax benefits whatsoever.

Acknowledge the Emotions, Then Separate from Them. It's perfectly normal to feel all kinds of things when a proverbial briefcase full of hundred-dollar bills drops into your lap. You may experience a range of emotions from sadness (if a loved one dies) to surprise (if you receive an inheritance from an unexpected source), or even guilt (if you make this money while friends and family are struggling). Of course, you may also feel exuberance that you'll be gaining some modicum of financial security. You may even feel all these emotions at the same time.

That cocktail of feelings is normal, but don't let them drive your decisions; this is part of the reason why you put that six-month rule into place. When emotions drive your financial decisions, that's when you get yourself into a jam. Don't feel guilty about feeling guilty. The trick is not letting your emotions chip away at your windfall—and the future earnings you can derive from them.

Example: You feel guilty, so you give your relatives money to pay off their debt. That's wonderful for you to consider them, but you also have to ask yourself if that makes the most financial sense for you and your family. What if your kindness means that you're left with virtually nothing or that the recipients of your gift use it on something other than that debt? That six-month breath keeps you from allowing the extreme emotions you may feel at the time to cloud your judgment.

Stash the Cash. So the question is, where do I put all that money before I make a decision on what to do with it? Great question, and one a professional wealth advisor can help you with. While I have spent a fair amount of time in this book telling you that you do not want to put any money in bank savings accounts, this would be one exception to that rule. Just put the lump sum in a FDIC insured bank account or a government money market account for those six months so you can take the time to assess your choices. You won't gain much in terms of interest over that time, and that's okay (it's similar to renting a house for six months while you assess the neighborhoods of a new city; renting isn't always the most financially savvy thing to do, but it helps give you time to make a better decision for the long run).

It's better to have it available to you for when you do decide how you want to invest it, rather than have it locked up in accounts that will make it difficult for you to choose other alternatives with it.

There are limits on how much you can put into traditional bank accounts and have it insured; if you exceed that amount, simply open several accounts. One thing you absolutely do not want to do is put the money in your checking account. It will be too tempting to simply use it and throw it away with frivolous purchases if the money is in an account tied to your everyday use. Once you hit that six months, that's when you take it from the bank account and place it where you want it to go.

Decide Where It's Going. After your six-month holding period, you'll have to decide how you want to allocate your assets. As is the case with any of your wealth (windfall or not), you need to establish goals and assess your risk level and all the things I've talked about throughout this book.

So above all, you should take your newfound cash and look at Chapter 5 on investing to figure out how you want to diversify your investments. Receiving a windfall is a bit different in that you may have a larger sum of money to work with and may be able to have a higher risk threshold than you would with your regular income. Of course, this all depends on your perspective as well. A million-dollar windfall would suggest that you can afford to put it in riskier asset classes (for greater opportunity for reward over the long term), as opposed to, say, a $100,000 windfall that you may want to use to build your nest egg and grow a bit more conservatively.

A smaller windfall may allow you to plug a hole in the dam by paying off credit card debt. Still, the amount of your windfall isn't the only factor you need to think about. Age is a biggie too. If you're close to retirement (or choose to retire early), you may want to invest in more conservative areas that will provide solid and steady income that can supplement your income. Note that your Social Security payments depend on your lifetime earnings, but it's certainly difficult to live on. If you're younger, you may be able to afford to take higher risks because you're in it for the long haul and don't need that income.

Keeping in mind that all situations are different because of these factors, here are my suggestions for things you should consider doing with your windfall, besides investing it in the places I refer to in Chapter 5.

If you don't already have one, start an emergency account that is equivalent to six months to a year of your lifestyles expenses (this account isn't to be touched, but is there as a backup fund if necessary). I would also encourage you to look at the performance of your retirement fund. No matter how much you have saved or how much you are earning in your retirement account, you can never be too safe when it comes to planning for your future. That's because we always underestimate how much it will take for us to live on when we retire. So what I would do is earmark a certain percentage of your windfall and put it toward retirement to plump up that nest even more than it already is. Another area to consider is educational programs for your children or grandchildren.

Keep It Quiet. Ooooh, I know what you want to do. You want to announce it, Tweet it, Facebook it, text all your friends. "Can u believe what luck? Won $200K in lotto!! #OMG!"

Don't do it. While the temptation is there to share your good fortune, it's best if you keep it private—for many reasons, but the main one is because when your windfalls become public, it's like everyone suddenly becomes your best friend in need of a handout. While some may be honest people who truly need help, others may just only be after your money. They can come in the form of relatives, charities, lawyers, even so-called personal finance advisors looking for a percentage of your good fortune.

You have to protect yourself against those looking to capitalize on your success, not because you don't want to help other people, but because the requests can be incessant and you can end up losing much of what you've earned if your pile of cash falls into the wrong hands. While there may be some cases you can't control—say, your relatives may learn of an inheritance, or if everybody sees you went on a sixty-seven-day win streak on *Jeopardy!*—but if you have the choice, keep news of your windfall out of the papers, off the Internet, and out of conversations.

Keep It in Perspective. If you're one of the lucky souls who do get an unexpected chunk of change, I'm happy for you. It's wonderful news, and it can help you have those sweet dreams that you've always wanted. Now, I don't want to pop all your balloons, but I do think that this is the exact type of situation that requires a level head. Any windfall also includes giving a significant percentage to your favorite uncle (Sam, that is and the state you reside in), so it's never the full amount you think it's going to be.

Your mind-set going in shouldn't be to spend the money you received but rather the income you earn off of that windfall, so you can keep your base amount of money intact. *That's* what will get you long-term financial independence. The biggest mistake that windfall recipients make is that they think the money will last forever. Spend it the wrong way (frivolously), and it certainly won't stretch to forever. So your frame of mind should be that the income made off the principal is there to balance and support you, while the principal itself is what will help your family for the rest of your life.

Keep Your Job. Here's what typically happens after someone gets their windfall. One, there's a scream of jubilation. Two, there's something said to the effect of "Sayonara, boss, I'm outta here!" The life of luxury may work for a few folks who find themselves on the receiving end of a big bucket of loot, but it's my experience that even when you think you have enough money to quit your job, you don't. So here's my advice: again, take that six-month holding period to really evaluate your situation. Then if you can afford to quit your job, consider it. There are many factors that need to be evaluated, such as age, goals, and investments before you can make that choice.

But here's what I think: if you enjoy what you do, why not keep going and build even more wealth? Don't use your windfall, but rather invest it and keep living on the money you're earning. That way, you can truly spend your extra money on things that are important to you (or fun for you) without having to worry that the money is going to run out.

Plus, think about all the other benefits that come from having your job: retirement plan matching, health benefits, mental stimulation, social connections, on and on. Maybe you can cut back or shift careers if you're in a situation you don't like. Or maybe what your windfall does is allow you more flexibility in your job to, say, take unpaid vacations or (if your company allows it) short sabbaticals and leaves of absence. That way, you get the best of both worlds—the income and benefits from having a job, but the flexibility and enjoyment that comes from having financial security.

I know I'm biased, because I love what I do, but I also think it makes the most financial sense to be able to keep your earnings coming, even if you're fortunate enough to be in a situation where you think you don't need to make any more money.

Splurge! Yes, I said it. Splurge. Spend. Buy a watch or a Winnebago. Go to Hawaii or the Hamptons. Take the grandchildren to Disney for a week. Depending on the amount of your windfall, you should treat yourself or your family to something that feels just a little extravagant—something you probably wouldn't spring for under normal circumstances, even though you've always wanted to do it and you know it will improve your life satisfaction.

But here's the trick: splurge, then stop. Don't buy the watch and then convince yourself you need the earrings, the bracelet, and the sports car. This is the real danger zone and the real question: can you manage your splurge so it's reasonable, so it doesn't chip away too much from your windfall, and so it doesn't domino from one splurge into one thousand splurges? This takes discipline, goal setting, patience, and budgeting. As I've said all along, wealth isn't just about the money; it's about opening up new options or time to do what you really want and enjoying the experiences you've always dreamed of.

So if this windfall allows you to carve out some more time or give you an experience (or thing) that will improve your quality of life, then go for it. Just keep the cost reasonable and in line with what you can afford. After all, the end game from any significant windfall is financial security for a long, long time.

> ## Question: What if my windfall is really big? Can't I just buy that private island?
>
> **Answer:** Well, maybe that's the case for a very select few, but I still would argue that no matter the amount of your big catch, you need to follow the principles I've outlined here in terms of being patient and being smart. Having that kind of money may allow you to better be able to get in touch with your passions, pay it forward to help people, and really invest it to give you the security you want. My general guideline is that if your windfall is more than $250,000, you need to work with a professional wealth advisor to make sure all of your bases are covered. (And certainly you can work with one if it's less than that amount!

The Reinvent Rich

21-Day Wealth Makeover

Sometimes, twenty-one days feels like forever—like if you're trying to plow through a season of record-breaking snow or a huge pile of paperwork. But in other ways, twenty-one days is just a blip on the timeline of your life. Snap your fingers and, *bam*, it's over like that. So now that you've read through my strategies for creating all kinds of wealth in your life, you have a good idea of where I stand on many money and life-related issues and decisions. So now the questions are: How do you put it all together? How do you take my strategies and integrate them into your life? How do you change your outlook to change your investment accounts? How do you reinvent rich?

Well, I believe that you can start taking my strategies and put them into action right now. Just go through the book, find the areas where you have trouble, and then work on creating those fixes that will best set you up for a lifetime of financial and emotional returns. That said, there could be a lot to learn and a lot to do. Admittedly, if you don't have much experience in this arena, you need a little more structure when it comes to creating a new series of values and tactics.

That's why I've created this 21-Day Wealth Makeover. No, no, no—this isn't a "get rich this month" scheme. You won't get wealthy in three weeks, but what you will do is re-create your systems and ways of life to set you up for a lifetime of success.

I know this process can be intimidating, so make no mistake: these three weeks aren't about doing *everything*. They're about establishing new baselines, new habits, new outlooks, and new ways of thinking and investing. Best of all, I've designed this plan so very few tasks will take more than a few minutes a day.

On each day, commit to this one action (even if it's just spending time thinking about a given topic), and you'll come out with the groundwork done to create a new kind of wealth, a new kind of you, and a new kind of opportunity to create the freedom and flexibility to enjoy life to the fullest.

The 21-Day Wealth Makeover

For each entry, you will find more details within the book. I've included the page numbers here so you can flip back for more detailed information.

Day 1

Activity: Write Down Your Values

Not what you want to buy or what you're saving for, but what you value in life—be it with family or work or free time or another goal. What are the five or six things you most value? This will serve as the foundation through which all of your decisions and strategies flow. (Page 30)

Approximate Time: 20 minutes

Day 2

Activity: Identify Your Team

Ask yourself two questions: Who is part of your financial planning team (i.e., your spouse)? Who would you like to be part of it (a professional, a lawyer, etc.)? Financial planning is private, but it's not a solo adventure. And the more you can communicate and trust in your team, the better off you will be. (Page 48)

Approximate Time: 5 minutes

Day 3

Activity: Go for a Walk and Make Exercise a Consistent Part of Your Daily Life.

You're only as rich as you are healthy. Your commitment to a wealthy future begins with a healthy now. (Page 61)

Approximate time: 30 minutes per day

Day 4

Activity: Make an Appointment

Schedule a time one week from today when you will sit down with your family partners (if this applies to you) and discuss the values that you came up with as well as financial priorities and concerns. Communication is key, and doing so when you're not trying to solve a conflict is important. (Page 35)

Approximate time: 15 minutes

Day 5

Activity: Do a Paperwork Checklist

Ask yourself this question: Do you have wills, living wills, and estate planning documents in order? If your answer is yes, make sure they are in the hands of a third party (like a lawyer or wealth manager to keep safe and close at hand in a document vault). If not, schedule a time to meet with a lawyer or wealth manager to make sure all of that paperwork is up to date in the last 5 years. (Page 121)

Approximate time: 5–10 minutes

Day 6

Activity: Set Up a Dollar-Cost Averaging Program

Set up a plan to to begin or expand dollar-cost averaging program. Make a phone call, set up a draft on your account, and watch your money grow for you and your family. (Page 82)

Approximate time: 30–45 minutes

Day 7

Activity: Plan Your Next Negotiation

Remember all of my discussion about negotiations? That has to be a mind-set you have if you want to create wealth in your everyday life. You never know when you'll be able to use those strategies in life. What is the next big (or semi-big) purchase you need to make? Think about strategies you can use to get a lower price or extra services, especially on all commodity items you purchase. (Page 96)

Approximate time: 10 minutes

Day 8

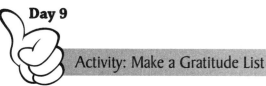

Activity: Make a Commitment for Retirement

Even if it's just a few more dollars per pay period, investing more now will set you up better for later. Call your employer's benefits department contact and find out the process and timeline for making that adjustment. Max out your annual allowable contribution to capture the full company match, even if it means using more of a spouse's income than you like. Take a leap of faith by going for the max, to make the most for yourself as well as growing the matching contributions from your employer.

Approximate time: 20 minutes

Day 9

Activity: Make a Gratitude List

Write down eight to ten things you are grateful for. Perspective is important and a good way to reinforce some of your key values. In addition, download an app called Win Streak, which is a fun system for allowing you to set three daily goals and aim to hit them. No matter what else may go right or wrong that day, your goal is to get those three things taken care of. It helps you keep plugging away, stay motivated, and not get sidetracked by the minutia that often derails our best intentions.

Approximate time: 5 minutes

Day 10

Activity: Draw a Picture

Sketch out your dreams, your goals, and what you want out of life. You can doodle it or create a masterpiece, but be creative and visualize something that's important to you. That image should stay in your mind while you're making decisions, having discussions, or having to make tough choices about budget. Bring your picture to tomorrow's talk. (Page 36)

Approximate time: 15 minutes

Day 11

Activity: Have the Talk

Have that discussion with your spouse, partner, or other team member about life values, financial issues, and priorities. You don't need to come to any decisions. You just need to agree on some next action steps, like evaluating your budget together, talking through investment portfolios, or making sure goals are aligned. Agree to another meeting about ten days from now. (Page 35)

Approximate Time: 90 minutes

Day 12

Activity: Review Your Bills, Part I

If you don't keep a monthly budget, gather all of your materials that will give insight into what you earn and spend every month. This can be a daunting task, so just take a few minutes every day for the next three days to gather the materials. If you already have a budget in good organizational order, then take this time and get in a workout! Use one of the online tools like mint.com to get yourself organized in an online system. (Page 40)

Approximate Time: 15–20 minutes

Day 13

Activity: Review Your Bills, Part 2

Repeat the previous day and finish the accumulation of your paperwork; or if you're done, fit in another vigorous walk or workout.

Approximate Time: 15–20 minutes

Day 14

Activity: Build Your Budget/Lifestyle Expense Overview

Using the data you've pulled over the last two days, create a spreadsheet (using some kind of financial-based software like Quicken or QuickBooks Professional makes it easier) so you can see how your income versus expenses works on a monthly and yearly basis. Make sure you carve out income that goes to retirement and other investments. (Page 42)

Approximate Time: 1 hour

Day 15

Activity: Take the Muffin Test

Do you have a daily habit that you can do without? Even if it's just a store-bought coffee, add up all of the little expenses that you think are inconsequential. Look at the total dollar amount over the course of a year. A lot, huh? Make a commitment to find ways to get the same fix (you can make your own coffee at home) for a fraction of the cost. That savings goes directly to your bottom line and, over time, compounds to thousands of dollars.

Approximate time: 15 minutes

Day 16

Activity: Make the Hard Decisions

Now that you have your budget and have cut some minor expenses (that can turn out to be major), ask yourself what you can do without. Make the decision (as a team), and then make the adjustment. Add this savings to your monthly dollar cost savings program.

Approximate time: 20 minutes

Day 17

Activity: Review Investment Principles

In most cases when the portfolio size becomes significant, I recommend using a professional to help guide you with investments, but even if you do, you should be aware of some of the major principles of smart investing—that is, asset allocation and diversification, saving ten cents from every dollar you earn, as well as having the courage to take risk over the long term.

Approximate time: 20 minutes

Day 18

Activity: Reorganize Your Files (Paper and Electronic)

If you're an ultra-organized keeper of paperwork, even the digital kind, great! But if not, it's worth doing a spring cleaning of your files to establish organized and sensible systems for you to reference and track your portfolio and files when needed. Even if this turns out to be a major time commitment, decluttering your files—and your mind—will benefit you in the long run. Turn a mess (no matter the degree) into order. (Page 40)

Approximate time: Varied, depending on the degree of your files

Day 19

Activity: Build (and Share!) Your Bucket List

Do it. Dream big. Share those things with your family. Give yourself and your family purpose, adventure, and moments. At family dinner tonight, everyone take a turn going around the table and naming two or three things on their list.

Approximate time: Varied and Priceless

Day 20

Activity: Have the Talk (Session Two)

Evaluate your monthly budget today. Agree on places where you can make adjustments. Talk about any reallocations of income, in terms of budget, retirement, or other investment accounts. This can be a fairly heavy-duty conversation, and if you've decided to bring in a wealth-management professional, this is a good time to have the discussion with that person. At this point, you really need to make some commitments, delegate responsibilities (perhaps to a professional), identify your weaknesses, and strategize about your future.

Approximate Time: 90 minutes

Day 21

Activity: Look Back and Look Forward

Take a moment to see all that you've accomplished in the last three weeks. Amazing strides! You now have the organizational and strategic infrastructure to build your wealth to places you've never dreamed of going. And if that's not enough to get you excited about the possibilities, I don't know what is.

REFERENCES

1   https://www.ssa.gov/news/press/factsheets/basicfact-alt.pdf
2   https://files.stlouisfed.org/files/htdocs/publications/es/14/ES_18_2014-07-18.pdf
3   https://en.wikipedia.org/wiki/Modern_portfolio_theory
4   https://en.wikipedia.org/wiki/Modern_portfolio_theory
5   http://www.cnbc.com/2017/05/12/warren-buffett-says-index-funds-make-the-best-retirement-sense-practically-all-the-time.html
6   https://www.sec.gov/investor/alerts/ib_fees_expenses.pdf
7   Morningstar
8   https://greenbackd.com/tag/equal-weight-index/
9   https://www.irs.gov/newsroom/irs-announces-2018-pension-plan-limitations-401k-contribution-limit-increases-to-18500-for-2018
10 http://www.willkie.com/~/media/Files/Publications/2017/12/2018_Estate_Gift_and_GST_Tax_Exemption_Increases.pdf
11 https://en.wikipedia.org/wiki/Life_insurance_trust
12 https://www.irs.gov/businesses/small-businesses-self-employed/estate-tax
13 https://www.irs.gov/businesses/small-businesses-self-employed/section-7520-interest-rates
14 https://www.fidelitycharitable.org/philanthropy/charitable-remainder-trusts.shtml
15 http://www.pgdc.com/pgdc/charitable-lead-trusts-primer
16 https://www.thebalance.com/what-is-a-qualified-personal-residence-trust-3505404
17 http://www.investorguide.com/article/11813/generation-skipping-trusts-and-why-they-are-advantageous-igu/
18 http://www.willkie.com/~/media/Files/Publications/2017/12/2018_Estate_Gift_and_GST_Tax_Exemption_Increases.pdf
19 http://www.finaid.org/savings/ugma.phtml
20 https://www.nytimes.com/2017/12/21/your-money/529-plans-taxes-private-school.html
21 http://www.savingtoinvest.com/500-non-child-dependent-or-flexible-credit-in-trump-gop-tax-reform-bill/

ABOUT THE AUTHOR

Irvin Schorsch is the visionary who founded Pennsylvania Capital Management in 1995. As a thought leader, his mission was to build an entrepreneurial firm to help people crystalize their thinking about their future and financial goals.

Irvin represents a new breed of wealth advisors who are passionate about providing the highest level of personalized service and attention to PCM's clients. He's committed to developing life-long, partnership style relationships with the multi-generational clientele PCM serves.

Irvin graduated with honors from the Commerce and Finance Division of Villanova University. He has earned three advanced certifications: Certified Financial Planner™ from the College for Financial Planning in Denver, Colorado; the Certified Investment Management Analyst CIMA® designation through the Wharton School of the University of Pennsylvania in conjunction with the Investments & Wealth Institute®; and the Accredited Investment Fiduciary® awarded by the Center for Fiduciary Studies, which is associated with the University of Pittsburgh.

Irvin is an in-demand author, speaker, and consultant on many topics from financial planning to wealth management for all demographics and age groups. Mr. Schorsch can be reached at 215-881-7700 or irvin@pcmadvisors.com.